T&T Clark Studies in Systematic Theology

Edited by

John Webster
Ian A. McFarland
Ivor Davidson

Volume 14

GOD IS A COMMUNICATIVE BEING

Divine Communicativeness and Harmony in the Theology of Jonathan Edwards

William M. Schweitzer

May God pour out His blessings and communicate His knowledge, love and joy to the students of WPTS.

BLOOMSBURY

LONDON • NEW DELHI • NEW YORK • SYDNEY

Bloomsbury T&T Clark
An imprint of Bloomsbury Publishing Plc

50 Bedford Square
London
WC1B 3DP
UK

1385 Broadway
New York
NY 10018
USA

www.bloomsbury.com

Bloomsbury is a registered trade mark of Bloomsbury Publishing Plc

First published 2012
Paperback edition first published 2013

British Library Cataloguing-in-Publication Data
A catalogue record for this book is available from the British Library.

ISBN: HB: 978-0-567-19522-7
PB: 978-0-567-51220-8

Library of Congress Cataloging-in-Publication Data
A catalogue record for this book is available from the Library of Congress

Typeset by Deanta Global Publishing Services, Chennai, India

To my Fidelia
a being familiar with communicative harmony

Contents

Introduction

"Though the parts are very various and innumerable, and distant one from another, yet all bear a relation one to another and all is united together so as to make one frame and to be all together, one building."

—Jonathan Edwards, "Approaching the End of God's Grand Design"[1]

I Perry Miller and the Beautiful Mind

The recent Jonathan Edwards revival owes much to the improbable encouragement of Harvard historian Perry Miller. Miller was not a theologian, nor was he a likely friend of the religion Edwards championed. In the years since his seminal 1949 work *Jonathan Edwards*, few of Miller's theological pronouncements have stood entirely without challenge. Indeed, one could take exception even to his warmest commendation: "The truth is, Edwards was infinitely more than a theologian. He was one of America's five or six major artists, who happened to work with ideas instead of poems or novels."[2] This was hardly an affirmation of Edwards' chosen discipline as queen of the sciences. However, we also see in this statement something of why Miller could ignite a movement—he had identified a beautiful mind. He had found a figure who, by the grace of God, could imagine the breathtaking reality behind and beyond mundane perception. Miller, in turn, was able to showcase the brilliance of Edwards' thought and the immensity of his vision. Little wonder he succeeded in capturing the imagination of scores of able scholars who would carry on the work.

The work since Miller has proceeded along two main lines. One has been the mammoth task of editing Edwards' writings for publication in the Yale Edition. The largest primary works project in American history was begun

[1] Primary citations taken from the Yale Edition of *The Works of Jonathan Edwards* will be referred to in the following abbreviated manner: Edwards, "Title," in *Works Vol. 1*, pp.1–2. Full bibliographic details, including the editor and the year of publication, appear in the bibliography. In this case, the reference is Edwards, "Approaching the End of God's Grand Design," in *Works Vol. 25*, p. 115.

[2] Perry Miller, *Jonathan Edwards* (New York: William Sloan Associates, 1949), p. xvi.

under Miller's own leadership in the 1950s and was not completed until 2008.[3] The other focus of effort has been in scholarship. Though open-ended by nature, this effort has also made Herculean progress, not least in raising Edwards' profile. The American colonial has belatedly taken his place among the great theologians, wherein virtually every feature of his thought is considered worthy of serious study. Indeed, one might get the impression that there are not many features of his thought that have yet escaped scholarly attention.[4] If there has been any shortcoming, it has perhaps been in a failure to maintain an awareness of the immense, unified vision Miller found so captivating. With some welcome exceptions, the forest has often been missed for the trees.[5]

This book is an effort to take another look at the forest. There are some good reasons to make such an attempt. We have said that Edwards' vision was beautiful, and for some, this is reason enough. Perhaps it is also the case that Edwards lived at the right moment in history to exert his particular gifts to best effect. The Reformed faith had been given its foundation by Calvin in the sixteenth century and was framed by the post-Reformation greats in the seventeenth century, but the house was not quite finished. There were some gaps that Edwards wanted to fill, ranging from the purpose for which God created the universe to answering the question of whether heaven was a static or progressive state. While Calvin was famously allergic to anything that hinted of speculation, Edwards thought it was his duty to solve every theological problem he encountered, a proclivity that enabled him to perhaps make some advances from within the system of doctrine he received.[6] Philosophically, no one had yet articulated the orthodox faith in terms familiar to the European Enlightenment that was then coming of age. His valiant attempt to do this was undeterred by the long list of failures that would follow in the years ahead. As those who live in a world defined by the outworking of radical ideas that were making their first public

[3] It should be noted that the letterpress volumes found on library shelves comprise only a sizeable fraction of Edwards' extant writings; the remainder are available in the Jonathan Edwards Center's online volumes beginning with "Volume 27."

[4] The work of M. X. Lesser is instructive here. See Lesser, *Reading Jonathan Edwards: An Annotated Bibliography in Three Parts, 1729–2005* (Grand Rapids, MI: Eerdmans, 2008).

[5] The most notable of these exceptions is probably Robert W. Jenson, *America's Theologian: A Recommendation of Jonathan Edwards* (New York: Oxford University Press, 1988).

[6] "Resolved, when I think of any theorem in divinity to be solved, immediately to do what I can towards solving it" (Edwards, 'Resolutions' 11, in *Works Vol* 16). The oft-repeated illustration of this contrast between Calvin and Edwards is that while Revelation was practically the only book of the Bible on which Calvin did not comment, it was the only book for which Edwards wrote anything like a commentary. Of course, such a proclivity came with the potential for problems as well as for advancement.

appearance in Edwards' time, we are amazed to find a Christian system so aware of, yet so unfettered by, the skeptical forces of modernity.[7]

The comprehensiveness of Edwards' thought is also attractive. Edwards wanted to unite theology, science, philosophy, and history under a single banner, one of the last great efforts to do so.[8] His "tri-world vision" depicted not only this present world but also heaven and hell as alive with the vivid detail typical of real places.[9] In terms of chronological scope, his vision sweeps from eternity past through the whole of human history and into eternity future. In all of these things, he was interested not only in truth but also in ethical and aesthetic valuation. In lesser hands, such wide-ranging pursuits might have yielded a forgettable mess, but in Edwards' beautiful mind, the result was something of enduring appeal.

II Explaining Edwards

Given the attraction of Edwards' vision, we naturally want to explain it. And, while much lies in attention to detail, this understanding can only be achieved holistically. No one has stated this better than Paul Ramsey: "A student's first effort must be to understand Edwards *whole*, in the integrity of all parts of his writings on theological subjects."[10] Yet, is Edwards' theology actually coherent enough for this to be a realistic approach?[11] Are there enough integral factors across Edwards' corpus that might enable us to arrive at this kind of unified understanding? Arguments could be made on

[7] For a plausible account of these forces, see Jonathan I. Israel, *Radical Enlightenment: Philosophy and the Making of the Modernity 1650–1750* (Oxford and New York: Oxford University Press, 2001).

[8] In his planned great work of apologetic theology entitled "A Rational Account of the Main Doctrines of the Christian Religion Attempted," Edwards wanted to show "how all arts and sciences, the more they are perfected, the more they issue in divinity, and coincide with it, and appear to be as parts of it" (Edwards, "Outline of a Rational Account," *Works Vol. 6*, p. 397). Miller was of the opinion that Edwards was indeed, ". . . the last great American, perhaps the last European, for whom there could be no warfare between religion and science, or between ethics and nature" (Perry Miller, *Jonathan Edwards* (New York: William Sloan Associates, 1949), p. 72).

[9] See Harry S. Stout, "Jonathan Edwards's Tri-World Vision," in D. G. Hart, Sean Michael Lewis and Stephen J. Nichols (eds.), *The Legacy of Jonathan Edwards: American Religion and the Evangelical Tradition* (Grand Rapids, MI: Baker, 2003), pp. 27–46.

[10] Paul Ramsey, "Editor's Introduction," in *Works Vol. 8*, p. 3.

[11] Amy Plantinga Pauw suggests that Edwards had a "high tolerance for theological tension," but her case in point is admittedly one of "complementary linguistic idioms" rather than real tension (Amy Pauw, *The Supreme Harmony of All: The Trinitarian Theology of Jonathan Edwards* (Grand Rapids, MI and Cambridge: Eerdmans, 2002), p. 11). Edwards, while willing to rest in mystery in a few intractable cases, was in fact highly sensitive to theological tension and worked tirelessly to resolve it. See Edwards, "Resolutions" 11, in *Works Vol* 16.

either side, but the prevailing direction of Edwards' thought certainly gives us encouragement to make the attempt. Consider this statement from one of his later sermons:

> God's design in all his works is one, and all his manifold and various dispensations are parts of one scheme . . . His works are various and manifold, but the end ultimately aimed at in all is the same. He han't different and separate designs that have no relation one to another in his various works, but has one great design in all. Indeed, there are different subordinate designs that God has in his different works, but not different independent designs . . . The scheme for the obtaining of this great end is but one: all the various works of God have relation one to another and are united one to another as different parts of one scheme, so that the contrivance is but one and the work is one . . . Though the parts are very various and innumerable, and distant one from another, yet all bear a relation one to another and all is united together so as to make one frame and to be all together, one building.[12]

The subject here is God's works rather than his own project, but consider the argument that Edwards makes. He thinks that God's works are so diverse that they could be mistaken for having no unifying purpose, but this would be impossible. Why? Because, "that he should act and have no end in acting . . . is inconsistent with the nature of an intelligent, voluntary and free agent."[13] Edwards believed that a diverse body of work united by an overarching purpose was a natural characteristic of *all* intelligent beings. Given such a belief, should we not at least hope to find evidence of some unifying factor among Edwards' own works, some hints of an overarching project?

I think that, beyond the biblical religion that Edwards held in common with many other thinkers, there is something that speaks of a core intuition underlying his "various and manifold" formulations. My proposal is that what is distinctive in Edwards is related to his insight that "God is a communicative Being."[14] The context of this statement is a problem that animated him throughout his life: why did a self-sufficient God create the world? His astonishing reply was "The great and universal end of God's

[12] Edwards, "Approaching the End of God's Grand Design," in *Works Vol. 25*, pp. 114–115.
[13] Edwards, "Approaching the End of God's Grand Design," in *Works Vol. 25*, p. 114.
[14] It should be understood that all such statements are intended to be observations or theories about the theology of Jonathan Edwards. While my perspective is largely sympathetic to Edwards, such observations and theories may not in every case reflect my own theology.

creating the world was to communicate himself. God is a communicative being."[15] To understand all that Edwards meant by this, in the final analysis, is to understand the Northampton pastor. For the moment, we can say he meant that God is fundamentally self-giving, and his dealings with his creatures reflect this all-important characteristic.

There are numerous manifestations of this core insight as it works back and forth throughout Edwards' thought. One important example would be how Edwards' doctrine of God begins squarely with the reality of the Trinity; the way to talk about God is to name Father, Son, and Spirit. With the Persons are the harmonious knowledge, love, and joy that are always *communicated* among them, and all other divine attributes are in some way descriptions of this eternal communication. God's project in creation and redemption then echoes the inter-Trinitarian communication in its multidimensionality as a communication of God's own knowledge, love, and joy. Thus, an adequate description of true religion demanded attention to the affections as well as to the intellect, and preaching must address itself to the heart as well as the head. These and other implications of Edwards' core theology defined the characteristic shape of his work.

Perhaps we can also describe an overarching project in Edwards' work. Edwards believed that God's "end" in creation and redemption was to communicate himself. He also believed this divine work was ordinarily carried on through the human agency of ministers like himself. Edwards self-consciously aligned himself with God's project by conveying divine communication to his fellow creatures through his preaching and writing. However, this project did not end with simple conveyance. The distinctive aspect of Edwards' project of furthering divine communication was in his method. God's self-communication bears the hallmark of Trinitarian "harmony." Indeed, the raison d'être of all created reality is so that human observers might appreciate this harmony. However, God's harmony is exceedingly complex and manifests itself in ways that may seem counterintuitive. Even supernaturally regenerate people need the help of Christ's ordained servants to recognize this harmony correctly. Edwards' work was fully consistent with such an understanding. As manifested by the united purpose of all three unfinished "Great Works," Edwards' lifelong project was to interpret the harmony of reality.[16]

If Edwards' characteristic insight had to do with God's communication, then it naturally follows that a book about his distinctive theology would

[15] Edwards, "Miscellany" 332, in *Works Vol. 13*, p. 410.
[16] See below, Chapter 6.

need to deal heavily with material concerning revelation. Thus, in between the first chapter explaining Edwards' core theology and the last chapter explaining his project, there are four chapters dealing with the media of revelation—nature, special revelation, Scripture, and history. Although Edwards' doctrine of revelation remains as one of the few major loci of systematic theology that has not yet been the subject of a fully comprehensive study, we shall learn from the many recent studies that interact with this area.[17] Through this scholarship and through the primary research presented here, the category of revelation looms so large in Edwards' corpus that it becomes possible to speak of his theology as a theology of divine communication.[18]

It is not terribly difficult to see why the category of revelation was so important to Edwards, given his situation in history. The Enlightenment was preoccupied with the range of issues under this broad heading, such as reason, revelation, biblical criticism, epistemology, natural science, and history. Edwards saw himself as a faithful minister responding to the challenges posed by the corrosive elements of this movement, and it makes sense that he would also focus on such issues. For an age in which the Scriptures were increasingly being conceived of as internally incoherent and irreconcilable with the data available from science, philosophy, and history, Edwards argued for the radical opposite: all of reality is the harmonious communication of the Triune divine mind.[19] In particular, Scripture and its teachings are in harmony with Scripture itself, with nature, and with history.

III The Roadmap

We have mentioned that the forest is often lost for the trees. It may be that in the course of our forays into the various aspects of Edwards' thought, readers may find themselves looking closely at various species of trees with no forest in sight. Perhaps, then, it would be good just to provide a

[17] A number of high-quality studies dealing with aspects of Edwards' doctrine of revelation have appeared in the last decade or so, including those by Stephen J. Stein, Gerald McDermott, Douglas Sweeney, Robert Brown, and John Carrick.

[18] Inasmuch as there is a meaningful difference between the terms "revelation" and "communication" in Edwards, there is in communication a greater emphasis on particularity; God reveals himself to all creation but he *communicates* his knowledge, love, and joy to believers only. See the discussion below, Chapter 1.

[19] On the issue of Edwards' occasionalism, see Oliver D. Crisp, "How Occasional was Edwards' Occasionalism?" in Paul Helm and Oliver D. Crisp (eds.), *Jonathan Edwards: Philosophical Theologian* (Aldershot: Ashgate, 2003), pp. 61–77.

large-scale roadmap, stating succinctly what it is this book is about. I intend to explain Edwards' work in terms of the *teleology* of divine communication and the *methodology* of interpreting harmony, paying attention to the *context* of the Enlightenment and the revivals.

Just to expand slightly, my intuition is that what marks out Edwards as a distinctive theologian is connected with his concept of God being "a communicative Being." Since God's means of communicating himself included nature and history as well as Scripture, Edwards was concerned to handle all three of these media in his work. And since what God communicates consists ultimately of his own knowledge, love, and joy, Edwards is therefore perennially interested in the affections as well as in bare knowledge. He was convinced that ministers in general—and one American colonist in particular—ought to convey these things through preaching, polemic theology, and apologetics. Edwards' *method* in carrying out this communicative task was the interpretation of Trinitarian harmony. Of course, what gave all these things shape was their historical context. Thus, a subplot throughout the book is Edwards' nuanced response to Enlightenment intellectual currents. While it is now widely accepted that Edwards did open warfare with the English Deists, Edwards was alert to the whole range of possible threats, including those coming from more subtle sources.[20] Finally, Edwards believed that he was living during a notable movement of God's communicative project and that it was his duty to covey this new material to the transatlantic church. So it was that the Awakenings provided the other main historical occasion for his work.

With this large-scale map in place, let us now summarize the contents of the chapters.

Chapter 1: The Communicative God. Edwards' theology of divine revelation originates with his doctrine of God. Partially in response to Deist critiques of the Trinity, Edwards formulated some concepts that offered insight into the beautiful rationality of the Christian God. The most important of these is *communicativeness*, whereby Edwards argued that the generally acknowledged attribute of God's goodness entails a disposition to share or "communicate" his good state, calling for an eternal plurality in the divine being. In a similar manner, communicativeness furnished the answer to a theological problem that intrigued Edwards throughout his career: why

[20] This recognition is largely attributable to the work of Gerald R. McDermott, particularly in McDermott, *Jonathan Edwards Confronts the Gods: Christian Theology, Enlightenment Religion, and Non-Christian Faiths* (Oxford and New York: Oxford University Press, 2000).

did God create? His answer was that God created the world to communicate himself to intelligent beings. At a time when the Deists were arguing persuasively for the sufficiency of human reason to know God, the concept of communicativeness provided the basis for a highly robust and comprehensive theology of divine revelation. Edwards could appropriate every aspect of reality—nature and history as well as special revelation—for its revelatory content. Moreover, as a repetition *ad extra* of Trinitarian communicative activity, the content of revelation corresponds to the content of the Trinity's own communication *ad intra.* Perhaps most determinative for the distinctive bent of Edwards' work, this correspondence means that revelation, like the Trinity's own multidimensional communication, consists of noetic (knowledge), affectional (love), and beatific (joy) components.

Chapter 2: Nature. Edwards' earliest intellectual pursuits were actually in science. Conserving an approach that was taken for granted in the past but one that was in decline by his time, Edwards did his science to the glory of the Triune God. This brand of science is to be understood as in self-conscious opposition to Hobbes' materialism and to mechanistic interpretations of Newton. Consistent with his larger interpretive project, he used his own observation and reflection upon nature to yield new revelatory content to disseminate to other intelligent observers of the universe. In later years, Edwards increasingly made use of typological interpretation of nature. These "types" were not merely illustrations, but contrivances made by God for the very purpose of pointing to their antitypes, such as Christ. As the centerpiece of the Deist agenda, natural theology was a crucial issue for Edwards. He argued that, although nature could never stand alone as a sufficient guide for religion, the joyful appropriation of creation by the regenerate was to fulfill the divine purposes of both.

Chapter 3: The Necessity of Special Revelation. Given the apparently boundless possibilities Edwards would seem to grant to general revelation in nature, one might possibly wonder whether special revelation was superfluous. On the contrary, as part of his larger campaign against hostile Enlightenment ideas, Edwards mounted a broad-spectrum apologetic for the absolute necessity of special revelation. This apologetic was developed in response not only to Deism but also to John Locke, as new evidence presented here would suggest. Edwards' distinctive theology of revelation is illustrated by his innovative arguments built around divine communicativeness. In polar opposition to rationalist sensibilities, Edwards did not reduce the issue to the mere need for data. Because he is a communicative being, God would still communicate with us even if exhaustive noetic information were available to us in nature. In other words, we were made to converse with our communicative maker.

Chapter 4: The Harmony of Scripture. In common with his theological inheritance, Edwards believed that the Scriptures shared the attributes of God. For Edwards, informed by his thoroughgoing Trinitarianism, the most significant of these attributes was its beautiful harmony. In an intellectual milieu bent on rebellion against the authority of this book as much as against its author, interpreting its harmony was for Edwards the preeminent apologetic method. Other topics explored include Edwards' belief structure as distinguished from his apologetics, his doctrines of inspiration, canon, and illumination, Locke's "Fundamentalism," and Edwards' attitude toward biblical criticism. Regarding this last topic, we shall see that although Edwards used the tools of the critical method, one cannot make too much from this concerning his larger attitude toward the modern critical project. The "freethinkers" wielded these tools to uncover the inconsistency and incoherence that their agenda demanded, while Edwards used them to demonstrate the perfect harmony that his theology assumed.

Chapter 5: The Harmony of History. History is an integral category of Edwards' theology of revelation. The infinite God's self-communication necessarily happens over time, meaning that the accurate record of this communication (history) becomes, in effect, a medium of communication. The object of our study of history is not, as some contemporaries might have thought, to demonstrate the ultimacy of human agency in the affairs of state but rather to display sovereign divine agency in the work of redemption. Edwards approached history as fundamentally supernatural and sought to demonstrate its harmony with Scripture. Some of the ways in which this thinking was manifested in Edwards' work are then illustrated, including not only the famous "History of the Work of Redemption" but also some lesser-known projects that likewise demonstrate how seriously Edwards took the implications of God revealing himself through the providential workings of redemptive history.

Chapter 6: Edwards' Project of Interpreting the Harmony of Reality. In the final chapter, we develop the proposal that Edwards' project was to interpret the harmony of God's self-communication in order to help his fellow "intelligent beings" better fulfill their purpose for existence. This theory is supported by the direction of his distinctive theology, the stated aims of his three projected "great works," the elements of the "Personal Narrative," and his understanding of the ministerial vocation. Edwards' high view of his office was emblematic of his understanding of the divine communicative project, whereby ministers were instruments to enable people to re-emanate divine revelation through the work of preaching, polemics, and apologetics. The role of the Awakenings in determining the actual shape of this project is also explored.

We turn now to consider a little more of what Edwards meant when he said that "God is a Communicative Being."

Chapter 1

The Communicative God

"The great and universal end of God's creating the world was to communicate himself. God is a communicative being."

—*Jonathan Edwards, "Miscellany"332*[1]

I Introduction

Our understanding of reality has a close relationship to our beliefs about its creator. The clockwork universe of uniform natural causation imagined by the English Deists, for instance, was implicit in the nature of their clockmaker Deity. So it is that the pattern for any coherent system of theology is set by its doctrine of God.[2] If we want to understand the character of Jonathan Edwards' system, then surely the best place to begin is with his theology proper. My proposal is that the distinctive qualities of Edwards' theology emanate from a single, powerful insight into the divine nature: "God is a communicative being."[3] We shall discuss various aspects of this insight, and its implications for Edwards' theology, beginning with his doctrine of the Trinity.

II The Trinity (Communicativeness *ad intra*)

Edwards was an orthodox Augustinian in his basic conception of the Trinity.[4] However, the particular expression of his Trinitarianism was prompted by a

[1] Edwards, "Miscellany" 332, in *Works Vol. 13*, p. 410.

[2] There is, of course, the potential for influence to flow in either direction. It is therefore useful to consider where any *a priori* commitments might lie, and how these commitments are mapped out on either side of this equation.

[3] Edwards, "Miscellany" 332, in *Works Vol. 13*, p. 410.

[4] The orthodoxy of Edwards' Trinitarianism has occasionally been challenged. See Paul Helm, "Editor's Introduction," in *Treatise on Grace and Other Posthumously Published Writings* (London: James Clark, 1971), pp. 1–5; and Richard M. Webber, "The Trinitarian Theology of Jonathan

creatively critical engagement with some less orthodox elements of his Enlightenment context.[5] Partially in response to charges by skeptics that the doctrine of the Trinity was flagrantly irrational and even unbiblical, Edwards developed a concept of necessary plurality that offered some rationale for this all-important doctrine.[6] This concept could be expressed in terms of love ("That in John, 'God is love,' shows that there are more persons than one in the Deity") or excellence ("One alone, without any reference to any more, cannot be excellent").[7] However, the concept seemingly took flight in terms of *communicativeness*, wherein Edwards argued that the mere fact that God is good—something even the most ardent Unitarian would affirm—implies a "disposition" to share or "communicate" that goodness. This, in turn, requires an eternal plurality in the divine being, for if God has no one to share with, how could his goodness have any exercise in eternity past? In Edwards' mind, this concept offered the doctrine of the Trinity its rightful place as a philosophic necessity rather than an embarrassing surd.

Edwards then employed the concept of divine communicativeness to solve a theological problem that fascinated him throughout his career: why did a self-sufficient God create? The answer is "God is a communicative being"; he

Edwards: An Investigation of Charges against Its Orthodoxy," in *Journal of the Evangelical Theological Society 44*, no. 2 (2001), pp. 297–318. For literature on Edwards' Trinitarianism, see Oliver D. Crisp, "Jonathan Edwards's God: Trinity, Individuation, and Divine Simplicity," in Bruce L. McCormack (ed.), *Engaging the Doctrine of God: Contemporary Protestant Perspectives* (Grand Rapids, MI: Baker Academic and Rutherford House, 2008), pp. 83–103; William J. Danaher Jr., *The Trinitarian Ethics of Jonathan Edwards* (Louisville, KY: Westminster John Knox); Stephen R. Holmes, *God of Grace and God of Glory: An Account of the Theology of Jonathan Edwards* (Edinburgh: T&T Clark, 2000); Sang Hyun Lee, "Editor's Introduction," in *Works Vol. 21*; Michael J. McClymond, *Encounters with God: An Approach to the Theology of Jonathan Edwards*, (Oxford: Oxford University Press, 1998); Amy Plantinga Pauw, *The Supreme Harmony of All: The Trinitarian Theology of Jonathan Edwards* (Grand Rapids, MI and Cambridge: Eerdmans, 2002); and Stephen M. Studebaker, "Jonathan Edwards's Social Augustinian Trinitarianism: An Alternative to a Recent Trend," *Scottish Journal of Theology 56*, (2003), pp. 268–85.

5 "Indeed, the fruitful tension between Enlightenment 'latitude' and Reformed traditionalism animated Edwards' entire career . . ." (Peter J. Thuesen, "Editor's Introduction," in *Works Vol. 26*, p. 3).

6 Edwards' first notebook entry on the Trinity refers to such criticism: "There has been much cry of late against saying one word, particularly about the Trinity. . . ." He then outlines an optimistic estimate of the doctrine's philosophic cogency: "I think that it is within the reach of naked reason to perceive certainly that there are three distinct in God, each of which is the same [God], three that must be distinct, really and truly distinct; but three, either distinct persons or properties or anything else; and that of these three, one is (more properly than anything else) begotten of the other, and that the third proceeds alike from both, and that the first neither is begotten nor proceeds" (Edwards, "Miscellany" 94, in *Works Vol. 13*, pp. 256–257).

7 Edwards, *Works Vol. 21*, p. 113; *Works Vol. 6*, p. 337. See Amy Plantinga Pauw, "'One Alone Cannot be Excellent': Edwards on Divine Simplicity," in Paul Helm and Oliver D. Crisp (eds.), *Jonathan Edwards: Philosophical Theologian* (Aldershot: Ashgate, 2003), pp. 115–25.

created the world "to communicate himself" to intelligent beings.[8] Also, at a time when the Deists (and others) were arguing endlessly for the sufficiency of human reason, communicativeness provided the basis for a compelling doctrine of divine revelation. In Edwards' communicative perspective, it was not that some formal knowledge of the Deity was the by-product of the Clockmaker's world machine; it was rather that the universe was designed expressly to be the vehicle of God's personal communication to men and angels. Thus, every aspect of reality—nature and history as well as Scripture—was infused with revelatory content and intended for joyful human appropriation. Moreover, as repetition *ad extra* of the eternal communication inside the Trinity, the content of revelation corresponds to God's own multidimensional sharing of knowledge, love, and joy. This multidimensionality was reflected in the nature of Edwards' work. Why, for instance, was the Northampton theologian so concerned with religious affections, not only in the famous book of that name but throughout his corpus? It was because in the midst of an age captivated by sterile Reason, Edwards believed that God communicates his love and joy as well as his knowledge, so that appropriate affections were as essential to authentic reception as correct beliefs.

To explore this theology, we should begin with the concept of communicativeness itself.[9] As a loose definition, communicativeness is the inclination (or disposition, in Edwards' terminology) to convey or transmit something of oneself. In Edwards' eighteenth century usage, one might "communicate" things like money or possessions as well as mere information; the language of military strategy still speaks of logistics supply routes as "lines of communication." Whether Edwards might have chosen a different term today is a moot point, but it is important to keep in mind that the potential content of communication was not limited to information. This is seen in how closely communicativeness is related to expansive Edwardsean concepts such as goodness, excellency, harmony, and beauty.[10] While Edwards sometimes uses these terms nearly synonymously in view of their inherent mutuality and other times uses them more precisely, communicativeness is perhaps best explained as the disposition continually

[8] This is the thesis of *The End for Which God Created the World.* This book was completed near the end of Edwards' life, but the main idea is found in his notebooks as early as "Miscellany" gg composed in April 1723, when he was 19 years old. See Thomas A. Schafer, "Editor's Introduction," in *Works Vol. 13*, p. 92.

[9] Edwards does not use the noun form of the word used here, "communicativeness." He does, however, use the verb "communicate" often and the adjective "communicative" not infrequently.

[10] The most important discussion of these terms occurs in "The Mind" entry 1, in *Works Vol. 6*, pp. 332–338.

arising in those who are good to share their own happy condition with others.[11] In any case, what is particularly significant for this study is that Edwards thought of communicativeness *as a divine attribute.*

Edwards sometimes took a fresh approach to aspects of the old Reformed orthodoxy, and one example would be in the area of divine attributes. A recent study has argued that Edwards inverted the long-standing privilege of simplicity (God is one) over triplicity (God is three) in theology proper.[12] It is questionable whether Edwards moved things to the opposite extreme, but there is little doubt that he wished to avoid the former imbalance.[13] Such a shift in emphasis, however, could hardly fail to have important implications for Edwards' understanding of divine attributes. Indeed, he thought it improper to posit real distinctions in God's character beyond the three persons:

> 'Tis evident that there are no more than these three really distinct in God: God, and his idea, and his love or delight. We can't conceive of any further real distinctions. If you say there is the power of God, I answer, the power of a being, even in creatures, is nothing distinct from the being itself, besides a mere relation to an effect. If you say there is the infiniteness, eternity, and immutability of God, they are mere modes or manners of existence. [. . .] there is no more than these three in God, but what even in creatures are nothing but the same with the very being, or only some mere modes or relations.[14]

It is important to recognize what Edwards is, and is not, saying. He is not denying the traditional divine attributes such as infinity, eternity, and immutability.[15] Rather, he wants to redress the priority that these attributes had accrued in the tradition by changing the language from terms that

[11] "These at first may appear to be entirely distinct things: but if we more closely consider the matter, they will all appear to be one thing" (Edwards, *The End for which God Created the World*, in *Works Vol. 8*, p. 527). Although written in a somewhat different context, these words give a sense of the ease, fully consistent with Trinitarianism, with which Edwards moved from distinction to ultimate unity among interrelated concepts.

[12] Amy Plantinga Pauw, "One Alone Cannot be Excellent: Edwards on Divine Simplicity," in Paul Helm and Oliver D. Crisp (eds.), *Jonathan Edwards: Philosophical Theologian* (Aldershot: Ashgate, 2003), pp. 115–125.

[13] Oliver D. Crisp, "Jonathan Edwards's God: The Trinity, Individuation and Divine Simplicity," in Bruce McCormack (ed.), *Engaging the Doctrine of God* (Grand Rapids: Baker Academic, 2008), pp. 83–103.

[14] "Miscellany" 259, in *Works Vol. 13*, p. 367.

[15] In another place, Edwards applies these very terms to God, but notice the grammar of this sentence "[I]t is evident, by both Scripture and reason, that God is infinitely, eternally, unchangeably, and independently *glorious and happy*" (Edwards, *Works Vol. 8*, p. 420). The philosophical attributes are not independent primary attributes but modify God's glory and happiness.

might imply primary existence to ". . . mere modes or manners of existence." Edwards insists that all that can be said to be truly distinct in God are the three persons, although we can yet speak in a secondary sense of their various characteristics as "modes or relations." If the Sabellian heresy thought of a unitary God and his unitary attributes as the "real" God and the three persons as mere modes, then Edwards is about as far away from this error as possible within the bounds of orthodoxy: the three persons of the Trinity are the real God, and the attributes are mere modes.[16]

Consistent with his rejection of tritheism no less than his distaste for the unwarranted priority assigned to divine simplicity, Edwards thinks that the character of God may be boiled down to one thing—goodness or glory—which may also be denominated by knowledge, love, and joy:[17]

> The whole of God's internal good or glory, is in these three things, viz. his infinite knowledge; his infinite virtue or holiness, and his infinite joy and happiness. Indeed there are a great many attributes in God, according to our way of conceiving or talking of them: but all may be reduced to these; or to the degree, circumstances and relations of these.[18]

"These three things" describe the shared "good or glory" of the Godhead but also indicate the diversity of the three Persons. For Edwards, the best way we can describe God is simply to restate in some way that he is Trinity. And as we shall see, it is precisely the threefold content of God's internal glory—knowledge, love, and joy—which constitutes the three elements or dimensions of God's communication to us.

With this introduction to Edwards' approach to attribute language, we are in a position to discuss communicativeness as a divine attribute. Beyond knowledge, love, and joy, Edwards leaves room for a "great many attributes" consisting of the "degree, circumstances and relations of these."[19] Communicativeness is one such attribute; as such, it describes the

[16] Oliver D. Crisp points out that Edwards' *a priori* argument for God in "Miscellany" 94 can actually be understood in a way that entails modalism. He also discusses Edwards' attribute language. See Crisp, "Jonathan Edwards's God: Trinity, Individuation, and Divine Simplicity," in Bruce L. McCormack (ed.), *Engaging the Doctrine of God: Contemporary Protestant Perspectives* (Grand Rapids, MI: Baker Academic and Rutherford House 2008, pp. 83–103).

[17] Much of *The End for Which God Created the World* is devoted to showing how God manifests in creation what he is in himself, and the Scriptures describe this summarily as being goodness or glory. Note also that in the *Nature of True Virtue*, Edwards thought that the nature of true "virtue" was holy "love," so that "virtue" and "love" become in this way functionally equivalent. See the whole of Edwards, *Works Vol. 8*.

[18] Edwards, *The End for Which God Created the World*, in *Works Vol. 8*, p. 528.

[19] Edwards, *The End for Which God Created the World*, in *Works Vol. 8*, p. 528.

overflowing and transmissional circumstances of God's knowledge, love, and joy. Observe how Edwards reasons from God's goodness to his plurality in "Miscellany" 96:

> It appears that there must be more than a unity in infinite and eternal essence, otherwise the goodness of God can have no perfect exercise. To be perfectly good is to incline to and delight in making another happy in the same proportion as it is happy itself, that is, to delight as much in *communicating* happiness to another as in enjoying of it himself, and an inclination to *communicate* all his happiness; it appears that this is perfect goodness, because goodness is delight in *communicating* happiness. Wherefore, if this goodness be perfect this delight must be perfect, because goodness and this delight are the same.[20]

We all know that God is good and that he must be so, but what exactly does that mean? Edwards thinks that to be perfectly good is "to incline to and delight in making another happy in the same proportion as it is happy itself, that is, to delight as much in *communicating* happiness to another as in enjoying of it himself." A unitary God would seem to have no means of exercising this inclination in eternity, and for this reason, "there must be more than a unity" in God. And the only "perfect exercise" of this inclination toward self-communication is "the Father's begetting of the Son," which "is a complete *communication* of all his happiness, and so an eternal, adequate, and infinite exercise of perfect goodness, that is completely equal to such an inclination in perfection."[21] Thus, God's goodness entails his communicativeness, and his communicativeness implies the plurality of the ontological Trinity.

III Creation and Redemption (Communicativeness *ad extra*)

What, then, does divine communicativeness mean for reality beyond eternal God himself? As previously mentioned, Edwards brings this understanding of God's nature to bear on the question of why God created the universe.[22] Though the mature formulation of his answer to this question would

[20] "Miscellany" 96, in *Works Vol. 13*, pp. 263–264; emphasis mine.
[21] "Miscellany" 104, in *Works Vol. 13*, p. 272.
[22] For a full discussion of this subject, see Stephen R. Holmes, *God of Grace and God of Glory: An Account of the Theology of Jonathan Edwards* (Edinburgh: T&T Clark, 2000), Chapter 2.

develop over time, the seed is clearly present in the early notebook entry that provides this study its title quotation, "Miscellany" 332:

> The great and universal end of God's creating the world was to *communicate* himself. *God is a communicative being.* This communication is really only to intelligent beings: the communication of himself to their understandings is his glory, and the communication of himself with respect to their wills, the enjoying faculty, is their happiness. God created the world for the shining forth of his excellency and for the flowing forth of his happiness. It don't make God the happier to be praised, but it is a becoming and condecent and worthy thing for infinite and supreme excellency to shine forth: 'tis not his happiness but his excellency so to do.[23]

This statement would make little sense if Edwards thought of God's communicativeness as merely economic.[24] In asserting that God is a communicative being, Edwards is referring to a logically and temporally prior theology whereby God is inherently communicative *ad intra* among the persons of the Godhead. It is this ontological theology that explains the existence of creation. As he makes explicit in a corollary to "Miscellany" 104, communicativeness is rightly understood as an essential attribute of God: ". . . for it is his essence to incline to communicate himself."[25] On this understanding, it makes perfect sense for Edwards to suppose that "The great and universal end of God's creating the world was to communicate himself"; God was continuing *ad extra* the communicative activity that is necessarily and eternally present *ad intra*.[26]

Notice also the emphasis Edwards places on the *intelligent* reception of God's communication. God could not truly communicate himself by the mere existence of a physical creation. "[H]is communication is really only to intelligent beings," so there must be creatures who have the capacity to know and understand God. Moreover, these intelligent creatures must have

[23] "Miscellany" 332, in *Works Vol. 13*, p. 410; emphasis mine.

[24] "The continuity of the immanent and economic Trinity is a hallmark of Edwards' theology" (Sang Hyun Lee, "Editor's Introduction," in *Works Vol. 20*, p. 31).

[25] Edwards, "Miscellany" 107[b], in *Works Vol. 13*, pp. 277–78. Whether there was any real disparity between essential and nonessential attributes in Edwards is doubtful, but his language here obviates any speculation regarding the propriety of describing his concept of communicativeness as an essential divine attribute.

[26] Edwards, "Miscellany" 332, in *Works Vol. 13*, p. 410. Edwards yet has the mighty task of explaining why the creation, though explained in terms of God's nature, is yet a non-necessary or voluntary action, a task undertaken in section IV of *The End for which God Created the World, in Works Vol. 8*, pp. 445–63.

"the enjoying faculty" or the capacity to enjoy God. Indeed, as Edwards makes very clear elsewhere, ". . . if there were not intelligent beings in the world, all the world would be without any end at all."[27] In Edwards' communicative theology, had there never been at least one angel or human who both knew *and* enjoyed God, all of created reality would have been without any purpose whatsoever. This teleology that entails the intelligent, joyful reception of divine communication will have wide-reaching implications for Edwards' project.

Consider the import of Edwards' distinction in the final sentence "'tis not his happiness but his excellency so to do." In this "Miscellany" entry, which would eventually feed into his full-scale treatise *The End for which God Created the World*, Edwards must avoid the basic error of making God somehow dependent upon his creation. God is a communicative being whether *ad intra* or *ad extra*, but the associated mode of this communication in these two cases must be somehow different. Hence the contrast between happiness and excellency. Happiness ". . . consists in the perception of these three things: of the consent of being to its own being; of its own consent to being; and of being's consent to being."[28] The happiness of Father, Son, and Holy Spirit entails that they be communicative one with another; they do so or they would not be God. God is communicative externally, however, in terms of "excellency." Edwards defines this term as "The consent of being to being, or being's consent to entity."[29] This definition of excellency seems to give little in way of meaningful differentiation from happiness, but judging from Edwards' usage, the nuance appears to be in terms of propriety and relative externality. Excellency can and perhaps *should* be seen from the outside: "it is a becoming and condecent and worthy thing for infinite and supreme excellency to shine forth."[30]

Edwards also saw the completeness of God's image being realized in the Son as a potential problem. If God the father had fully communicated everything he was to the Son, and thus had satisfied his disposition to communicate himself, what was left to explain creation? Edwards' solution is, "But yet the Son has also an inclination to communicate himself, in an image of his person that may partake of his happiness: and this was the end of the creation, even the communication of the

[27] Edwards, "Miscellany" gg, in *Works Vol. 13*, p. 185.
[28] Edwards, "The Mind" entry 1, in *Works Vol. 6*, p. 338.
[29] Edwards, "The Mind" entry 1, in *Works Vol. 6*, p. 336.
[30] Edwards, "Miscellany" 332, in *Works Vol. 13*, p. 410.

happiness of the Son of God."[31] The subject of the Son's desire to communicate himself was, of course, elect humanity who would bear his image.

With these potentially troublesome difficulties solved to his satisfaction, Edwards can answer the question he would pose many years later in *The End for Which God Created the World*: what moved God to create the world? Answer: a "disposition to communicate himself."[32] And it is this disposition that provides the basis for all revelation, both general and special. God's project is ever to communicate himself. He does this ontologically in his eternal Triune existence, and he continues this economically by also communicating himself to his intelligent creatures in creation and redemption. Just as this communication is ongoing throughout time, so are the works of creation and redemption. In polar opposition to deistic conceptions of a divine clockmaker setting things in motion and then absenting himself, Edwards believed in a *continuous* creation: "It [is] most agreeable to the Scripture, to suppose creation to be performed new every moment."[33] Of course, Edwards thought that that creation was not an end to itself but rather the backdrop for the even more glorious work of redemption.[34] Here again Edwards thought that this work was continuous, not only in relation to sanctification and glorification but also in what might otherwise be considered the momentary event of the second birth: ". . . a new work of creation [must be enacted] on every heart, and this power must be continued [as] a kind of continual creation."[35] This is not at all to imply that Edwards thought that justification was gradual, but only that the once-and-for-all action of God can never be detached from continuing divine agency. As we shall see in the next section, Edwards thought that all of reality is the ongoing communication of the divine mind; torn asunder from God, creation itself would fall into nothingness, and, it appears, so would twice-born saints. Thus, in Edwards' communicative theology, we have not only a continuous creation but also a continuous redemption.

[31] Edwards, "Miscellany" 104, in *Works Vol. 13*, p. 272.

[32] Edwards, *The End for which God Created the World*, in *Works Vol. 8*, p. 433.

[33] Edwards, "Miscellany" 346, in *Works Volume 13*, p. 418. Such a doctrine is entirely consistent with Edwards' radical anti-Deist agenda. See my "Rage against the Machine: Jonathan Edwards vs. The God of Deism," *Scottish Bulletin of Evangelical Theology* 25, no. 1 (2007), pp. 70–71.

[34] "It may be further argued that the creation of the visible world was in order to the work of redemption, that not only the things made so shadow forth things that appertain to this work, but the work of creation itself seems to be so done that it should shadow forth the work of redemption in the manner of doing of it" (Edwards, "Miscellany" 702, in *Works Vol. 18*, p. 284).

[35] Edwards, "Approaching the End of God's Grand Design," in *Works Vol. 25*, p. 126.

IV The Content of Divine Communication

For Edwards, the content of what God communicates to his intelligent beings is, ultimately, *himself.* Everything that angels and humans receive by divine revelation is first to be found in the eternal communication between the persons of the Godhead. And in Edwards' analysis, there is ultimately nothing in this eternal communication other than God's knowledge, love, and joy. This correlation between the intertrinitarian knowledge, love, and joy and the content of revelation is one that has far-reaching implications for Edwards' theology and work as a minister. Though the tridimensional conception of divine revelation as conveying noetic, affectional, and beatific elements is the most important implication, some others—such as the basic ideas of Edwards' metaphysics—likewise demand attention.

Edwards' philosophy is not a topic to be broached casually, but there is a foundational concept within it that provides the broadest possible metaphysical warrant for his theology of divine communication. As a rough sketch, Edwards formulated a Christian version of idealism that incorporated certain aspects of Locke as well as Malebranche.[36] In general agreement with Locke, he thought ". . . all existence is mental, that the existence of all exterior things is ideal."[37] But in failing to account for the real substance of these ideas, Locke's philosophy was found wanting by Edwards. In dramatic contrast to Locke's "I know not what," Edwards found the substance of the world of ideas directly in the Triune God's reflective knowledge of himself:[38]

> And indeed, the secret lies here: that which truly is the substance of all bodies is the infinitely exact and precise and perfectly stable idea in God's mind, together with his stable will that *the same shall gradually be communicated to us*, and to other minds, according to certain fixed and exact established methods and laws.[39]

[36] The genealogy of Edwards' philosophy has been debated. See, for example, Norman S. Fiering, "The Rationalist Foundations of Jonathan Edwards's Metaphysics," in Nathan O. Hatch and Harry S. Stout (eds.), *Jonathan Edwards and the American Experience* (New York and Oxford: Oxford University Press, 1988), pp. 73–101; Paul Copan, "Jonathan Edwards's Philosophical Influences: Lockean or Malebranchean?" *Journal of the Evangelical Theological Society* 44, no. 1 (2001), pp. 107–24; and William J. Danaher Jr., *The Trinitarian Ethics of Jonathan Edwards* (Louisville, KY and London: Westminster John Knox Press, 2004), pp. 19–26.

[37] Edwards, "The Mind" entry 9, in *Works Vol. 6*, p. 341.

[38] Locke, *Essay*, II.23.15.

[39] Edwards, *Works Vol. 6*, p. 344; emphasis mine.

This "secret" that the Unitarian Locke found so unreasonable[40] came quite naturally to the deeply Trinitarian Edwards, as it no doubt came to the Augustinian Catholic Malebranche.[41] All ideas have their origin and substance in God's idea he has of himself, which is indeed the second person of the Trinity.

It is important to recognize what this signal passage from "The Mind" quoted above means for Edwards' communicative theology. All reality resides in the divine mind, and there can be nothing in creation that did not come from, and forever remains grounded in, the Trinity. But this divine "idea" is "gradually *communicated* to us, and to other minds."[42] There is thus a real correlation between our knowledge and God's. The difference between our situation and God's at this point would seem merely to be that this divine idea is known immediately and comprehensively by God, whereas it is only gradually conveyed to our finite minds over the course of time "according to certain fixed and exact methods and laws."

However, Edwards elsewhere explains that the difference between our knowledge and God's knowledge is also beyond temporal finitude. This is found in an early "Miscellany" on the Trinity:

> The Almighty's knowledge is not so different from ours, but that ours is the image of [it]. It is by an idea, as ours is, only his [is] infinitely perfect. . . . None will suppose that God has any such ideas as we [have], that are only as it were the shadow of things and not the very things. We cannot suppose that God reflects on himself after the imperfect manner we reflect on things, for we can view nothing immediately.[43]

Unlike in the case of the Father begetting the Son, our ideas are not so perfect as to beget some ontologically real image of them. God's knowledge

[40] Edwards was familiar with Locke's *An Examination of P. Malebranche's Opinion of Seeing All Things in God*; see *Works Vol. 26*, p. 193. See also Charlotte Johnston, "Locke's Examination of Malebranche and John Norris," *Journal of the History of Ideas 19*, Oct 1958 pp. 551–58.

[41] While the personal religious views of John Locke are controversial, a conclusion that he was at least a Unitarian seems probable. See Victor Nuovo, "Locke's Theology"; and John Marshall, "Locke, Socinianism, 'Socinianism,' and Unitarianism," both in M. A. Stewart (ed.), *English Philosophy in the Age of Locke* (Oxford: Oxford University Press, 2000); Dewey D. Wallace, Jr., "Socinianism, Justification by Faith, and the Sources of John Locke's The Reasonableness of Christianity," *Journal of the History of Ideas*, Jan 1984, pp. 49–66; and Maurice Wiles, *Archetypal Heresy: Arianism Through the Centuries* (Oxford: Oxford University Press, 1996), Chapter 4.

[42] Edwards habitually includes the angels in his discussion of the human situation, often using the blanket term "intelligent creatures" to cover both. Here, "other minds" would seem to serve as the philosophic equivalent.

[43] Edwards, "Miscellany" 94, in *Works Vol. 13*, pp. 257–58.

is "by an idea" but one that is "infinitely perfect" and ours, quite simply, is not. For unlike God, "we can view nothing immediately." Edwards' statements on immediacy must be interpreted in terms of their specific context, but when he is writing with philosophic precision, he denies emphatically that we can have truly immediate knowledge.[44] What we have is, "as it were the shadow of things." Such a caveat would seem to preserve the creator–creature distinction endangered by the otherwise identical idea given to creatures in revelation.[45] This inherent restriction of creative minds to mediate knowledge also has important implications for the necessity of Christ as the mediator of divine communication.

The idea that our knowledge of God is ectypal of God's archetypal knowledge of himself is a fairly standard feature in the history of orthodox theology. Edwards' ontology was fully consistent with this theology when he said that the universe itself is nothing other than the ongoing realization of the divine idea.[46] Perhaps less standard, however, Edwards also held a fully consistent epistemology:

> Our perceptions, or ideas that we passively receive by our bodies, are communicated to us immediately by God while our minds are united to our bodies; but only we in some measure know the rule. We know that upon such alterations in our bodies there follow such ideas in the mind.[47]

Not only do our ideas necessarily originate from God's idea, they are also "immediately" communicated to us by God while our bodies "passively receive" them. Here "immediately" seems to mean that, despite appearances to the contrary, there is no real causation of our ideas through sensory input but only a concurrence according to God's "rule." In signature Edwardsean style, the counterpoint to Deist philosophy predicated on the autonomy of human reason and implying the epistemological dispensability of God, is utterly complete.[48] Far from being the epistemic masters of our

[44] See also Edwards, "Miscellany" 777, in *Works Vol. 18*, pp. 427–28.
[45] Edwards develops this reasoning in "Miscellany" 777, in *Works Vol. 18*, pp. 427–34.
[46] See above, and Edwards, "Of Being," in *Works Vol. 6*, p. 204. See also "Miscellany" 697, in *Works Vol. 18*, p. 282.
[47] Edwards, "The Mind" entry 3, in *Works Vol. 6*, p. 339.
[48] For Edwards' response to Deism, see Gerald R. McDermott, *Jonathan Edwards Confronts the Gods: Christian Theology, Enlightenment Religion, and Non-Christian Faiths* (Oxford and New York: Oxford University Press, 2000), and my "Rage Against the Machine: Jonathan Edwards vs. The God of Deism" *Scottish Bulletin of Evangelical Theology* 25, no. 1 (2007), pp. 61–79.

own universe, we are nothing more than the "passive" recipients of God's communication.[49]

With these philosophic parameters in mind, we consider the content of divine communication. Returning to Edwards' psychological model of the Trinity, the "idea" God is communicating is not at all something outside of or apart from God, but the Word of God himself:

> Again, that which is the express image of God, in which God enjoys infinite happiness, and is also the Word of God, is God's perfect idea of God. The Word of God, in its most proper meaning, is a transcript of the divine perfections. This Word is either the declared Word of God or the essential: the one is the copy of the divine perfections given to us, the other is the perfect transcript thereof in God's own mind.[50]

This "perfect idea" is identical with the Word of God, which is also the "transcript of the divine perfections." What is being communicated to intelligent beings is not just knowledge *about* God, but is in some way the Son of God himself. He is the transcript, the perfect representation of the divine perfections that God was disposed to share outside of himself. And this self-giving continues on for eternity, as more and more of the infinite "transcript" is read and understood by intelligent minds but never exhausted.[51]

In this sense, the incarnation was not the first time God shared his Son with humanity: the Son of God has been "gradually communicated to us" throughout all reality since the creation.[52] However, there were elements of God's communicative project that could come only with the incarnation. Edwards points to the unique revelatory role given to the incarnate Christ in terms of its inherent propriety:

> Who can be so properly appointed to be [the] revealer of God to the world, as that person who is God's own perfect idea or understanding of himself? Who can be so properly appointed to be the light by which God's glory shall appear to creatures, as he is that effulgence of his glory by

[49] In a manner somewhat akin to how God's sovereignty in salvation does not entail human inactivity in Reformed theology, the ultimate passivity in human reception of divine communication did not seem to restrict Edwards' activism in promoting the divine project of self-communication.

[50] Edwards, "Miscellany" 94, in *Works Vol. 13*, p. 259.

[51] See, for example, Paul Ramsay's discussion of the eternal state in Appendix III, entitled "Heaven is a Progressive State," in Edwards, *Works Vol. 8*, pp. 706–38.

[52] See Edwards, "Miscellany" 554, in *Works Vol. 18*, pp. 98–99.

> which he appears to himself? And this is intimated to us in the Scripture to be the reason why Christ is the light of the world and the revealer of God to men, because he is the image of God.[53]

Thus, in concert with the Reformed orthodox tradition, Christ is the "revealer of God to the world" as well as the content of that revelation.[54]

We have been focusing on God's communication of his knowledge as the Word, the Second Person. But as we have already mentioned, Edwards' theology of divine communication is fully Trinitarian. The same concept therefore applies to the communication of love: God communicates to humanity his Holy Spirit. In the context of discussing the *charismata*, Edwards explains that the Spirit gives more than mere gifts in the sense of detached entities:

> [When] the Spirit by his ordinary influences bestows saving grace, he therein imparts himself to the soul in his own holy nature; that nature on account of which he is so often called in Scripture the Holy Ghost, or the Holy Spirit. By his producing this effect the Spirit becomes an indwelling vital principle in the soul, and the subject becomes a spiritual being, denominated so from the Spirit of God which dwells in him and of whose nature he is a partaker [II Pet 1:4]. Yea, grace is as it were the holy nature of the Spirit of God imparted to the soul.[55]

Just as the believer does not get a detached word from God but the very Word, what is "imparted" to the believer spiritually is not mere gifts but the Holy Spirit himself. God's communication of his Triune self is necessarily multidimensional.

What, then, of the of the third Edwardsean component, God's goodness? If the communication of divine knowledge is particularly associated with the Son, and love with the Spirit, what of joy? Here things are not so neat. Edwards, for instance, will link the Son with God's "name" and the Spirit with God's "glory," but refrains from making any similar link for the First Person.[56] The fundamental problem is simply that the Father could never be communicated in the way that the Son and the Spirit are. Edwards was,

[53] Edwards, "Discourse on the Trinity," in *Works Vol. 21*, p. 121.
[54] See Richard Muller, "Christ—the Revelation or the Revealer? Brunner and Reformed Orthodoxy on the Doctrine of the Word of God," *Journal of the Evangelical Theological Society* 26, no. 3 (1983), p. 307.
[55] Edwards, *Works Vol. 8*, p. 158.
[56] Edwards, "Miscellany" 1084, in *Works Vol. 20*, p. 467; emphasis mine.

after all, an Augustinian, and his doctrine of the Trinity featured role diversity as well as ontological equality. In the case of the Father, this diversity is articulated in terms of authority: "... the Father [is] first in order, fountain of Godhead, sustains dignity of Deity, sends forth the other two. All is from him, all is in him originally."[57] As the Father is the "fountain of Godhead" he "sends forth the other two," while he ever remains the unsent one. Thus there are only two persons available to map onto the transmission of the three elements of Trinitarian revelation.

In light of these parameters, Edwards assigns the Spirit double duty:

> It may be thus expressed: the Son is the Deity generated by God's understanding, or having an idea of himself; the Holy Ghost is the divine essence flowing out, or breathed forth, in infinite love and delight. Or, which is the same, the Son is God's idea of himself, and the Spirit is God's love to and delight in himself.[58]

In this scheme, the Son communicates knowledge and the Spirit communicates both love and joy. However, it should also be noted that Edwards thought that the effective communication of ideas should cause the receiver to have affections corresponding to that idea: "For a very clear *idea* of sorrow, or joy, or any act, exercise or passion of the mind, is the very same thing in a degree existing in the mind that it is an idea of."[59] So if the idea of joy is clearly communicated to us, we are made joyful. In this way, it is possible that Edwards could have conceived of the Son as well as the Spirit as involved in communicating joy.

In any case, Edwards was certain that there were three aspects or dimensions of divine self-communication: knowledge, love, and joy. Edwards says this in various places and contexts, but the most comprehensive statement is no doubt to be found in *The End for which God Created the World*:

> As there is an infinite fullness of all possible good in God, a fullness of every perfection, of all excellency and beauty, and of infinite happiness. And as this fullness is capable of communication or emanation *ad extra*; so it seems a thing amiable and valuable in itself that it should be communicated or flow forth, that this infinite fountain of good should send forth abundant streams, that this infinite fountain of light should, diffusing

[57] Edwards, "Discourse on the Trinity," in *Works Vol. 21*, p. 143.
[58] Edwards, "Miscellany" 405, in *Works Vol. 13*, p. 468. See also Edwards, "Miscellany" 448, in *Works Vol. 13*, p. 495.
[59] Edwards, "Miscellany" 621, in *Works Vol. 18*, p. 152; emphasis mine.

its excellent fullness, pour forth light all around. . . . From this view it appears another way to be a thing in itself valuable, that there should be such things as the knowledge of God's glory in other beings, and an high esteem of it, love to it, and delight and complacence in it: this appears I say in another way, viz. as *these things are but the emanations of God's own knowledge, holiness and joy.*[60]

God possesses a fullness of "all possible good," and this fullness is "capable of communication or emanation." It is not necessary but rather "amiable and valuable" that such a communication might occur. The content of this communication is "God's own knowledge, holiness and joy."[61] Very much like the Trinity's eternal communication *ad intra*, the tridimensional content of revelation is "the knowledge of God's glory," "love to it," and "delight and complacence in it."

V The Manner of Divine Communication

We now consider the *manner* by which Edwards thought God communicates himself. Recall Edwards' psychological representation of the Trinity, consisting of the Father, the ontologically real idea of himself (the Son), and the love between them (the Holy Spirit). In a cognate way, the process of revelation consists of imparting God's idea to human persons, inculcating them with a love for this idea, and thereby bringing them into a joyful state approaching ever closer—but never fully attaining—to that of God. Such a process is characteristically tridimensional, consisting of interrelated noetic, affectional, and beatific elements.

Edwards establishes this analogy between God's glorious existence as Trinity and the process of God's glorification of himself in intelligent creation in "Miscellany" 448:

God is glorified within himself these two ways: (1) by appearing or being manifested to himself in his own perfect idea, or, in his Son, who is the brightness of his glory; (2) by enjoying and delighting in himself, by flowing forth in infinite love and delight towards himself, or, in his Holy Spirit. So God glorifies himself towards the creatures also two ways:

[60] Edwards, *The End for which God Created the World*, in *Works Vol. 8*, pp. 432–33; emphasis mine.

[61] Again, as shown in the next sentence quoted, "holiness" for Edwards is at least sometimes functionally equivalent to love.

> (1) by appearing to them, being manifested to their understandings; (2) in communicating himself to their hearts, and in their rejoicing and delighting in, and enjoying the manifestations which he makes of himself.[62]

Keeping in mind that the thesis of *The End For Which God Created the World* is that God's great "end" is self-glorification through self-communication, Edwards makes a significant statement when he says that this glorification comes about in parallel ways whether *ad extra* or *ad intra*. As "God is glorified within himself these two ways," so "God glorifies himself towards the creatures also two ways: (1) by appearing to them, being manifested to their understandings; (2) in communicating himself to their hearts, and in their rejoicing and delighting in, and enjoying the manifestations which he makes of himself. Thus, it is not merely the content of self-communication that is closely analogous to God's own eternal situation; it is also the manner by which this communication operates in elect creatures."

Moreover, Edwards makes it very clear that this communication involves emotive as well as rational involvement on the part of the recipient:

> God is glorified not only by his glory being seen, but by its being rejoiced in, when those that see it delight in it: God is more glorified than if they only see it; his glory is then received by the soul, both by the understanding and by the heart.[63]

Noetic and beatific elements are thus both indispensable to the communication of God's glory. God is glorified merely in being known but is "more glorified" in being delighted in. Indeed, Edwards concludes, "God made the world that he might [be] received both by the mind and the heart."[64]

The Trinitarian cooperation between noetic and affectional elements is highly useful for understanding the distinctive aspects of Edwards' theological project as well as his preaching.[65] The necessity of appropriate cooperation between knowledge and the affections is manifested implicitly throughout the corpus. This concept is, however, occasionally stated explicitly, as it is in this 1739 sermon on Hebrews 5:22:

[62] Edwards, "Miscellany" 448, in *Works Vol. 13*, p. 495.
[63] Edwards, "Miscellany" 448, in *Works Vol. 13*, p. 495.
[64] Edwards, "Miscellany" 448, in *Works Vol. 13*, p. 495.
[65] On Edwards' larger project, see below, Chapter 6. On Edwards' Trinitarian preaching, see Edwards, "Subjects to be Handled in the Treatise on the Mind," in *Works Vol. 6*, p. 388.

> No speech can be any means of grace, but by conveying knowledge . . . He that doth not understand, can receive no faith, nor any other grace; for God deals with man as with a rational creature; and when faith is in exercise, it is not about something he knows not what . . . So there can be no love without knowledge. It is not according to the nature of the human soul, to love an object which is entirely unknown.[66]

There is not much in Edwards' practical theology that is not summarized in the simple words, "there can be no love without knowledge." God's self-communication to us operates in parallel to the way that it does within the Trinity: God knows himself, and he loves what he knows. Likewise, when we come to know God, our "affections" are not something extraneous but indispensable elements in the process of God communicating himself to us. We must know God in order to love him, and if we know God, we should love him.

Edwards also conceived of God's revelatory project as *holistically* analogous to the Trinity. In a way perhaps suggested by Augustine's psychological "trinities" or possibly Mastricht's conception of the church's inclusion into the divine family, Edwards shows how God's self-communication to people results in something like a repetition of the Trinity *ad extra*:[67]

> As the Father loveth the Son as a communication of himself, as begotten in pursuance of his eternal inclination to communicate himself; so the Son of God loveth the church, or the saints, as the effect of his love and goodness, and natural inclination to communicate himself. In this also there is a trinity, an image of the eternal Trinity; wherein Christ is the everlasting father, and believers are his seed, and the Holy Spirit, or Comforter, is the third person in Christ, being his delight and love flowing out towards the church. In believers the Spirit and delight of God, being communicated unto them, flows out toward the Lord Jesus Christ.[68]

[66] Edwards, "The Importance and Advantage of a Thorough Knowledge of Divine Truth" sermon on Heb 5:12, in *Works Vol. 22*, p. 88.

[67] "Miscellany" 482, entitled "CONCERNING THE ECONOMY OF THE PERSONS OF THE TRINITY AND THE CHURCH'S COMMUNION WITH GOD," consists entirely of a reference to Mastricht, namely, "See Mastricht, Lib. II, cap. 24, § 11." Schafer explains, "In this chapter of the Theorectico-practica theologia, § 11, the Trinitarian 'oeconomia' is described after the analogy of a household: there is the Father's love of and delight in the Son, the Son's honoring of the Father, and the Spirit's searching of the deep things of both and glorifying of both. Of particular interest to JE was Mastricht's representation of God as having taken up the church into the 'communion' and 'society' of this family (p. 238)." (Schafer, editorial note in *Works Vol. 13*, p. 524 n.1)

[68] Edwards, "Miscellany" 104, in *Works Vol. 13*, pp. 273–74.

God is triune. Therefore, a real communication of God will image trinitarian life, including the all-important reality of three persons living in loving union. In Edwards' conception, God's communicative project to intelligent beings results in "... a trinity, an image of the eternal Trinity; wherein Christ is the everlasting father, and believers are his seed [the Son], and the Holy Spirit, or Comforter, is the third person in Christ." From this vantage point, Edwards' communicative theology/ecclesiology is a description of God's project to create through Christ, the church, and the Spirit an image of the Trinity.[69]

With this analogy in mind, we consider Edwards' concise—and somewhat provocative—statement of the end goal of the process of divine communication:

> There are many reasons to think that what God has in view, in an increasing communication of himself throughout eternity, is an increasing knowledge of God, love to him, and joy in him. And 'tis to be considered that the more those divine communications increase in the creature, *the more it becomes one with God.*[70]

God's communication to his elect creatures consists of God actually imparting himself to them, so that they know God, love him, and enjoy him in an eternally upward moving spiral. The product of this process is, according to Edwards, asymptotic union with God.[71]

VI The Medium and Media of Divine Communication

Because we are incapable of truly immediate knowledge, God makes use of *media* in his work of self-communication. In the chapters ahead, we shall focus on what are, in effect, the subordinate media of revelation, but we cannot lose sight of the priority Edwards' gives to Christ as the singular *medium* of divine communication. The great statement of this doctrine is in a late sermon, "Approaching the End of God's Grand Design":

> The one grand medium by which he glorifies himself in all is Jesus Christ, God-man ... 'Tis by this one grand medium that God communicates

[69] In other places, Edwards emphasizes the more ordinary language of the church being the *bride* of Christ rather than an image of the Trinity. See Edwards, "Approaching the End of God's Grand Design," in *Works Vol. 25*, p. 116.

[70] Edwards, *The End for Which God Created the World*, in *Works Vol. 8*, p. 443; emphasis mine.

[71] See also Walter Shultz, "Jonathan Edwards's End of Creation: An Exposition and Defense," *Journal of the Evangelical Theological Society* 49, no. 2 (2006), p. 255.

> himself to all his elect creatures in heaven and on earth: all fullness dwells [in Christ], a fullness not only to fill man but to fill angels . . . Jesus Christ, and that as God-man, is the grand medium by which God attains his end, both in communicating himself to the creatures and [in] glorifying himself by the creation.[72]

There are times in Edwards' writings in which he seems to speak of one of the subordinate media as being the central method of God's communication to humanity. Yet, this must be understood in light of the statement we have here: ultimately, Jesus Christ is the "one grand medium" of God's communicative project.

Underneath this grand medium, God employs three "means" or media: "revealed religion" or Scripture, "creation" or nature, and "providence" or history.[73] In Edwards' understanding as articulated in "Approaching the End," these are not ultimately detached from Christ himself but simply the modes of Christ's own revelation in space and time.[74] Again, the radical counterpoint to eighteenth century skeptical conceptions about the Bible, science, and history is discernable. However, rather than entering now into an abstracted discussion of these media, we shall simply conclude this outline of Edwards' core theology and proceed to explore how each of them functions in the middle four chapters of this book.

VII Conclusion

In this chapter, we have focused on Edwards' perspective on God as "a Communicative Being" both in terms of the doctrine of the Trinity and in terms of God's great project to communicate himself to elect creatures in love, knowledge, and joy. This communicative concept is the foundation of Edwards' distinctive theology and perhaps provided the inspiration for his own life's project in interpreting and conveying this communication. The middle chapters of this book explore nature, special revelation, and history as the media God uses to communicate himself in creation and redemption. In the next chapter, we explore how Edwards approached the medium of nature.

[72] Edwards, "Approaching the End of God's Grand Design," in *Works Vol. 25*, pp. 116–17.
[73] Edwards, "Miscellany" 706, in *Works Vol. 18*, p. 324.
[74] Edwards, "Approaching the End of God's Grand Design," in *Works Vol. 25*, pp. 113–26.

Chapter 2

Nature

"[I]ntelligent beings are created to be the consciousness of the universe, they that may perceive what God is and does."

—Jonathan Edwards, "Miscellany" 87[1]

I Introduction

Edwards' doctrine of God leads on directly to his interrelated doctrines of revelation and of creation. Consistent with his insight into God's communicative character, these doctrines were woven together in a theology of nature that explained not merely what the world was like but, more importantly, what it was *for*. For Edwards, creation was an intricate vehicle built by a communicative God to deliver divine revelation to intelligent beings:

> 'Tis most certain that if there were not intelligent beings in the world, all the world would be without any end at all . . . What would this vast universe of matter, placed in such excellent order and governed by such excellent rules, be good for, if there were no intelligence that could know anything of it? Wherefore it necessarily follows that intelligent beings are the end of the creation, that their end must be to behold and admire the doings of God, and magnify him for them, and to contemplate his glories in them . . . If it were not for men, this world would be altogether in vain, with all the curious workmanship of it and accoutrements about it.[2]

The universe exists for no other reason than to provide the means for God to communicate his own knowledge, love, and joy to angels and human

[1] Edwards, "Miscellany" 87, in *Works Vol. 13*, p. 252.
[2] Edwards, "Miscellany" gg, in *Works Vol. 13*, p. 185.

beings. This chapter explores the ways in which Edwards interpreted the creation as a medium of harmonious divine communication.

As with virtually everyone else of his day, Edwards was influenced by the Newtonian revolution then dominating the intellectual landscape. However, the metaphysical and theological implications of Newton's impressive scientific achievements were hotly contested. The Deists appropriated the new science to promote a mechanistic vision of reality in which the great Architect set in motion a maintenance-free world machine governed by impersonal laws of nature.[3] Edwards, guided by his conviction that the world was the ongoing communication of a personal God, could never cede this strategic territory to the enemy. In his own exegesis of nature Edwards showed how that, far from teaching Deism, science and philosophy actually confirmed orthodox Christian doctrine.

Because our own ideas about science in relation to Christianity are dominated by the recent history of mutual opposition and exclusion, it might be worthwhile to understand that Edwards' situation was different. Scientists were often devout Christian laymen if not clergymen, and clergymen were often competent amateur observers if not scientists.[4] That does not mean that they always integrated their science and their religion; even by the early eighteenth century, these were increasingly enterprises to be pursued separately.[5] Edwards, however, saw theology and science as utterly complementary elements of his unitary project to interpret the harmony of all reality.[6] There is nothing in the natural world that is without its significance, and it is the duty of human observers to recognize

[3] I am indebted here to Robert W. Jenson, ". . . the God of the eighteenth century's reception of Newton was an omniscient and omnipotent Engineer, who had fashioned a universal machine for his own pleasure and to be the maintenance-free mill of his blessings for others" (Robert W. Jenson, *America's Theologian: A Recommendation of Jonathan Edwards*. New York: Oxford University Press, 1988, p. 25). A similar idea has been recently expressed by John Carrick: "Just as, in the early twentieth century, Einstein's theory of relativity was misconstrued by the popular mind as justifying relativism, so, in the late seventeenth and early eighteenth centuries, Newton's confirmation of the Copernican system was misconstrued by certain minds as a confirmation of Deism" (John Carrick, *The Preaching of Jonathan Edwards*. Edinburgh: Banner of Truth, 2008. pp. 21–22).

[4] Colonial minister and theologian Cotton Mather, for example, was elected a Fellow of the Royal Society in 1726 for his work on small pox inoculation.

[5] Somewhat in contrast to the earlier days of the Royal Society, while the *Philosophical Transactions* of the first quarter of the eighteenth century feature numerous clergymen as authors, there are relatively few references to God or to divine causation.

[6] Anderson rightly notes that ". . . Edwards found no conflict between his scientific interests and his religious convictions and vocation, and his interest in science did not flag after his conversion. On the contrary, the major body of notes and discussions in 'Natural Philosophy' were written after his conversion, and he wrote the 'Spider' letter and began to plan his treatise at the very time that he was actively seeking a pulpit, during the summer and autumn of 1723" (Wallace E. Anderson, "Editor's Introduction," in *Works Vol. 6*, p. 37).

this meaning as completely as possible, using all the tools they have available.[7] For Edwards, these tools included observation, theorizing, and—far less familiar today—typological interpretation. Through these means, people are enabled to carry out their function as intelligent observers of the universe and, thereby, to fulfill the purpose of the communicative phenomena they observe.[8]

We shall discuss Edwards' thought in this area under the headings of science, "mysticism," and natural typology.[9] After discussing these aspects of nature in Edwards' writings, we shall briefly consider the larger issue of harmony in nature.

II Edwards as Scientist

Edwards labored under the limitations of early modern science and, in common with other scientists of his day, some of his observations and theories now appear untenable while others remain plausible.[10] Edwards showed enough aptitude in this discipline that his unfulfilled promise has been a source of regret for some nineteenth-century and early twentieth-century scholars.[11] However, Edwards was no more an abortive scientist than he was a failed psychologist or historian. These activities were all part of being an intelligent observer of God's works, and although he focused more on this discipline in his earlier years there was never any question of pursuing one of them to the exclusion of others. Edwards' purpose for the

[7] See, for example, Edwards, "Miscellany" 1218, in *Works Vol. 23*, p. 153.

[8] See Edwards, "Miscellany" 87, in *Works Vol. 13*, p. 252; and "The Great Concern of a Watchman for Souls," in *Works Vol. 25*, p. 66.

[9] Mystical is a concept having real continuity with Edwards' religious experience, yet one that also implies a religious epistemology that would be anathema to him. Therefore, "mystical" and its cognates will appear in quotation marks.

[10] Astronomer Edmund Halley, for instance, believed the earth consisted of three concentric hollow shells and a core each separated by an atmosphere, in order to explain observed magnetic anomalies. See Halley, "An Account of the Cause of the Change of the Variation of the Magnetic Needle with an Hypothesis of the Structure of the Internal Parts of the Earth," *Philosophical Transactions*, Vol. 16 (1692) pp. 563–578.

[11] "Critics filled with the spirit of modern positivism rashly declare that . . . he was a potential scientist thwarted by his environment and forced into the uncongenial wastes of theology." Perry Miller, *Jonathan Edwards* (New York: William Sloan Associates, 1949), p. 46. Clarence H. Faust cites Moses Coit Tyler and Carl Van Doren among such critics in Faust, "Jonathan Edwards as a Scientist," *American Literature* 1 (1930), p. 393. Clyde A. Holbrook adds Benjamin Silliman and Rufus Suter in Holbrook, "Jonathan Edwards and His Detractors," *Theology Today* 10 (1953), pp. 391–2. The estimation of Edwards' scientific potential began with Sereno Dwight: "Had his life been devoted to these pursuits . . . he would have met with no ordinary success, in extending the bounds of human knowledge in the most important and interesting fields of Physical Science" (Dwight, *Life of President Edwards*, in Edwards, *Works in Two Volumes* I, p. 54).

"Rational Account" project was to show ". . . how all arts and sciences, the more they are perfected, the more they issue in divinity, and coincide with it, and appear to be as parts of it."[12] Implicit even in this purpose, however, is the recognition that bare observation never stands alone but is capable of multiple readings. Edwards thought that materialist and mechanistic *interpretations* of scientific data were threatening to undermine true religion, and his scientific work should be understood as a self-conscious attempt to do the opposite.[13] His work as a scientist consists of some ambitious theoretical physics found in his notebooks and a couple of naturalist essays.[14] We begin with the latter.

a. Edwards as naturalist

The famous "Spider Letter," written by Edwards in 1723, was apparently intended for submission to the *Philosophical Transactions of the Royal Society.* [15] Frequent American correspondent to the Society Paul Dudley had recently included in his published correspondence an account of a remarkable pumpkin vine as related to him by Timothy Edwards. Dudley had given the elder Edwards an open invitation to tell him of other items of interest.[16] It was, however, the younger Edwards who took up the invitation, taking as his subject the amazing "flying" spider. It seems that Jonathan hoped not merely to have his observations included second hand in Dudley's next correspondence, but given the careful composition and plain intimations of the letter, to have his entire letter forwarded on for publication. This did not happen, probably because—unbeknownst to Edwards—someone else had already treated the subject, so the letter remained unpublished during his lifetime.[17]

[12] Edwards, "Preface to the Rational Account," in *Works Vol. 6*, p. 396.

[13] For the best statement of this issue, see Robert W. Jensen, *America's Theologian: A Recommendation of Jonathan Edwards* (Oxford: Oxford University Press, 1988), p. 27.

[14] "On Insects" covered the same ground, and fed directly into, the "Spider Letter."

[15] Edwards' first biographer, Sereno E. Dwight, proposed a pre-Yale matriculation date for the draft letter, or about age 13. This was followed by Egbert C. Smyth in "The Flying Spider—Observations by Jonathan Edwards when a Boy," *Andover Review* Vol. 13 pp. 5–13, and others up until Thomas A. Schafer's meticulous manuscript dating work cast doubt upon it and the discovery of the actual dated letter disproved it. See Anderson, *Works Vol.* 6, pp. 3 n.4, 6, 147.

[16] Edwards recounts this in the first line of his letter. See Edwards, The "Spider" Letter, *Works Vol. 6*, p. 163.

[17] The original letter bears the word "Lister" on it, apparently written by the recipient indicating that the English naturalist Martin Lister had earlier published three accounts of spiders in the *Philosophical Transactions* covering some of the same data, which probably explains why Edwards' letter was never published. Anderson, "Editor's Introduction" in *Works Vol. 6*, pp. 151–53. See also *Works Vol. 26*, p. 168.

Even if Edwards' idea had not already been taken, it is highly questionable whether the theologically charged "Spider Letter" would have been in step with the usual fare of the *Philosophical Transactions* even of that day.[18] Edwards begins conventionally enough with an account of his curiosity and his patient experimentation that enabled him to understand how spiders can "fly." Using colorful description aided by his own line drawing, he reveals the answer: the spider first lowers itself into the air by one line of its web and then issues a separate line that catches the wind like a sail. However, Edwards then moves on to less standard territory. He explains how the "flying" spider's amazing characteristics were intended to exhibit aspects of God's glorious character: "Hence the wisdom of the Creator in providing of the spider with that wonderful liquor with which their bottle tail is filled. . . ."[19] On the supposition that spiders take to the air simply for fun, Edwards adds "Hence the exuberant goodness of the Creator, who hath not only provided for all the necessities, but also for the pleasure and recreation of all sorts of creatures, even the insects."[20] Edwards closes the letter with the telling statement, "Pardon me if I thought it might at least give you occasion to make better observations on these wondrous animals, that should be worthy of *communicating* to the learned world, from whose glittering webs so much of the wisdom of the Creator shines."[21] This much is already more than enough to propel the "Spider Letter" to the top of the theological content charts for the *Transactions* of the time, had it been published. In the years 1720–1725, there are but four articles that make any reference to God at all, and only one that is at all comparable—an article written the previous year by the aforementioned Paul Dudley, which Edwards might well have taken as partial inspiration.[22]

[18] David S. Wilson is of the opinion that Edwards' paper was perfectly consonant with the science of his day. See Wilson, "The Flying Spider," *Journal of the History of Ideas* 32 (1971), pp. 447–58. Wilson does not give sufficient weight to the noticeable de-theological shift from the early years of the Society to the 1720s, nor to how Edwards' paper was significantly more theological (and more speculative) than its predecessors.

[19] Edwards, "The Spider Letter," in *Works Vol. 6*, p. 167.

[20] Edwards, "The Spider Letter," in *Works Vol. 6*, p. 167.

[21] Edwards, "The Spider Letter," in *Works Vol. 6*, p. 169; emphasis mine.

[22] "A Rattlesnake creeps with his Head close to the Ground, and is very slow in moving, so that a Man may easily get out of his Way: This ought to be remarked as an Instance of the Goodness of God, who preserves Man and Beast" (Paul Dudley, "An Account of the Rattlesnake," *Philosophical Transactions* Vol. 32 (1722–1723), p. 292). The most sustained interaction with theological material during this time is certainly Edmund Halley's "Some Considerations about the Cause of the Universal Deluge, laid Before the Royal Society on the 12th of December 1694," *Philosophical Transactions* Vol. 33 (1724–1725), pp. 118–123. However, not only was this a 30-year-old paper, but the reason for this belated publication was because Halley's conclusions were so heterodox—disregarding the specifics of the

However, Edwards does not stop here. He wants to know not only how, but also *why* the spiders fly.[23] In all of his writings, Edwards is preoccupied with searching out the purpose of things, and this was as true for individual natural phenomena as it was for acts of providence or the creation itself. Edwards once reminded his congregation that "The particular end and use of many of the works of creation are yet unknown, though the late searches of learned men into the works of nature have served to discover the wonderful wisdom of God in many things whose use was formerly wholly unknown . . . ."[24] This sermon was among Edwards' latter writings, but it explains rather well what he was doing many years earlier in the teleological speculation that forms the second half of the "Spider Letter": he was searching into the works of nature to find out their purpose, in order to "discover the wonderful wisdom of God."

What purpose, then, does Edwards propose that flying spiders serve in God's creation? "But yet, Sir, I am assured that the chief end"—notice the term— "of this faculty that is given them is not their recreation but their destruction . . ."[25] This is because, as Edwards relates, the prevailing winds always blow from the inland toward the sea, and so the majority of flying spiders must therefore end up in the ocean. This being the apparent case, what possible use might be their destruction?

> *Corol.* 1. Hence [there] is reason to admire at the wisdom of the Creator, and to be convinced that it is exercised about such little things in this wonderful contrivance of *annually carrying off and burying the corruption and nauseousness of the air,* of which flying insects are little collections, in the bottom of the ocean where it will do no harm; and especially the strange way of bringing this about in spiders, which are collections of these collections, their food being flying insects, flies being the poison of the air, and spiders being the poison of flies collected together.[26]

Genesis account as deficient tradition and advancing a theory about a preexisting world destroyed for our benefit, predicated on the mechanism of death—he was ". . . apprehensive that he might incur the Censure of the Sacred Order" ("Some Further Thoughts upon the same Subject," *Philosophical Transactions* Vol. 33 (1724–1725), p. 125). There is a reference to God as "Great Author" in Halley's 1720 paper "Some Remarks . . . on the Refraction of the Air" (Vol. 31 (1720–1721), p. 172), and there is only one passing reference to the divine among Leeuwenhoek's numerous papers during these years.

[23] Anderson thinks, "Edwards' primary and original concern was to discover the physical principles that would account for the flight of the wingless insect" (*Works Vol. 6*). I think Edwards' primary concern actually goes beyond this, however.

[24] Edwards, "Approaching the End of God's Grand Design," in *Works Vol. 25*, p. 114.

[25] Edwards, "The Spider Letter," in *Works Vol. 6*, p. 167.

[26] Edwards, "The Spider Letter," in *Works Vol. 6*, p. 167; emphasis mine.

Flying insects are "little collections" of the "poison" or "corruption" of the air? Spiders are "collections of these collections," designed by God to be blown into the sea every year? These are rather puzzling statements, and, perhaps understandably, there have not been many attempts to explain what Edwards might have meant.

However, let us just go on with Edwards for a little while longer. He reasons ". . . spiders and flies are such exceedingly multiplying creatures, that if [they carried on in some ordinary way] it would not be many years before we should be *plagued* with as vast numbers *as Egypt was.*"[27] This appears to indicate that Edwards' frame of reference was the plagues on Egypt found in Exodus, where we read "and there came a grievous swarm of flies into the house of Pharaoh, and into his servants' houses, and into all the land of Egypt: the land was corrupted by reason of the swarm of flies." (Exodus 8:24, KJV) No doubt this connection between flies and "corruption" in the Bible—apparently taken by Edwards to mean noxious vapors—was in some way confirmed by Edwards' observation. What exactly do flies eat but things that smelled bad, like manure and rotting carcasses? Since you are what you eat, they were thus "little collections" of the "corruption" of the air. And because spiders eat flies, they were "collections of these collections." Thus, the paper describes (brilliantly but somewhat mistakenly) God's amazing corruption removal system, consisting of flies and flying spiders being blown into the ocean every year.

We might note that even in the midst of a paper Edwards hoped to publish in a scientific journal, the influence of Scripture is conspicuous. Indeed, where might Edwards have gotten the idea that problematic flying insects are to be swept into the ocean? Quite possibly from another place in the Exodus account, where ". . . the LORD turned a mighty strong west wind, which took away the locusts, and cast them into the Red sea . . ." (Exodus 10:19, KJV).[28] If so, this early and largely unsuccessful attempt foreshadows later, more plausible efforts to integrate the media of revelation that were the output of Edwards' project to interpret the harmony of reality.

In any case, working from his speculation as to the useful purpose God might have in providing wingless insects the ability to fly, Edwards concludes,

[27] Edwards, "The Spider Letter," in *Works Vol. 6*, p. 168; emphasis mine.

[28] There are no Blank Bible entries on either of these passages in Exodus, but of course, Edwards did not yet have this book in his possession in 1723. He could have afterward annotated a reference to the "Spider Paper" at the relevant place as he often did, but this did not happen. Whether he simply neglected to do so, or more probably, had lost confidence in his youthful opinion, is unknown.

> *Corol.* 2. The wisdom of the Creator is also admirable in so nicely and mathematically adjusting their plastic nature, that notwithstanding their destruction by this means and the multitudes that are eaten by birds, that they do not decrease and so by little come to nothing; and in so adjusting their destruction to their multiplication they do neither increase, but taking one year with another, there is always an equal number of them.[29]

The world needs spiders, but neither too many nor too few of them, and so the Creator has devised the perfect means of maintaining the right population. God's goodness and wisdom are constantly on display in the theater of his creation.[30] Edwards thought that every significant detail was ". . . worthy of communicating to the learned world."[31]

Finally, the "Spider Letter" also includes the affectional dimension that Edwards was concerned to convey, in his science no less than in his preaching. It is not merely that God is good and wise, but that his goodness is "exuberant" and his wisdom is "admirable." This appreciation of what Edwards termed God's "excellency" was predicated upon "the new sense of the heart" given to the regenerate, but it demanded some object of God's universe, some content, to admire.[32] And it was this *affectional* appreciation of reality that was the ultimate goal of all God's revelation: God wants us to love him and enjoy him in his works. Likewise, affectional appreciation was the ultimate goal of Edwards' science.

b. Edwards as physicist

The bulk of Edwards' scientific work was actually in theoretical physics. While many American colonials of his time engaged in naturalist observations and applied science, Edwards was perhaps alone in his pursuit of this field.[33] Moving beyond the kind of indirect apologetic seen in the "Spider Letter,"

[29] Edwards, "The Spider Letter," in *Works Vol. 6*, pp. 168–69.

[30] This theme was very much present in the Reformed tradition, originating with Calvin. See Susan Schreiner, *The Theater of His Glory: Nature and the Natural Order in the Thought of John Calvin* (Grand Rapids, MI: Baker Academic, 2001).

[31] Edwards, "The Spider Letter," in *Works Vol. 6*, p. 169.

[32] See, for example, Perry Miller, "Jonathan Edwards on the Sense of the Heart," *Harvard Theological Review* 41 (1948), pp. 123–45; and William J. Wainwright, "Jonathan Edwards and the Sense of the Heart," *Faith and Philosophy* 7 (1990), pp. 43–62.

[33] "Edwards appears to be nearly unique among colonial scientists in the early eighteenth century, in that while their contributions were overwhelmingly in the fields of natural history, agriculture, and medicine, his primary interests and efforts were directed to problems in physics" (Anderson, "Editor's Introduction," in *Works Vol. 6*, p. 39). Anderson's assessment is readily confirmed as far as the contents of the *Philosophical Transactions* might indicate.

his physics were intended to formally disprove mechanistic conclusions as part of the planned "Rational Account." Yet Edwards' overall purpose in these labors remained the same—to exegete the physical universe in ways that would glorify the Creator, convey communicative truth to the reader and provoke the appropriate affectional response.

Beyond a foundation in Newtonian mechanics, the central component in Edwards' physics was atomism.[34] As derived from the theory of Henry More, Edwards' atoms were not the microcosmic solar systems of modern chemistry. Rather, they were defined as utterly solid, perfectly uniform, and simple units of matter. Edwards found in atomic theory a likely avenue to work against the prevailing mechanistic conceptions of nature he found to be so corrosive of orthodox theology, and thus counter to God's actual purposes in creation.[35] In his reasoning, atoms required constant, intelligent, and infinite power to keep them in existence and in functioning order: ". . . it is God himself, or the immediate exercise of his power, that keeps the parts of the atoms or two bodies touching . . . it follows that the constant exercise of the infinite power of God is necessary to preserve bodies in being."[36] Atoms were not self-existing mechanistic transferals of inertia but were necessarily the subject of God's direct and immediate action.

What specifically, then, did Edwards believe his atomic speculation could demonstrate about God? Consider a selection of his corollaries:

> '*Corol.* 4. Since, by the foregoing corollary, the exercising of the infinite power of God is necessary to keep the parts of atoms together, and since, by the first corollary of [Prop. 1], the dissolution of them would be annihilation, it follows that the constant exercise of the infinite power of God is necessary to preserve bodies in being.
>
> *Corol.* 15. Hence we see what's that we call the laws of nature in bodies, to wit: the stated methods of God's acting with respect to bodies, and the stated conditions of the alteration of the manner of his acting.
>
> *Corol.* 16. Hence we learn that *there is no such thing as mechanism*, if that word is taken to be that whereby bodies act each upon other, purely and properly by themselves.'[37]

[34] My discussion here follows Anderson, *Works Vol. 6*, pp. 44–45.

[35] "The contrasts between Edwards' early metaphysical conclusions and the claims of the materialists deserve careful study, not only because he himself often calls attention to them, but because he consciously undertook to develop a metaphysics that would be a conclusive answer to materialism" (Anderson, "Editor's Introduction," in *Works Vol. 6*, p. 54).

[36] Edwards, *Works Vol. 6*, p. 214.

[37] Edwards, *Works Vol. 6*, pp. 214, 216; emphasis mine.

In other words, if we reason rightly about nature, we will arrive at a conclusion precisely opposite of what Hobbes and many Deists thought. They imagined that science revealed a universe of autonomous machinery, operating independently and everlastingly according to fixed laws of nature such as inertia. As Edwards was acutely aware, this relegated God to the distant role of clockmaker. Edwards' retort was that atomic physics actually taught the precise opposite: the universe is the moment-by-moment display of God's "acting with respect to bodies." There is therefore "no such thing as mechanism." In the context of the milieu in which Edwards wrote, this was a hugely important statement to make.[38]

Even though Edwards emphatically denied pure "mechanism," he yet believed the universe was so minutely interconnected that one could extrapolate nearly everything merely from the data of any one atom:

> 'Tis only for want of sufficient accurateness, strength and comprehension of mind, that from the motion of any one particular atom we can't tell all that ever has been, [all] that now is in the whole extent of the creation (as to quantity of matter, figure, bulk and motion, distance), and everything that ever shall be. *Corol.* What room for improvement of reason is there, for angels and glorified minds![39]

Since everything in the universe impinges upon everything else through gravity in precise relationship to its mass and distance, we ought to be able to work backward from the track of a single atom through space—if only we had the infinitely improved powers of observation and reason needed to carry out the experiment. Characteristically for the tri-world thinker, Edwards' corollary for his scientific theory is something applicable ". . . for angels and glorified minds" in heaven. In any case, the thrust of his point illustrates how he conceived of nature as brimming with revelatory content waiting to be observed, interpreted and communicated.

[38] Among other aims accomplished by this maneuver, Edwards was concerned to stave off the inevitable ethical breakdown he saw implied by a mechanistic universe (see *The Nature of True Virtue*, in *Works Vol. 8*). Edwards' concerns were not entirely without cause: "Contemporary theories of human behavior have been fashioned after the deterministic model of classical physics in that human behavior is considered the product of antecedent events. Each psychological event is viewed as fully determined by its antecedent, in the same manner as physical events are by theirs. Under this view, it is entirely natural for a criminal to act as he does, since his criminality is a natural product of prior events. Punishment becomes inappropriate . . ." (G. Roy Sumpter, "Crime, Individual Culpability and Punishment," *Journal of the Evangelical Theological Society* (1973), pp. 223–27).

[39] Edwards, "Miscellany" 272, in *Works Vol. 13*, p. 374.

Incidentally, Edwards was not alone among the eighteenth-century philosophers either in his approach to physics or in some of his conclusions. The notion of extrapolating the past, present, and future of the universe from a single entity (whether an atom or a monad) is, for instance, also to be found in Leibniz's 1714 "Monadology":

> For everything has been regulated in things, once for all, with as much order and agreement as possible; the supreme wisdom and goodness cannot act except with perfect harmony. The present is great with the future; the future could be read in the past; the distant is expressed in the near. One could learn the beauty of the universe in each soul [dominant monad] if one could unravel all that is rolled up in it but that develops perceptibly only with time.[40]

We would forgive the reader if the statement "the supreme wisdom and goodness cannot act except with perfect harmony" were mistaken for a quote from Edwards. The two figures are certainly thinking along similar lines. Yet, it does not appear that Edwards had read Leibniz on this point; rather, it would seem that similar ideas about the nature of the universe led to similar conclusions.[41]

c. Edwards' approach to science

How did Edwards approach science in relation to the other media of divine revelation, particularly Scripture? One of the notes he made to himself on the cover-leaf of his early scientific notebook provides some candid insight:

> Lest I may mention a great many things, and places of Scripture, that the world will judge but frivolous reasons for the proof of what I drive at, not to mention such as I fear it of as what I depend on for proof, but to bring 'em in so that the force of reasons will naturally and unavoidably be brought to the mind of the reader.[42]

[40] Leibniz, "The Monadology" paragraph 13, in Leroy E. Loemaker (ed.), *Philosophical Papers and Letters* (Chicago: University of Chicago Press, 1956), p. 640.
[41] There is no indication that Edwards read Leibniz in his "Catalogues of Books," in *Works Vol. 26*.
[42] Edwards, "Cover-Leaf Memoranda," in *Works Vol. 6*, pp. 194–95.

Notice how far down the modernist road Edwards perceived the early eighteenth-century learned culture to be. He is concerned that "the world" will consider things such as Scriptural exegesis to be "frivolous reasons" for his theories. They might suspect ("as I fear it") that such things are what really stand behind Edwards' conclusions, implying that the culture would find this source of authority unconvincing. "The world" has some prejudices against biblical religion, but rather than a frontal attack Edwards wants to at least appear to play by their rules for a while. He does not share the anti-Scriptural bias of his audience, but he thinks he can win them over through the "force of reasons" that conform to their standards of rationality.

As Edwards apparently judged the situation, "the world" thought that the Bible was either inaccurate or merely irrelevant, but either way, to be excluded from the scientific and philosophical discussion. Religious bias, or any bias, was disallowed. Anderson warns us to be "wary of leaping to the conclusion that Edwards' scientific efforts were prejudiced by the doctrine of his Calvinist theology."[43] But I think we would have to say that it certainly was prejudiced—in Edwards' view, *correctly* prejudiced, but prejudiced nonetheless. Indeed, if the standard is disinterested, fully open-ended scientific observation, then Edwards' work would seem to be closer to the very opposite.[44] Now, we might just note that science itself has never really conformed to the ideals of disinterested and open-ended observation, as Kant would predict and as Kuhn has shown to in fact be the case.[45] But more importantly, Edwards' theology taught that all the media of revelation were inherently harmonious and coherent. Edwards thus believed that the study of nature would inevitably agree with the conclusions of theology derived from Biblical exegesis.[46] No doubt, Edwards' science in various ways confirmed what he already knew, if not in detail then at least in gist. As Perry Miller remarked in his inimitable style, ". . . Edwards went to nature and experience, not in search of the possible, but of the given, of that which cannot be controverted. . . ."[47] This assurance that everything would

[43] Anderson, "Editor's Introduction," in *Works Vol. 6*, p. 50.

[44] "The whole thing is to be something of a dialectical game, and the very first rule he registers is: 'Try not only to silence, but to gain.' This is hardly what we commonly think of the scientific attitude" (Clarence H. Faust, "Jonathan Edwards as a Scientist" *American Literature* 1, pp. 398–99).

[45] See Immanuel Kant, *The Critique of Pure Reason* (Cambridge: Cambridge University Press, 1998) and Thomas S. Kuhn, *The Structure of Scientific Revolutions* (Chicago: University of Chicago Press, 1962).

[46] Edwards thought that "... all arts and sciences, the more they are perfected, the more they issue in divinity, and coincide with it, and appear to be as parts of it" (Edwards, "Outline of a Rational Account," in *Works Vol. 6*, p. 397). See also Edwards, "Miscellany" 1, in *Works Vol. 13*, p. 197.

[47] Miller, *Jonathan Edwards*, p. 46.

harmonize does not, however, imply that Edwards could not engage in scientific observation; in theory, at least, the evidence would end up in the right place without any pressure.

Edwards did plan in his notebook to conceal his internal procedures from the audience of his science and to appear as if he were proceeding only according to the canons of secular Enlightenment rationality. Yet, we must keep in mind the fact that the early "Rational Account" project never saw the light of day. None of Edwards' published works actually follow such a procedure—indeed, almost all of the published works contain an explicit prior commitment to Scripture—and thus it seems that he must have decided against this possibility.[48]

Finally, Edwards' approach to science did not in any case revolve around the mere quest for information. Edwards thought that the best use of science issues not only in statements of fact, but also in an appreciation of God's glory as displayed in the given phenomenon. Thus the aim of natural science is not to learn new things for their own sake, nor even to improve our lives through practical advances; but in keeping with the "end" of creation, it is to promote our knowing, loving, and joyful worship of the Creator.

III Edwards as "Mystic"

We turn now to Edwards' reflections on nature as the "mystical" or direct apprehension of the divine.[49] By this we mean the experience of nature, not as interpreted by rational reflection (as in science), nor as interpreted as types for something else (as in typology), but as a relatively immediate communication of God's presence and nature.[50] The "Personal Narrative" contains an account of Edwards' postconversion experience that bears some resemblance to classical mysticism, in that Edwards perceived God's presence and attributes through natural phenomena and responded with the appropriately delightful affections. However, the "Narrative" also makes clear that such an experience is available only to regenerate minds looking

[48] An example of this occurs in the conclusion to Edwards' formidable *Freedom of the Will*, where, after demonstrating the incoherence of the Arminian position on philosophical grounds, he underscores his prior commitment to Scriptural evidence. See Edwards, *Freedom of the Will*, in *Works Vol. 1*.

[49] I again note that the term denotes a kind of experience that is basically consonant with Edwards' situation but also implies a religious epistemology that is not, so "mystic" appears in quotation marks.

[50] Edwards does not think there is any truly immediate (nonmediated) apprehension of God. See Edwards, "Miscellany" 777, in *Works Vol. 18*, pp. 427–34.

at nature through the perfect lens of Scripture. Similarly, Edwards also displayed a certain affinity with the American Romantic tradition that, on closer examination, turns out to be more formal than real. However, while Edwards was neither a mystic nor a Romantic, his theology perhaps addresses some legitimate concerns that were operative in these schools.

Let us quote at length the most sustained example of this genre in Edwards' corpus, the "Personal Narrative."[51] Here, Edwards is recounting his experiences just after his conversion:

> And when the discourse was ended, I walked abroad alone, in a solitary place in my father's pasture, for contemplation. And as I was walking there, and looked up on the sky and clouds; there came into my mind, a sweet sense of the glorious majesty and grace of God, that I know not how to express. I seemed to see them both in a sweet conjunction: majesty and meekness joined together: it was a sweet and gentle, and holy majesty; and also a majestic meekness; an awful sweetness; a high, and great, and holy gentleness . . . God's excellency, his wisdom, his purity and love, seemed to appear in everything; in the sun, moon and stars; in the clouds, and blue sky; in the grass, flowers, trees; in the water, and all nature; which used greatly to fix my mind. I often used to sit and view the moon, for a long time; and so in the daytime, spent much time in viewing the clouds and sky, to behold the sweet glory of God in these things: in the meantime, singing forth with a low voice, my contemplations of the Creator and Redeemer. And scarce anything, among all the works of nature, was so sweet to me as thunder and lighting . . . I felt God at the first appearance of a thunderstorm. And used to take the opportunity at such times, to fix myself to view the clouds, and see the lightnings play, and hear the majestic and awful voice of God's thunder: which often times was exceeding entertaining, leading me to sweet contemplations of my great and glorious God.[52]

Notice first of all the *novelty* of the experience. This was obviously not the first time that Edwards had seen the sun or the clouds in the sky. But now, under the power of supernatural regeneration, the appearance of these things was greatly "altered." Edwards now had the ability to perceive

[51] See the discussion on the reliability and theological usefulness of the "Personal Narrative" below in Chapter 6. In sum, the "Narrative" can, at the very least, be taken to provide an account of what Edwards thought *should* happen to the regenerate and is therefore of great theological significance.

[52] Edwards, "Personal Narrative," in *Works Vol. 16*, pp. 793–94.

something that was always there but left unappreciated: the communication of God's glory in nature. And moreover, this ". . . sense of divine things gradually increased." God is gradually removing the scales from his eyes to permit a progressively greater comprehension of the revelatory content in nature.

Then there is the *ineffability* of the affectional content of the experience. He was taking in things that, at one level, he knew ". . . not how to express." It would seem to be a common feature of mystical experience that certain aspects of the communication are simply beyond the capacity of human language.[53] One must add immediately, however, that Edwards has just said virtually the same thing regarding his experience reading the Bible: "The whole book of Canticles used to be pleasant to me, and I used to be much in reading it, about that time; and found from time to time an inward sweetness, that would carry me away in my contemplations. This I know not how to express."[54] So ineffability is not something belonging to natural revelation as inherently inarticulate; it is rather indicative of the overwhelming affectional response that comes with the experience, whatever the media.

On the other hand, there is also the *intelligibility* of the experience. Edwards may not have been able to explain everything precisely, but there was enough there for him to make an attempt: "I seemed to see them both in a sweet conjunction: majesty and meekness joined together: it was a sweet and gentle, and holy majesty; and also a majestic meekness; an awful sweetness; a high, and great, and holy gentleness." Even so, his description mingles affectional and noetic attributes that do not seem to go together, an example perhaps of why Edwards could never have been satisfied with an understanding of revelation that did not account for this Trinitarian complexity.[55]

Read in isolation, Edwards' "Personal Narrative" could sound almost like Romantic poetry. Indeed, the possibility of Edwards either influencing or partially anticipating the American Transcendental movement has occurred to some scholars.[56] But would Edwards really have been at home at Thoreau's Walden Pond? For a small sampling of the Transcendentalist agenda,

[53] See, for example, St. Teresa: "But as to what I then felt, I do not know where to begin, if I were to describe it; it is utterly inexplicable . . . I cannot see how it is possible to describe it." St. Teresa, "A Vision of Hell," in Paul De Jaehger (ed.), *An Anthology of Mysticism*, (London: Burns & Oates, 1977), p. 85.

[54] Edwards, "Personal Narrative," in *Works Vol. 16*, p. 793.

[55] Such a statement, while superficially reconcilable with Avihu Zakai's interpretation of Edwards having a *theologia gloriae*, would seem at another level to accord with a *theologia crucis*. See Zakai, *Jonathan Edwards's Philosophy of History: The Reenchantment of the World in the Age of Enlightenment* (Princeton, NJ: Princeton University Press, 2003), p. 72.

[56] See, for instance, Perry Miller, "Jonathan Edwards to Emerson," *The England Quarterly*, Vol. 13 no. 4 (Dec 1940), pp. 589–617.

consider this emblematic sentence from Emerson's famous Divinity School address: "But now the priest's Sabbath *has lost the splendor of nature*; it is unlovely; we are glad when it is done; we can make, we do make, even sitting in our pews, a far better, holier, sweeter, for ourselves."[57] We find in these sentiments both continuity and discontinuity with Edwards. Emerson, reacting against the sterility of the same formalist, rationalist religion that Edwards himself opposed, wanted to reestablish the individual, personal connection with the divine through the contemplation of nature.[58] Such sentiments would find some degree of resonance with Edwards' "Personal Narrative," and Edwards would be sympathetic to Emerson's aesthetic categories. At a deeper level, however, Transcendentalism was itself a continuation of the larger Enlightenment project Edwards fought so fiercely against: the project of putting the individual human at the center of the universe, though now in the guise of the mystic rather than of the rationalist. As Emerson put it, "Man is the wonderworker. He is seen amid miracles."[59] It is clear that this direction is something Edwards would have rejected out of hand; his experiences of nature are radically theocentric.[60] Thus, rather than any real anticipation, Harold P. Simonson has rightly concluded that there was actually an antithesis between Edwards' Christianity and Emerson's "romantic mysticism" vying for predominance in the nineteenth-century American soul.[61] One can only lament the fact that the stuffy formalism passing for Christianity against which Emerson framed his attack had not been more indelibly marked by Jonathan Edwards' own balanced approach.

Before we leave this subject, we might say a brief word on the larger subject of mystical tendencies in Edwards. Going back to Victorian biographer of Edwards A. V. G. Allen, interpreters have seen a strain of "intuitive mysticism" in Edwards' religious epistemology, whereby "all who accept the truth, that divine things are known to be divine because humanity is endowed with the gift of direct vision into divinity, are accepting what

[57] Ralph Waldo Emerson, *Divinity School Address* 1838 [cited 8 Mar 2010], available from http://www.emersoncentral.com/divaddr.htm; emphasis mine.

[58] "Whenever the pulpit is usurped by a formalist, then is the worshipper defrauded and disconsolate" (Emerson, *Divinity School Address* 1838 [cited 8 Mar 2010], available from http://www.emersoncentral.com/divaddr.htm).

[59] Emerson, *Divinity School Address* 1838 [cited 8 Mar 2010], available from http://www.emersoncentral.com/divaddr.htm.

[60] Edwards' theocentricity is the specific thesis of Michael J. McClymond's *Encounters with God: An Approach to the Theology of Jonathan Edwards* (Oxford: Oxford University Press, 1998) but is assumed in many places throughout the literature.

[61] See Harold P. Simonson, *Radical Discontinuities: American Romanticism and Christian Consciousness* (Madison, NJ: Fairleigh Dickinson University Press, 1983).

Edwards proclaimed."[62] And going back to Clyde Holbrook, others have pointed out that such tendencies must be understood only in light of everything else Edwards said.[63] More recently, Sang Hyun Lee has given us a concise statement of the correct understanding of Edwards' "mysticism":

> The new 'sensible knowledge' that the Holy Spirit makes possible is not some new information separate from the human words in Scripture but rather a new apprehension of what already was in Scripture. Finite, creaturely ideas, including concrete ideas of the physical universe, are all necessary 'stuff' in and through which the transcendent is experienced and known . . . . Edwards is not a 'mystic,' if the term denote one who contends that the true knowledge of ultimate reality involves a departure from the sensible and mundane.[64]

There is nothing out there in "mystical" experience, of nature or of anything else, that is "new information" beyond Scripture. For Edwards, there are no direct visions of God. Edwards' apprehension of the divine in nature is rooted precisely in the sensible experience of a "mundane" universe inherently embedded with God's self-communication.[65]

In summary, the *Personal Narrative* provides a portrait of Edwards' use of nature in the "mystical" mode. Like all other media of divine revelation, there is objective content waiting to be apprehended by the regenerate observer. This content is ineffable in some respects but is yet intelligible. And although Edwards' theology of revelation indeed made room for the main things the mystically inclined would like to affirm, particularly by paying attention to nature and to the affections, his stress on Trinitarian harmony (authoritative unity as well as diversity) throughout the media of revelation had the effect of reigning in the potential imbalances.

IV Nature as Types

While the "Personal Narrative" was a later retelling of an early experience, and the scientific notebooks were all written early on, Edwards' use of

[62] Clyde A. Holbrook, "Jonathan Edwards and His Detractors," *Theology Today* 10 (1953), p. 391. See also Alexander V. G. Allen, *Jonathan Edwards* (Edinburgh: T&T Clark, 1889).

[63] Clyde A. Holbrook, "Jonathan Edwards and His Detractors," *Theology Today* 10 (1953), p. 391.

[64] Sang Hyun Lee, "God's Relation to the World," in Sang Hyun Lee (ed.), *The Princeton Companion to Jonathan Edwards* (Princeton and Oxford: Princeton University Press, 2005), p. 69.

[65] Of course, Edwards thought that our ideas were in any case communicated to us by God "immediately," but that sensible reality concurred with our ideas. See above, Chapter 1.

natural typology was a constant feature throughout his works. For Edwards, "types" such as the Sun were not merely convenient illustrations, but contrivances created by God for the very purpose of pointing to their antitype, primarily Christ. In fact, Edwards thought that one could learn the principles established by Scripture for understanding natural types—the very "language of God"—and thus become enabled to interpret virtually any aspect of nature as a semiotic message conveying divine revelation.[66] No new truth unheard of in Scripture would be discovered by doing this; the sun, for instance, would not reveal to us a new Christology. However, thinking of the sun as a Christological type might enable us both to see and to *feel* in a new way the old truth of Christ being the source of all goodness.

Typology was once regarded—when it was considered at all—as an arcane hermeneutic connected with allegorical interpretation, lying alongside it in deserved obscurity. But as Hans Frei reminds us, typology is actually ". . . a natural extension of literal interpretation" and a tool that once dominated orthodox hermeneutics.[67] Typology was particularly important to Edwards, and accordingly, there has arisen a host of fairly recent scholarship dealing with this subject.[68] The native province of typology was in the Christian interpretation of the Old Testament, where it identified various cultic elements as intentional "types" pointing to Christ or other "antitypes." However, "In Edwards' hands . . . typology took on a broadened significance that comprehended not only Scripture but also nature and history."[69] While it is unclear as to exactly how much an innovation Edwards' use of typology really comprised, Anderson and others believe that Edwards knowingly

[66] See Stephen Daniel, *The Philosophy of Jonathan Edwards: A Study in Divine Semiotics* (Bloomington, IN: Indiana University Press, 1994).

[67] Hans W. Frei, *The Eclipse of Biblical Narrative: A Study in Eighteenth and Nineteenth Century Hermeneutics* (New Haven and London: Yale University Press, 1974), p. 2.

[68] See, for example, Conrad Cherry, "Symbols of Spiritual Truth: Jonathan Edwards as Biblical Interpreter," *Interpretation* 39, no. JI (1985), pp. 263–71; Nelson D. Kloosterman, "The Use of Typology in Post-Canonical Salvation History: An Orientation to Jonathan Edwards' *A History of the Work of Redemption*," *Mid-America Journal of Theology* 14 (2003), pp. 59–96; Janice Knight, "Learning the Language of God: Jonathan Edwards and the Typology of Nature," *William and Mary Quarterly* 48 (1991), pp. 531–51; Mason I. Lowance, "Images or Shadows of Divine Things: The Typology of Jonathan Edwards," *Early American Literature* 5, no. 1 (1970), pp. 141–81; Kenneth P. Minkema, "The Other Unfinished 'Great Work': Jonathan Edwards, Messianic Prophecy, And 'The Harmony of the Old and New Testament,'" in *Jonathan Edwards's Writings: Text, Context, Interpretation* (Bloomington, IN: Indiana University Press, 1996) pp. 52–65; and William J. Wainwright, "Jonathan Edwards and the Language of God," *Journal of the American Academy of Religion* 48, no. D (1980), pp. 519–30.

[69] Anderson, "Editor's Introduction," in *Works Vol. 11*, p. 3.

departed from the mainstream of his tradition by finding types in natural phenomena not explicitly identified as such in Scripture.[70]

Edwards' formulated his robust approach to typology early on in his career, in "Miscellany" 362:

> For indeed the whole outward creation, which is but the shadows of beings, is so made as to represent spiritual things. It might be demonstrated by the wonderful agreement in thousands of things, much of the same kind as is between the types of the Old Testament and their antitypes, and by spiritual things being so often and continually compared with them in the Word of God. And it's agreeable to God's wisdom that it should be so, that the inferior and shadowy parts of his works should be made to represent those things that are more real and excellent, spiritual and divine, to represent the things that immediately concern himself and the highest parts of his work.[71]

Consider the import of Edwards' claims here. We are not merely permitted to find in nature the occasional sermon illustration. No, *all of nature* is nothing less than God's intentional representation of spiritual reality. Notice also the "wonderful agreement" between type and antitype, which reminds us of why Edwards was so drawn to the use of typology. Typological exegesis of nature, as was the case with Scripture and history, allowed Edwards to interpret the beautiful, Trinitarian harmony he believed permeates all reality. Finally, we see something of Edwards' ontological hierarchy, whereby spiritual things are what is "real" and are represented by the "shadowy" physical creation.

Edwards devoted a sizable notebook exclusively to types in nature.[72] Immediately before the first entry in this notebook, Edwards places the reminder: "Under the head of Creation." Given Edwards' usual care in organization, it is significant that he thought of his catalogue of natural types as a subheading under the doctrine of creation. This is further confirmation of how his typology was no accidental feature but one fully integrated into his doctrine of creation. His "Types" notebook, the fascinating details of

[70] Anderson holds this view despite his familiarity with Cotton Mather, whose *Agricola* (1727) might seem to constitute a precedent for Edwards' typology. Anderson's case rests upon his distinction between the *metaphorical* usage allowed by Mather and others for phenomena not designated as types in Scripture and Edwards' explicitly *typological* usage, and upon Edwards' careful defense of his typology from presumed detractors in the "Types" notebook. See Anderson, "Editor's Introduction," in *Works Vol. 11*, pp. 6–33.

[71] Edwards, "Miscellany" 362, in *Works Vol. 13*, p. 434.

[72] See Edwards, "Types" notebook, in *Works Vol. 11*.

which unfortunately shall not detain us here, represents the outworking of a doctrine of creation in which material things exist only to serve as revelatory media in God's project of self-revelation. Specific phenomena were thus always pregnant with meaning. As William J. Wainwright put it, "A world in which things resemble one another, in which lower species imitate higher species, and the physical shadows forth the moral, is the sort of world in which types and emblems are to be expected."[73] In brief, Edwards thought that the entire creation was embedded with typological meaning waiting to be interpreted by those who had learned the "language of God."

V The Harmony of Nature

At this point, we pause to consider the Edwardsean concept that holds great significance for this study as a whole: harmony. Edwards describes the essence of divine beauty or "excellency" as consisting in symmetry, mutual agreement, or, more comprehensively, "harmony."[74] Harmonies may be simple or complex, physical or spiritual, but the paradigm of harmony is to be found ". . . among the persons of the Trinity, the supreme harmony of all."[75] As the manifestation of Trinitarian communication, the physical universe exhibits harmony throughout but is particularly illustrated on the macroscopic scale by our solar system:

> The beauty of the world consists wholly of sweet mutual consents, either within itself, or with the Supreme Being. [. . .] This beauty is peculiar to natural things, it surpassing the art of man. Thus there is the resemblance of a decent trust, dependence and acknowledgment in the planets continually moving round the sun, receiving his influences by which they are made happy, bright and beautiful, a decent attendance in the secondary planets, an image of majesty, power, glory and beneficence in the sun in the midst of all.[76]

Edwards' description of "the beauty of the world" explains how harmony operates at a couple of levels. At one level, the world is simply beautiful because of the symmetries "within itself." At another, there is an agreement

[73] William J. Wainwright, "Jonathan Edwards and the Language of God," *Journal of the American Academy of Religion* 48 (1980), p. 522.
[74] See Edwards, "The Mind" entry 1, in *Works Vol. 6*, pp. 332–38.
[75] Edwards, "Miscellany" 182, in *Works Vol. 13*, pp. 328–29.
[76] Edwards, "Beauty of the World," in *Works Vol. 6*, p. 305.

with spiritual things that surpasses "the art of man," seen in how the planets are made "bright and beautiful" by their faithful revolving around the sun.

Edwards thought that beholding the beauty of the natural universe would naturally lead one to recognize the spiritual beauty of its creator:

> When we see beautiful airs of look and gesture, we naturally think the mind that resides within is beautiful. We have all the same, and more, reason to conclude the spiritual beauty of Christ from the beauty of the world; for all the beauties of the universe so as immediately result from the efficiency of Christ, as a cast of an eye or a smile of the countenance depends on the efficiency of the human soul.[77]

Just as a beautiful countenance leads one to believe that there is a beautiful mind behind it, so a beautiful universe should lead one to think about the "spiritual beauty of Christ" who stands behind it. There is therefore immense theological and apologetic potential in demonstrating the beauty or harmony in nature. Edwards leveraged this potential in his scientific work, seeking "To shew how all nature consists in things being precisely according to strict rules of justice and *harmony*."[78]

I will soon enough point out how Edwards responded negatively to Locke's philosophy and theology on points he thought to be problematic for the biblical faith. But at least in formal terms, the two figures had much in common regarding the harmony in nature:

> And when we consider the infinite Power and Wisdom of the Maker, we have reason to think, that it is suitable to the magnificent Harmony of the Universe, and the great Design and infinite Goodness of the Architect, that the Species of Creatures should also, by gentle degrees, ascend upward from us towards his infinite Perfection, as we see they gradually descend from us downwards . . .[79]

The great philosopher and the young Jonathan Edwards were entirely convinced that there was harmony in the universe. The subtle but significant difference was that Locke saw this harmony as reflecting the "great Design and infinite Goodness" of the (unitary) "Architect," whereas Edwards saw the "spiritual beauty" stemming from the "immediate efficacy" of the Son of God.

[77] Edwards, "Miscellany" 185, in *Works Vol. 13*, p. 330; emphasis mine.
[78] Edwards, "Things to be Considered" (Long Series) entry 15, in *Works Vol. 6*, p. 231.
[79] Locke, *Essay*, III.6.12.

VI Conclusion

Edwards mined the natural creation for revelatory treasure. He did so in ways that could only offend modern sensibilities—using his science as a vehicle to demonstrate what he already knew and declaring that the deeper purpose of every feature in this "material" world was to exhibit Trinitarian harmony and/or to serve as a type of the spiritual realm. And to a degree that might seem a bit excessive even to the contemporary incumbents of his ecclesiastical tradition, Edwards made the Psalmist's musings on the heavens declaring the glory of God his own vivid experience.

The profound aspect of Edwards' thought on natural revelation, however, was not in what he thought nature could give us notionally. When Christians behold nature, joyfully recognizing the work of God in all its glorious detail, they act in fulfillment of the very reason for the existence of the universe. There are no new notional propositions to be found in nature. Yet, Edwards teaches that the active appreciation of nature by believers is an important aspect of the Christian life. Without this doxological participation, Christians as God's intelligent worshippers and the creation as God's communication both fall short of their divinely ordained purpose. This teaching was of course part and parcel of Edwards' larger theology of revelation, wherein all reality serves as the noetic, affectional, and beatific communication of God to intelligent creatures. We turn now to investigate more fully the intersection of nature and Scripture, and particularly Edwards' arguments for the necessity of special revelation.

Chapter 3

Special Revelation

"And therefore we stand in the greatest necessity of a divine revelation."
—Jonathan Edwards, "Miscellany" 837[1]

I Introduction

This chapter has three purposes. First, it provides a necessary counterbalance to the almost limitless revelatory potential Edwards would seem to grant to nature. Second, it advances our historical narrative of Edwards' campaign against problematic Enlightenment currents, seen not only in terms of the obvious threat of Deism but also in terms of the subtler dangers posed by more moderate figures. Thirdly and most importantly, it shows how Edwards' distinctively Trinitarian theology of divine communication made a difference in the way he carried out his apologetic campaign, as epitomized by his communicative argument for the necessity of special revelation.

Few orthodox theologians allowed more space for general revelation than did Jonathan Edwards. His ontology alone—which, in sum, is that all reality is the continual manifestation of ideas from the divine mind—might give the impression that human observers should have all the data required to know true religion by the mere study of the universe.[2] Moreover, not only did he seek to maintain a symbiotic alliance between science and religion, he actually thought that he could show how all the main doctrines of the Christian faith were perfectly compatible with human reason.[3] However,

[1] Edwards, "Miscellany" 837, in *Works Vol. 20*, p. 53.

[2] See Edwards, "The Mind," in *Works Vol. 6*, p. 344.

[3] Ava Chamberlain describes Edwards' planned "Rational Account" thus: ". . . another of Edwards' proposed titles for the treatise [was] 'A Rational Account of Christianity, or, The Perfect Harmony between the Doctrines of the Christian Religion and Human Reason Manifested.' This formulation of the title describes more precisely the aims of the 'Rational Account.' Edwards intended this treatise to be not simply a systematic theology but a demonstration of the rationality or reasonableness of Christian doctrine" (Chamberlain, "Editor's Introduction," in *Works Vol. 18* p. 25).

this expansiveness regarding general revelation was only one aspect of the great American theologian's comprehensive and integrative project. In a no less ambitious manner, Edwards also insisted upon the absolute necessity of special revelation. If his lifelong warfare with the Deists and their allies had a central front, it was here at this crucial question of whether nature and reason were sufficient to bring people into right relationship with God. Edwards thus took to himself the difficult and *prima facie* contradictory task of affirming the almost unbounded extent of revelatory content in the "book of nature" while also arguing for the absolute necessity of a supernatural Word of God.

Such a "both/and" approach to thorny theological problems, perhaps a signature feature of Edwards' thought, tended to breed in his formulations a creative insight that went beyond the superficial point at issue to the deeper, more basic concerns that lay behind them. His advocacy for the necessity of revelation is a perfect example of this feature at work. The Deists thought that humans did not *need* information from special revelation because they have all the data they require from nature and reason. Like the other anti-Deist apologists of his time, Edwards never tired of enumerating the ways in which natural reason is either theoretically or practically inadequate for valid religion. But in a paradigmatic application of the concept of divine communicativeness discussed in Chapter 1, Edwards also affirmed that God is personal and communicative and that the entire universe exists as nothing other than a structure for his communication to personal, relational, and communicative intelligent beings. Whether or not we *need information* is entirely beside the point; the point is that God has determined to engage with us in relational conversation. This line of reasoning was for Edwards no mere ad hoc apologetic device but a foundational aspect of reality rooted deep within the Trinity and in God's purposes for creation.

Our discussion will center on this communicative argument for special revelation. In order to set the stage for this discussion, we need to first observe Edwards interacting with contemporary Deist teachings arguing for the redundancy of special revelation. However, as we shall see, Edwards was alert to the dangers posed by a whole spectrum of Enlightenment thought—not only the Deists but also some figures operating under more mainstream auspices. This means that along with the predictable characters such as Tindal and Chubb, we will examine evidence that Edwards' proximate antagonist for his relational model may have been none other than John Locke. Finally, we discuss the role of Edwards' defense of special revelation within his program of planned master works of apologetic theology.

II Natural Theology, No; Natural Revelation, Yes

Edwards stood squarely in the stream of the orthodox Reformed faith, and his position on natural revelation is essentially that of Calvin.[4] Yet, Edwards also lived during the Enlightenment, and he self-consciously assumed the task of formulating orthodoxy in terms that were intelligible—if not always attractive—to the contemporary intellectual milieu. In response to Deists such as Tindal and Chubb, Edwards subjected "natural divinity" (natural theology) to a tireless, creative, and withering critique.[5] Yet, he would not deny any grain of truth that could be found in his opponents, and he granted natural revelation itself the highest of epistemic standings.[6] Most aspects of Edwards' apologetic agenda were driven by the contemporary Deist threat, but this is particularly so in the case of natural theology. We shall therefore consider briefly the writings of Tindal and Chubb.

a. Tindal and Chubb

Matthew Tindal (1657–1733) was the most influential Deist thinker of Edwards' time, and it was to him that Edwards was primarily responding on the issue of natural theology. Tindal spoke as if he were merely making clear the implications of what was already widely accepted among prominent Church of England clergy (indeed, the title of his major work *Christianity as Old as the Creation* was a quote from a Bishop), and this probably reflected more than a modicum of truth.[7] Archbishop Tillotson's statements on nature and reason were so useful to the Deist position as to make him one of the most widely quoted figures in freethinking literature.[8] It might even be argued that Deism, or at least some forms of it, was simply the more

[4] Some of the relevant literature includes Diana Butler, "God's Visible Glory: The Beauty of Nature in the Thought of John Calvin and Jonathan Edwards," *Westminster Theological Journal* 52, no. 1 (1990): pp. 13–26; Edward A. Dowey Jr., *The Knowledge of God in Calvin's Theology*, third ed. (Grand Rapids, MI: Eerdmans, 1994); T. H. L. Parker, *The Doctrine of the Knowledge of God: A Study in the Theology of John Calvin* (Edinburgh: Oliver and Boyd, 1952); and Susan Schreiner, *The Theater of His Glory: Nature & the Natural Order in the Thought of John Calvin* (Grand Rapids, MI: Baker Academic, 2001).

[5] See Edwards, "Miscellanies" 1170, 1126, 1239, 1298, 1301, 1302, 1304, 1313, 1337, 1338, 1340, and 1350; all in *Works Vol. 23*.

[6] See Edwards, "Images of Divine Things" entry 70, in *Works Vol. 11*, p. 74.

[7] "The Religion of the Gospel, is the true original Religion of Reason and Nature . . . And its Precepts declarative of that original Religion, which was as old as the Creation," quoting a sermon by Bishop Sherlock of Bangor. See Tindal, *Christianity as Old as the Creation* (London: 1730).

[8] See J. O'Higgins, "Archbishop Tillotson and the Religion of Nature," *Journal of Theological Studies* n.s.: 24, no. 1 (1973), pp. 123–142.

consistent outworking of rationalist tendencies already present in Latitudinarianism.[9]

In any case, it was on the doctrine of revelation that Tindal sought to establish his foundation for Deism, and the priority of natural theology was his pièce de résistance. The character "A," who represents Tindal in this dialogue, declares:

> I think, too great a stress can't be laid on natural religion, which as I take it, differs not from revealed, but in the manner of its being communicated: the one being the internal, as the other the external revelation of the same unchangeable Will of a Being . . .[10]

To this, "B," the thoughtful Anglican whom Tindal is trying to win over, replies "Surely, sir, this must be extremely heterodox. Can you believe, that *Natural* and *revealed* religion differ in nothing but the Manner of their being conveyed to us?"[11] Yet, as Tindal's proposal is developed, it begins to sound more reasonable to "B." After all, these two media of revelation come from the same source, and no doubt they must contain the same information necessary for right relationship with God. If this is what God already gave in natural religion, asks "A," "Can revelation, I say, add anything to a religion thus absolutely perfect, universal, and immutable?"[12] Revelation is simply superfluous to natural religion. From this foundation on natural revelation alone, Tindal builds his Deist theology.

Thomas Chubb (1679–1747) was a developer and popularizer of Deist doctrine formulated by Tindal and others. Chubb's main work on revelation was *A Discourse Concerning Reason with Regard to Religion and Divine Revelation: Wherein It Is Shown That Reason Is, or Else That It Ought to Be, a Sufficient Guide in Matters of Religion.*[13] The book does what its long title suggests, making the simple but highly subversive point that human reason is sufficient to determine religious faith. Chubb's thesis is that mankind is universally accountable before God and therefore must have universal access to essential religious truth:

[9] Or that Latitudinarianism was a less consistent outworking of the rationalistic tendencies of Deism. Both were manifestations of an age universally "bent upon a rational religion" (Thomas Sprat, 1667, quoted in Robert E. Brown, *Jonathan Edwards and the Bible* (Bloomington, IN: Indiana University Press, 2002), p. 31).

[10] Tindal, Christianity as Old as Creation, p. 3.

[11] Tindal, *Christianity as Old as Creation*, p. 3; emphasis original.

[12] Tindal, Christianity as Old as Creation, p. 3.

[13] Chubb, *A Discourse Concerning Reason with Regard to Religion and Divine Revelation* (London: T. Cox, 1733).

> Man in his natural state, when destitute of divine revelation, is supposed to be an accountable creature, who is answerable to God for his actions, and who will be amply rewarded or severely punished in another world, according as he behaves himself in this. Now, admitting this to be the case, then, I say, that man has a right, by the laws of common equity, to be invested with such a capacity or power, as is sufficient (when duly exercised) to discover what it is he is accountable for . . .[14]

The point has force because it hits the ordinary people where it matters: we will all be held accountable in the next life for the things we know now. If God is good, then we all surely ought to have been furnished with what is needed to acquire the relevant knowledge.

Chubb then addresses the Christian claim that reason must be insufficient since God has seen fit to provide special revelation. To put this another way, the orthodox could argue that reason alone must not have been enough or God would not have provided something additional. Chubb turns the tables, finding in this argument an opportunity to point to an uncomfortable fact about the provision of divine revelation:

> If it should be further urged, that reason is not a sufficient guide in matters of religion, and that *divine revelation* was kindly given of God to man, to supply the defects, or insufficiency of reason in that respect; for if reason had been a sufficient guide in matters of religion, then there would have been no need of revelation: I answer; that if this were the case, then the original constitution of things must have been very defective, as I observed above; because then, there would have been a whole species of beings, made accountable for their actions, without being furnished with capacities and powers sufficient to answer the purposes of such creatures; and then numberless millions of our species would have been very unequally and unkindly dealt with, because they have been destitute of such a divine revelation . . .[15]

Chubb resorts to what McDermott and others have called the "scandal of particularity."[16] As the Deists saw it, the most problematic issue in the notion

[14] Chubb, *A Discourse Concerning Reason with Regard to Religion and Divine Revelation* (London: T. Cox, 1733), pp. 4, 6.

[15] Chubb, *A Discourse Concerning Reason with Regard to Religion and Divine Revelation* (London: T. Cox, 1733), p. 12.

[16] "The scandal of particularity, then, was an important stimulus to Deism. It was a principle reason why they judged the orthodox God to be a monster in whom they could not believe" (McDermott, *Jonathan Edwards Confronts the Gods*, p. 25).

of special revelation is simply that it was not given to everyone but to a certain limited number of people located in particular times and places. The problem was made all too clear by the discoveries of the Age of Exploration, wherein Europeans realized that most (the oft-quoted figure was 5/6th) of the world's population did not have access to the Bible. For an age in which universal accessibility to truth had become virtually sacrosanct, this was a most powerful objection.

b. Edwards' response

Edwards had no inclination to deny the Deists' key premise that God truly reveals himself in nature. Doing so would run counter to his entire theology of divine communication, not to mention his project of interpreting the harmony of reality. Edwards was likewise committed to upholding God's justice; if God holds all people accountable for their failure to respond to some kind of revelatory message, then surely such knowledge must be available to all mankind.[17] Edwards thus had to affirm that natural theology is theoretically possible but that for various reasons, it is practically insufficient for any purpose beyond condemnation or perhaps a proto-evangel.[18]

Edwards responded to Tindal's case for natural theology in "Miscellany" 1337, at a length that suggests Edwards intended to eventually publish these thoughts. His first point is to draw attention to the gap between objective perfection and *subjective sufficiency*:

> Tindal's main argument against the need of any revelation is that the law of nature is absolutely perfect. But how weak and impertinent is this arguing that, because the law of nature . . . is perfect, that therefore the light of nature is sufficient. . . . how far is this from having any reference to that question whether we have by mere nature, without instruction, all that light and advantage that we need clearly and fully to know what is right, and all that is needful for us to be and to do in our circumstances as sinners, etc., in order to the forgiveness of sin, the favor of God and

[17] The "Blank Bible" note on Romans 1:32-2:1 includes the statement ". . . they all have that light that is sufficient to teach them that those that commit such things deserve the condemnation and wrath of God, and so death and destruction, which they are very ready to acknowledge and declare in the case of others when they see their wickedness." Edwards, "Blank Bible," in *Works Vol. 24*, p. 986.

[18] See, for example, the unpublished sermons on Romans 1:20 of June 1743 (Jonathan Edwards Center, Yale University).

> our own happiness. What according to the nature of things is fittest and best may be most perfect, and yet our natural discerning and knowledge of this may be most imperfect.[19]

Yes, Edwards affirms, the "light of nature" is as "perfect" as Tindal claims, but we in "our circumstances as sinners, etc." are definitely *not* perfect observers of this light. In our fallen situation, we are radically flawed observers and need something far more explicit and instructive than what nature alone can provide.

There is, moreover, a crucial distinction to be made between our religious duties as creatures and our requirements as fallen sinners. One might expect that Edwards would affirm the former possibility and deny the latter. However, Edwards thinks that nature is insufficient for *either* kind of religion:

> In order the more clearly to judge of this matter of the sufficiency of the light of nature, to know what is necessary to be known of religion in order to their happiness, we must consider what are the things that must be known in order to this, which are these two things: 1. the religion of nature . . . as creatures; 2. the religion of a sinner, or the religion and duties proper and necessary for us considering our state as depraved and guilty creatures, having incurred the displeasure of our Creator. As to the former, 'tis manifest from fact that nature alone is not sufficient for the discovery of the religion of nature . . . No, nor does it appear to have proved sufficient so much in a single instance. And as to the latter, viz. the religion of a sinner, or the duties proper and necessary for us as depraved, guilty and offending creatures, 'tis most evident the light of nature cannot be sufficient for our information by any means, or in any sense whatsoever . . . it affords no possibility of it.[20]

In Edwards' estimation, natural revelation has never "proved sufficient so much in a single instance" even for creaturely religion. Perhaps he has in mind how God employed special revelation even to inform the unfallen Adam and Eve of their religious duties.[21] As for the religion of a sinner, it is "most evident" to Edwards that the light of nature "affords no possibility" of being sufficient.

[19] Edwards, "Miscellany" 1337, in *Works Vol. 23*, p. 342.
[20] Edwards, "Miscellany" 1337, in *Works Vol. 23*, pp. 344–45; emphasis mine.
[21] Genesis 2:16–17.

In common with Calvin and the mainstream Reformed tradition, Edwards thinks that natural revelation is, however, sufficient to condemn unbelievers: "They have light sufficient for that judgment and condemnation which they shall be the subjects of. For their condemnation shall proceed no further than so far as to be proportioned to their light."[22] Those who remain obstinate under greater "light"—as, say, those in officially Christian nations—will receive greater condemnation, but no one is so removed from God's creation as to be excused. So with regard to Chubb's "scandal of particularity," Edwards would affirm one premise (that God holds people accountable for what they know through nature) while he would deny the other (that God is obliged to provide everyone the gospel).

Edwards would also point out the inadequacy of natural revelation to inform acceptable worship. Whatever we may know about God through reason alone, Edwards argues that we cannot know how to worship him as he desires without special revelation. In particular, we lack instructions on how to worship as a community:

> 'Tis easily provable, that the highest end and happiness of men is to view God's excellency, to love him and receive expressions of his love; and that therefore their greatest business is to meditate [on] and use means to understand God's bounty, and to express suitably their love; this love including all those other affections which depend upon it and are necessarily connected with it, which we call worship. The highest end of society, therefore, must be to assist and join with each other in this. But how comes it to pass, that this end of society was never yet obtained? When was there any social worship performed by Deists? And if there should be a society of Deists that were disposed socially to express their love to God, and honor of him, which way would they go to work? They have nothing from God to direct them.[23]

In a context in which almost everyone was agreed about the importance of the community worshiping God aright, Edwards' apologetic seizes upon an important vulnerability in his adversary: Deist communal worship was virtually unheard of.[24] Lacking the sort of instructions provided by Scripture, the Deists had no guidelines for how to worship God.

[22] Edwards, "Miscellany" 1338, in *Works Vol. 23*, p. 355.
[23] Edwards, "Miscellany" 127, in *Works Vol. 13*, p. 291.
[24] See Chubb, *Discourse Concerning Reason*, pp. 14–15.

Edwards also took a more Christological approach to the necessity of revelation. In the "Miscellany" quoted below, Edwards points not so much to the notional inadequacy of natural reason but to its inherent theological poverty resulting from a lack of relation to Christ:

> The whole of Christian divinity depends on divine revelation; for though there are many truths concerning God and our duty to him that are evident by the light of nature, yet no one truth is taught by the light of nature in that manner in which it is necessary for us to know it. For the knowledge of no truth in divinity is of any significance to us any otherwise that it, some way or other, belongs to the gospel scheme, or has relation to Christ the Mediator. It signifies nothing for us to know anything of any one of God's perfections, unless we know them as manifested in Christ; and so it signifies nothings to us to know any part of our duty, unless it will [bear] some relation to Christ . . . . And therefore we stand in the greatest necessity of a divine revelation.[25]

Once again, Edwards affirms "there are many truths concerning God and our duty to him that are evident by the light of nature." The problem is that since these truths come to us in this way, they lack the vital connection to Christ that makes them salvific. Though people could know the many doctrines that Edwards thought he could demonstrate through reason alone in the "Rational Account," it would ultimately do them no good outside the Christological perspective provided by Scripture. Thus, "we stand in the greatest necessity of a divine revelation."

Thus Edwards argued for the inadequacy of natural revelation. In a more positive direction, however, we have already seen how Edwards thinks that natural revelation provides tools for interpreting the great riches available in nature to the regenerate. Indeed, the intelligent and affectional reception of God's self-communication in nature is precisely the purpose for which nature exists: "What would this vast universe of matter, placed in such excellent order and governed by such excellent rules, be good for, if there were no intelligence that could know anything of it?"[26] Edwards theorizes that, in and of itself, the natural universe would have no purpose in being—it exists only to facilitate God's self-communication to elect intelligent beings. And this purpose demands not only the bare existence of intelligent creatures but also their actual apprehension of the beauty of God's work

[25] Edwards, "Miscellany" 837, in *Works Vol. 20*, pp. 52–53.
[26] Edwards, "Miscellany" gg, in *Works Vol. 13*, p. 185.

in creation. Edwards continues, "Wherefore it necessarily follows that intelligent beings are the end of the creation, that their end must be to behold and admire the doings of God, and magnify him for them, and to contemplate his glories in them."[27] The creation exists for the purpose of intelligent beings, and intelligent beings exist for the purpose of glorifying God in the multidimensional (loving and enjoying as well as knowing) appreciation of his works.

Only after saying all this does Edwards return to the original subject of his "Miscellany," which was "religion":

> Wherefore religion must be the end of the creation, the great end, the very end. If it were not for this, all those vast bodies we see ordered with so excellent skill, so according to the nicest rules of proportion, according to such laws of gravity and motion, would be all vanity, or good for nothing with no purpose at all. For religion is the very business, the noble business of intelligent beings, and for this end God has placed us on this earth. If it were not for men, this world would be altogether in vain, with all the curious workmanship of it and accoutrements about it.[28]

Perhaps we could say that Edwards had a "natural religion" after all, in the sense that the very "end of the creation" is religion. The purpose of the natural universe and of all its human and angelic inhabitants is to participate in a religion that contemplates the "curious workmanship" and "accoutrements" of God's glorious creation. Humanity exists to glorify God by recognizing God's work in creation, and as Edwards goes on to say, this function necessarily continues for eternity.[29] Characteristically, Edwards responds to the error of natural religion by constructing a theology that, while emphatically denying its errors, goes far beyond the Deists in affording nature the noblest of ultimate purposes.

c. Miller and Butler on nature in Edwards

Having discussed some of Edwards' thoughts on natural revelation, perhaps it might be useful to discuss a relevant debate in the secondary literature as a means of consolidation. Perry Miller thought there was a radical discontinuity between Edwards and his predecessors on the status he

[27] Edwards, "Miscellany" gg, in *Works Vol. 13*, p. 185.
[28] Edwards, "Miscellany" gg, in *Works Vol. 13*, p. 185.
[29] Edwards, "Miscellany" gg, in *Works Vol. 13*, p. 185.

granted to natural revelation, which he characterized as Edwards' elevating "nature to a level of authority coequal with revelation."[30] As with so many of Miller's colorful but unguarded statements, this assertion has been subjected to scrutiny. In her critique of Miller, Diana Butler makes the needed correction, but her qualification exposes the complexity of the problem:

> If God's glory is visible in nature, did Calvin or Edwards set nature next to Scripture as a separate form of revelation? The answer in both cases is no. If natural theology is an ability to arrive at a saving knowledge of God derived from creation, then neither Calvin nor Edwards promoted natural theology. However, in the theological context of both the sixteenth and eighteenth centuries, most theologians believed that nature testified to God's existence as Creator. Following Paul in Romans, both Calvin and Edwards assented to this limited use of natural revelation. Humanity is given enough knowledge of God through nature to make them responsible for their refusal to acknowledge and worship God. The deepest lessons of nature, however, are reserved for the regenerate.[31]

Butler is no doubt correct in her assessment that both Calvin and Edwards denied natural theology as an independent means of attaining saving knowledge. As we have just seen, the emphatic refutation of this position was an important item on Edwards' anti-Deist agenda. Butler is possibly correct in saying that Miller did not fully understand Calvin on this point and thus exaggerated the extent of Edwards' apparent discontinuity.[32] But Butler does not explain sufficiently how Edwards might have thought his emphatic statements against natural theology were to be reconciled with equally strong statements (". . . we look on these shadows of divine things as the voice of God") that would seem to support Miller's assertion.[33] This is no trivial disparity, so let us propose a solution.

The solution involves definition with regard to case. We must be careful to distinguish the *means* of revelation available (nature) and the *effects* of this revelation. Likewise, we must distinguish the effects with regard to the *unregenerate* (where it can only condemn) and to the *regenerate* (where it can

[30] Miller, "Introduction," in Perry Miller, ed. *Images or Shadows of Divine Things* (New Haven: Yale University Press, 1948), p. 28.
[31] Diana Butler, "God's Visible Glory: The Beauty of Nature in the Thought of John Calvin and Jonathan Edwards," *Westminster Theological Journal* 52, no. 1 (1990), p. 22.
[32] Rather than discontinuity, it would seem to us that Edwards' thought constitutes a development of Calvin on this issue.
[33] Edwards, "Types" entry 70, in *Works Vol. 11*, p. 74.

do much more). Returning to Butler's primary source of evidence in the Hebrews 5:12 sermon, Edwards says, "Indeed there is what is called natural religion or divinity. There are many truths concerning God, and our duty to him, which are evident by the light of nature."[34] Here we have an affirmation of the *means* of natural revelation; God does in fact convey information about himself and even our duty to him (which was Tindal's main point) through nature. Edwards then explains its effects, or lack thereof, with regard to the unregenerate:

> But Christian divinity, properly so called, is not evident by the light of nature; it depends on revelation. Such are our circumstances now in our fallen state, that nothing which it is needful for us to know concerning God, is manifest by the light of nature in the manner in which it is necessary for us to know it . . .[35]

Notice how Edwards makes it clear that this is a condition involving "our fallen state," indicating that this condition need not obtain in all circumstances. Notice also Edwards' qualification that nature cannot inform fallen humanity "in the manner in which it is necessary to know it," thus preserving the objective reality of nature's content while taking up the issue of its *subjective perspicuity*. Now in other places already cited, Edwards affirms the positive effects of natural revelation with regard to the regenerate Christian. Thus, Edwards' statements can be reconciled simply by taking into account that they refer to radically different subjective circumstances. Butler probably knew this, but a clear statement of the matter was lost in her effort to refute Miller's thesis.

Let us now synthesize Edwards' position on natural revelation. Natural revelation is, in various ways, less than, equal to, and greater than special revelation in Scripture. For unregenerate fallen humanity, natural revelation is *less* than special revelation, in that, although it says enough to condemn, it can never produce the things ". . . needful for us to know concerning God."[36] For regenerate humanity, it is *equal* to special revelation, in that it confirms and illumines the truths that are taught clearly in Scripture. For them, it is also in some highly qualified sense *greater* than special revelation;

[34] Edwards, "A Thorough Knowledge of Divine Truth," sermon on Heb 5:12, in *Works Vol. 22*, p. 86.
[35] Edwards, "A Thorough Knowledge of Divine Truth," sermon on Heb 5:12, in *Works Vol. 22*, p. 86.
[36] Edwards, "A Thorough Knowledge of Divine Truth," sermon on Heb 5:12, in *Works Vol. 22*, p. 86.

not at all that it reveals any new truth, but that the intelligent recognition and worshipful contemplation of God's works are precisely the joyful task elect humanity was created to undertake. Given this complexity, it is entirely understandable how one could miss Edwards' complete position by looking at individual parts of the corpus.

III The Communicative Argument

We mentioned that the truly original part of Edwards' thought on the necessity of revelation was his argument based on his theology of divine communication. To this subject we now turn. The Deists had framed the debate over revelation as if God and men were functionally no different from machines; the only question was whether or not the man-machine required a download of information from the clockmaker-god's database. For them, the discussion was confined to the sufficiency of purely notional information available from natural sources. In stark contrast to such reductionist and mechanistic ideas, Edwards' understanding of revelation was relational and multidimensional. Revelation is the personal communication of a personal God to his beloved intelligent creatures, as the expression of his eternal disposition to share his knowledge, love, and joy.

a. Communicative revelation

Edwards first makes the point that had so completely escaped the Deists: God and man are not like robots requiring only some kind of data exchange to fulfill their purposes. God is a relational and intelligent being characterized by the attribute of communicativeness, who exists in eternal communication between Father, Son, and Spirit. Human beings, created in God's image, were designed to be in communication with their maker. Here, we again direct our attention to "Miscellany" 332:

> The great and universal end of God's creating the world was to communicate himself. God is a communicative Being. This communication is really only to intelligent beings: the communication of himself to their understandings is his glory, and the communication of himself with respect to their wills, the enjoying faculty, is their happiness.[37]

[37] Edwards, "Miscellany" 332, in *Works Vol. 13*, p. 410.

As we have seen, Edwards' statement "God is a communicative Being" means that communicativeness is for him an essential divine attribute. This attribute amounts to a restatement of Edwards' doctrine of the Trinity as the eternal communication between the three Persons. God simply cannot be God without his *ad intra* communication.[38] And in a way that is at least analogical to the inter-Trinitarian situation, God's subordinate purpose in creation is to be in communion—and thus conversation—with "intelligent beings," angels as well as humans. The implications of this line of reasoning for Edwards' theology of revelation are wide-ranging and will require some unpacking from several different perspectives.

God and his intelligent creatures are *not* machines, and therefore the supply of notional information is only one part, and indeed the lesser part, of the picture involved in revelation. Edwards makes the crucial point that communication is far more than the impersonal exchange of information; it is a natural act between intelligent beings living in community with one another. God has obviously made us with the ability and desire to communicate with one another. But even this feature is in some way incidental to his making us with the ability for, and purpose of, communication with himself. We ought therefore to expect God to communicate with us. Edwards says:

> If man's natural reason were never so perfect, and however little need we had of revelation for the enlightening our darkness and correcting our errors, yet it would be most unreasonable to suppose that there never should be any revelation made to man . . . . God made spirits to have communication; and will he not have any communion with them himself, although they are made for this very end, to meditate on him and to love [him]? How unreasonable is it then to suppose, that God will so abscond himself from these his understanding creatures, that were made to be conversant about him![39]

So the question of whether or not we *need* revelation to supply data, which was the endless preoccupation of the Deists, becomes entirely secondary if not irrelevant. What is primary is that God is by nature a communicative being and would certainly communicate with us *even if we possessed exhaustive notional knowledge.*

[38] See the discussion on Edwards' definition of "communication" above, Chapter 1.
[39] Edwards, "Miscellany" 204, in *Works Vol. 13*, p. 339.

Verbal communication is therefore to be expected as an essential part of God's dutiful reign over his intelligent creation:

> It seems to me a kind of unreasonable thing, to suppose that there should be a God without any word of his; that there should be a God, an intelligent voluntary being, that has so much more concern with [us], and with whom we have infinitely more concern than with any other being, and yet that he should never speak. It is a property of all intelligent beings, that God has made in his own image, to speak; they are hereby distinguished from inferior creatures. It is therefore strange that any should imagine that the supreme intelligence should never speak, that there should be no word of his.[40]

Here again, Edwards is grounding his argument on an implicit understanding of communication as a characteristic of God. Specifically, speech is "a property of all intelligent beings." If this is true of lesser intelligent beings such as humans, certainly it must be true of the greatest intelligent being, God.

b. Conversational revelation

With the outline of Edwards' thought in place, and some notion of its import in view, let us now consider the *conversational* element taught by Edwards' relational doctrine of revelation. As "Miscellany" 1337 is Edward's definitive statement on the insufficiency of natural revelation in terms of notional content, "Miscellany" 1338 is Edward's definitive statement about the intentional element that is requisite in conversational revelation:

> By CONVERSATION I mean intelligent beings expressing their minds to each other in words or other significations equivalent, being signs intentionally directed to us for our notice, whose immediate and main design is to be significations to or expressions of the mind of him or them who causes or gives them to the knowledge or notice of him or them to whom they are directed; wherein those signs are evidence distinguished from works done by them, from which we may argue their minds, though the first and most immediate design of the work be something else besides as mere signification to us of the mind of the efficient. Thus I distinguish

[40] Edwards, "Miscellany" 544, in *Works Vol. 18*, pp. 89–90.

> God's communicating his mind to us by word or conversation from giving us opportunity to learn it by philosophical reasoning. By the latter I mean arguing the nature and will of God by God's works, which we observe in the natural world.[41]

The key point of Edwards' definition of conversation is that it describes the intentional transmission of an individual's mental activity through the medium of meaningful signs. Edwards makes the crucial distinction between the intentional communication involved in conversation and the mere reconstruction of thought based on the evidence of actions. What the Deists had—a forensic reconstruction of the Prime Mover's intentions based upon natural reasoning—was patently not conversation.

With this said, Edwards goes on to make the case that what is desired and expected in any society is friendship. And friendship manifestly requires the kind of conversation that is possible only in special revelation:

> The special medium of union and communication of the members of the society, and the being of society as such, is conversation. And the well-being and happiness of society is friendship. 'Tis the highest happiness of all moral agents. But friendship above all other things that belong to society, requires conversation. 'Tis what friendship most naturally and directly desires. 'Tis maintained and nourished by that, and the felicity of friendship is tasted and enjoyed by that. The happiness of God's moral kingdom consists, in an inferior degree, in the member's enjoyment of each others' friendship, but infinitely more in the enjoyment of the friendship of their head. Therefore, here especially, and above all, is conversation requisite.[42]

There could seemingly be no greater contrast possible between the Deist's clockmaker, who long ago set a mechanical universe into motion and subsequently left it to his human cogs to infer information about himself, and the God whom Edwards describes above, who appears as the head of a community in which he holds ongoing conversation with his people *for the sake of friendship*. Edwards' distancing from mechanistic conceptions of God and our knowledge of him is now logically complete and, if we might say so, astonishingly beautiful.

[41] Edwards, "Miscellany" 1338, in *Works Vol. 23*, p. 345.
[42] Edwards, "Miscellany" 1338, in *Works Vol. 23*, p. 350.

c. Conversational scripture

Thus far we have been examining Edwards' line of reasoning that it would be expected, if not inevitable, for God to converse with his intelligent creatures in some kind of special revelation. But we have not yet spoken of the actual means of so doing. Though Edwards obviously had in mind the Scriptures, his arguments are mainly concerned to establish the *principle* of special revelation rather than the reasonability of God using a particular method to do so. However, the notion that such communication should take the form of a written book is by no means a necessary inference from the theoretical inevitability of God engaging his creatures in conversation. The example of our normal mode of personal conversation, which is primarily oral, would indeed seem to militate against it. If God wanted to have a conversation with us as intelligent beings, why would he not just talk to us, instead of giving us a book?

Edwards is aware of the problem and is at pains to demonstrate how a book—the Bible—is not merely a legitimate means of conversation but is in fact the best possible method for God to converse with humans in our current condition. Once again, the entry is quoted at length in order to leave Edwards' argument intact:

> And the way of God's holding communion with men that the Christian religion supposes, is the most congruous that can possibly be thought of towards men in a fallen estate and in a wicked world, viz. to have his word written in a volume: where the matter is so various, so exceeding comprehensive and diversified, and suited to every circumstance; the texts having so many different aspects, respects, aptitudes and senses, as beheld in different lights and compared with God's providences or other parts of his Word. And there are such influences and teachings of the Spirit of God accompanying it to exhibit this Word thus in its various lights, continually bringing forth something new suited to the present stream of our thoughts, affections, and our case; that it is just as if God held up a continual conversation by word of mouth to those that read, understand and believe. And God doth indeed hold communion with [them]; and yet this is done in a secret way hidden from the wicked world, who it is not proper should see and intermeddle, nor is it exposed to their abuse and mockery—pearls are not cast before swine—for though they can read the Bible, there is nothing of this communion with God enjoyed by them, but all is to them as a dead letter. What other way can be thought of, so congruous as this?[43]

[43] Edwards, "Miscellany" 204, in *Works Vol. 13*, pp. 339–340.

Edwards begins by setting the theological parameters for his reasoning. A written book is the best conceivable means, not for sinless people in perfect circumstances—as in Eden or in heaven—but for "... men in a fallen estate and in a wicked world."

Edwards then points to the nature of the Bible's diverse content as being able to cope with the vastly differing circumstances of the untold multitudes who read it, thus highlighting the noetic dimension (the Logos) of special revelation. But as we might expect from Edwards' Trinitarian doctrine of revelation, Edwards immediately balances this with an equal affirmation of this affectional dimension (the Spirit) that accompanies it ". . . to exhibit this Word thus in its various lights." In concert, Word and Spirit are ". . . continually bringing forth something new suited to the present stream of our thoughts, affections, and our case." This leads up to Edwards' grand statement that Biblical communication is ". . . just as if God held up a continual conversation by word of mouth to those that read, understand and believe." Finally, it is worth noticing an element that would otherwise be considered something to minimize that Edwards instead celebrates. As we have seen, the Deists leveraged the "scandal of particularity" because they knew that the contemporary intellectual climate abhorred the notion of privileged religious information. But Edwards thinks this privileging is a good thing and even introduces a new, spiritual layer of particularity: "God doth indeed hold communion with [them]; and yet this is done in a secret way hidden from the wicked world . . . for though they can read the Bible, there is nothing of this communion with God enjoyed by them." This is a private conversation, inaccessible both to those without access to the Scriptures and also to the unregenerate, for whom it remains ". . . as a dead letter."

d. Two-sided conversation

True conversations have two sides. We have discussed how Edwards defends one side of the divine conversation—that God speaks to us in special revelation—but the more consistent Deists denied the other side of the conversation—prayer and worship—as well.[44] Edwards replies that the nature of God as an intelligent being no less requires human response in prayer, confession, and worship:

[44] Earlier Deists such as Toland sometimes held, with apparent philosophic inconsistency but in accordance with contemporary cultural sensibilities, that the worship of God and some manner of prayer were reasonable. Eighteenth-century figures such as Chubb would move in more consistent directions away from worship and prayer.

> Hence how rational is it to suppose, contrary to the principles of the Deists, that God ought to be worshipped by prayer, confession, praise and thanksgiving, and those duties in which we speak to God, and have to do with [him] as a properly intelligent being, or one that perceives and knows what we say to him that we ought to show respect to him by voluntary acts, as expression of our thoughts and volitions and motions of our hearts, purposely expressed before him and directed to him, as all intelligent creatures do to all other intelligent beings with whom they are concerned, or have intercourse. Never to go to God, or to purpose to exhibit our thoughts to him, or to direct any expression of any motion of our hearts to him, as we naturally do to all properly intelligent beings with whom we are concerned, certainly is not to treat him as a properly intelligent being.[45]

The principle of God being an intelligent, relational, and communicative Being works both ways regarding the reasonableness of the divine-human conversation. Edwards thus concludes, "And as 'tis hence rational to suppose that it should be required of us that we should speak to God, so 'tis as rational to suppose that he should speak to us."[46] Notice also that just as God's communication to us includes affectional as well as noetic content, so Edwards thinks our communication to God should convey the "expression of our thoughts and volitions and motions of our hearts."

We have already noted that Edwards qualifies his defense of written special revelation as being the most appropriate mode of conversation *in this world*. But in heaven, the mode of conversation changes to become yet more intimate:

> When the saints get to heaven they shall not merely see Christ, and have to do with him as subjects and servants with a glorious and gracious Lord and Sovereign, but Christ will most freely and intimately converse with them as friends and brethren. This we may learn from the manner of Christ's conversing with his disciples here on earth . . . .Though Christ be in a state of exaltation at the right hand of God, and appears in an immense height of glory, yet this won't hinder his conversing with his saints in a most familiar and intimate manner.[47]

[45] Edwards, "Miscellany" 749, in *Works Vol. 18*, p. 397.
[46] Edwards, "Miscellany" 749, in *Works Vol. 18*, p. 397.
[47] Edwards, "Miscellany" 571, in *Works Vol. 18*, p. 107.

We see that Edwards did not think that a written Bible was the ideal format for divine-human conversation *in absolute terms*, but only as our imperfect situation on earth requires. In the ideal environment of heaven, the glorified saints get to converse orally with Christ "in a most familiar and intimate manner." In fact, as Edwards states elsewhere, this perfecting of the divine-human conversation is one of the great benefits of the incarnation: "For Christ being united to the human nature, we have advantage for a far more intimate union and conversation with him, than we could possibly have had if he had remained only in the divine nature."[48] This approach to the incarnation is consistent with a theology that supposed God created the world in order to communicate himself personally.

Edwards' conversational principle, invoked periodically throughout his writings, was a centerpiece of his arguments for the necessity of special revelation. But this principle could be used in a radically different direction as well. Edwards usually began as if the existence of God was a given—he was, after all, replying to Deists who believed at least this much—and goes on from there to argue for special revelation. But at least on one occasion, Edwards also experimented with the idea of trying to prove God's existence *from* his conversational revelation.

> Suppose all the world had otherwise been ignorant of the being of God before, yet they might know it; because God has revealed himself, he has shown himself, he has said a great deal to us and *conversed much with us.* And this is every whit as rational a way of being convinced of the being of God, as it is of being convinced of the being of a man who comes from an unknown region, and shows himself to us, and converses with us for a long time: we have no other reason to be convinced of his being, than only that we see a long series of external concordant signs of an understanding, will and design, and various affections—the same way God makes himself known to us in his word.[49]

It is perhaps understandable why Edwards did not pursue this line any further as a public apologetic for the existence of God. Although the reasoning is cogent enough, the conclusion follows from a premise that no atheist would accept: that God has, in fact, spoken to us. It yet merits notice in our discussion because it demonstrates just how deep went Edwards' conviction that special revelation was a personal, relational, and

[48] Edwards, "Miscellany" 571, in *Works Vol. 18*, p. 110; emphasis mine.
[49] Edwards, "Miscellany" 254, in *Works Vol. 13*, p. 364; emphasis mine.

conversational word from God. To his mind, divine revelation was so akin to personal conversation that it *ought* to prove God's existence to an atheist.

IV Locke as a Possible Antagonist for the Communicative Argument

Whenever we encounter an intriguing theological development, we naturally want to identify possible influences. In the case of the communicative argument for the necessity of special revelation, there are some cognate ideas in Calvin and Turretin that might have planted seeds in the fertile mind of Jonathan Edwards.[50] Yet, it seems that such limited precursors are probably insufficient in themselves to account for some of the distinctive features, particularly the conversational element, of Edwards' model. Although we would readily admit that Edwards was a theologian of original genius, his apologetic and polemic works were almost inevitably framed in response to specific figures.[51] Based on both internal and external evidence, it appears that Edwards was in this case replying to John Locke. Specifically, it seems Edwards took exception to Locke's delimiting of man's endowment of communicative capacity to fellow humans in Book III of the *Essay*. This might appear at first glance to be an innocuous point, but, as Locke himself makes clear enough, Edwards knew it could only prove devastating for any orthodox understanding of special revelation.

Edwards' relationship to Locke has been a debated issue in Edwards scholarship since at least the time of Perry Miller.[52] Recently, Robert E.

[50] "Despite this [general revelation], it is needful that another and better help be added to direct us aright to the very Creator of the universe. It is not in vain, then, that he added the light of his Word by which to become known unto salvation; and he regarded as worthy of this privilege those whom he pleased to gather more closely and intimately to himself" (Calvin, *Institutes* I.6.i, Battles translation, Volume I, pp. 69–70). "Therefore it was necessary that the defect of the former revelation (made useless and insufficient by sin) should be supplied by another more clear (not only as to degree, but also as to species), not only that God should use mute teachers, but that his own sacred voice should also not only declare the excellence of his attributes, but open to us also the mystery of his will in order to our salvation" (Turretin, *Institutes of Elenctic Theology* (ed. James T. Dennison Jr.; trans. George Musgrave Giger; 3 vols, Phillipsburg, NJ: P&R Publishing 1992–97), p. 56).

[51] For example, *Freedom of the Will* was written to counter the specific arguments of Chubb, Whitby, and Watts, while *Original Sin* was in response to Taylor and Turnbull. See Paul Ramsey, "Editor's Introduction," in *Works Vol. 1*, p. 65; and Clyde A. Holbrook, "Editor's Introduction," in Edwards, *Works Vol. 3*, p. 23.

[52] Some of the more significant examples after Miller include Claude Smith, "Jonathan Edwards and 'the Way of Ideas,'" *Harvard Theological Review* 59, no. 2 (1966), pp. 153–73; Paul Helm, "John Locke and Jonathan Edwards: A Reconsideration," *Journal of the History of Ideas* 7 (1969), pp. 51–61; Norman S. Fiering, "The Rationalist Foundations of Jonathan Edwards's Metaphysics," in Nathan O. Hatch and Harry S. Stout (eds.), *Jonathan Edwards and*

Brown has argued that ". . . at critical points the estimations of Edwards and Locke regarding the epistemological status of biblical revelation were markedly similar," and that they both sought to maintain ". . . the philosophical prerogative of biblical revelation for religious discourse."[53] Brown also points to how Locke is not named in Edwards' polemic against rationalistic epistemology: "It can hardly be coincidence or mere omission that Edwards nowhere specifically mentions Locke or the *Essay* in his extensive criticisms of those who would 'make reason a higher rule than revelation.'"[54] This is an interesting absence, but we must at least allow for the possibility of another explanation. It is known, for instance, that *Freedom of the Will* was at least partially written against Isaac Watts.[55] Yet, Edwards' polemic against Arminianism never actually mentions the name of this celebrated hymn writer and minister to whom Edwards owed his initial foray into trans-Atlantic notoriety.[56] Just perhaps, Edwards would similarly avoid naming someone who carried such enormous philosophical prestige and to whom he was also, in some ways, indebted.[57]

Our reconsideration of this issue begins with Book III of Locke's *Essay*, which is largely concerned with the philosophy of language. The introduction posits a basis for human communication in divine creation:

> God having designed Man for a sociable Creature, made him not only with an inclination, and under a necessity to have fellowship with those of

the American Experience (New York and Oxford: Oxford University Press, 1988), pp. 73–101; Robert E. Brown, "Edwards, Locke, and the Bible," *The Journal of Religion* 79, no. 3 (1999), pp. 361–84; and Paul Copan, "Jonathan Edwards's Philosophical Influences: Lockean or Malebranchean?" *Journal of the Evangelical Theological Society* 44, no. 1 (2001), pp. 107–24.

[53] Brown, "Edwards, Locke, and the Bible," p. 362.

[54] Brown, "Edwards, Locke, and the Bible," p. 373.

[55] See Paul Ramsey, "Editor's Introduction," in *Works Vol. 1*, p. 65.

[56] Edwards does, however, specify Watts' name 17 times in the "Controversies" notebook (Edwards, *Works Vol. 27*). On Edwards' omission of Watts' name in the published work, see Paul Ramsey, "Editor's Introduction," in *Works Vol. 1*, pp. 94–95. The possible role of Watts' publishing anonymously would, of course, not be applicable to Locke's Essay. However, official anonymity has been more a convenient occasion for Edwards' omission than the core explanation. On Edwards' debt to Watts regarding the publication of "The Faithful Narrative," see C. C. Goen, "Editor's Introduction" to *Works Vol. 4*, pp. 33–45.

[57] Edwards acknowledged a great appreciation for Locke (Samuel Hopkins, *Life of President Edwards*, p. 3, quoted in Wallace Anderson, "Editor's Introduction," in *Works Vol. 6*, p. 17). Perhaps this appreciation, in conjunction with Locke's virtually unassailable contemporary reputation, might explain why Edwards would have been reluctant to criticize him by name in material that was probably intended for inclusion in the "Rational Account." This would be all the more plausible if Edwards planned to somehow leverage Locke's prestige—he could hardly claim that the Christian religion conformed to the great man's philosophy while also critiquing him by name on a fundamental point.

> his own kind; but furnished him also with Language, which was to be the great Instrument, and common Tye of Society.[58]

Locke explains our ability and "inclination" for verbal communication as a design feature given by God. Yet for Locke, the *objects* of such communication are "those of his own kind"—other human beings. Given Edwards' strongly theocentric, teleological doctrine of creation, Locke's omission of the vertical component of communication must have struck him as fundamentally wrongheaded; why would we restrict man's divinely designed communicative capacity to "his own kind"?

We are therefore not surprised to find Edwards responding to just such an "unreasonable" assumption in one of his notebook entries:

> And 'tis evident, God made spirits to have communication; and will he not have any communion with them himself, although they are made for this very end, to meditate on him and to love [him]? How unreasonable is it then to suppose, that God will so abscond himself from these his understanding creatures, that were made to be conversant about him![59]

Edwards is reacting to some specific statement he had encountered, and Locke's statement in the *Essay* fits perfectly. Edwards agrees that "understanding creatures" are made to have communication, but he scorns the "unreasonable" notion that this communication should be restricted to the horizontal component.[60] Returning for a moment to the larger reason for this discussion, notice that this particular notebook entry is the aforementioned "Miscellany" 204—the first instance of the communicative argument in the corpus.

We have suggested that Edwards would have been uncomfortable with Locke's statement lacking allowance for the God-man communicative relationship. However, in the course of Book III, there appears something more obviously problematic. Locke will go on to argue that language is inherently deficient due to the arbitrary human process of linking words with mental ideas.[61] Where might he be leading with this line of thought? Locke reveals all near the end of Book III:

[58] Locke, *Essay*, III.1.1.

[59] Edwards, "Miscellany" 204, in *Works Vol. 13*, p. 339.

[60] Note the change in terminology. Unlike Locke, Edwards is always careful to make room for angels as well as men by using terms such as "understanding creatures" or "intelligent beings."

[61] Locke makes this case throughout Book III, but particularly Chapters 1–22. Notice that Locke seems to think that intrapersonal communication, using proprietary language to call

> Since then the Precepts of Natural Religion are plain, and very intelligible to all Mankind, and seldom come to be controverted; and other revealed Truths, which are conveyed to us by Books and Languages, are liable to the common and natural obscurities and difficulties incident to Words, methinks it would become us to be more careful and diligent in observing the former, and less magisterial, positive, and imperious, in imposing our own sense and interpretations of the latter.[62]

Locke's point is that "revealed Truths, which are conveyed to us by Books and Languages" (special revelation) are "liable to the common and natural obscurities and difficulties incident to Words." Therefore, since special revelation is so woefully mired in problematic human language, and since on the other hand natural revelation is so "plain" and "intelligible," he argues that we should give precedence and emphasis to "Natural Religion." In other words, Locke completely undermines the philosophical prerogative of biblical revelation. It is therefore hardly remarkable that Edwards would critique Locke on this matter.

Lest we leave such an important point—that Edwards was not uncritical of Locke's explicit subordination of revelation to reason—without adequate evidence, there is also some external evidence to bolster this connection between Miscellany 204 and Locke's *Essay.* Thomas A. Schafer, the dean of "Miscellany" scholarship, dates this entry to between December 1725 and January 1726.[63] This is the very same time that Schafer indicates Edwards was writing "The Mind" entry numbers 40–45. The subject of "The Mind" entry 41 was a topic in Book II of Locke's *Essay*, while entries 42 and 43 deal with topics in Book III.[64] There is therefore little doubt that "Miscellany" 204 was written while Edwards was reading and reflecting upon Books II and III of the *Essay.*

In light of this evidence, we conclude that Locke's theory of human language and subsequent undermining of special revelation prompted Edwards to conceive of his communicative argument. God did not merely create human beings with the ability to speak with one another but also—and more importantly—furnished them the ability to converse with their

to mind one's own thoughts, is the one exception to this situation. Edwards could have replied that, no matter what the situation with human language, our reception of special revelation is just such a case. The "divine and supernatural light" is predicated on the presence of the Holy Spirit within the believer, and thus God is in fact speaking to himself using his own proprietary words.

[62] Locke, *Essay*, III.9.23.

[63] Thomas A. Schafer, "Editor's Introduction," in *Works Vol. 13*, p. 96.

[64] Edwards, "The Mind" entries 41–43, in *Works Vol. 6*, pp. 359–62.

communicative creator. This feature enables mankind to fulfill the "end" of creation as well as vouchsafes the epistemic priority of special revelation. Our discussion of this issue has again demonstrated Edwards' sensitivity to the threat posed by a wide range of philosophic currents, not only to left-of-center Deism but also to aspects of mainstream Lockean philosophy.

V The Necessity of Revelation in Edwards' Apologetic Program

We finally consider how the forgoing discussion relates to one of the more intriguing issues for interpreters of Edwards' theological and philosophical project: his apparent shift in apologetic approach from the "Rational Account" to the "History of the Work of Redemption."[65] The basic facts of the matter are these: from 1724 until around 1740, Edwards planned as his main work a comprehensive rational apologetic of orthodox theology called the "Rational Account."[66] By the time he writes to the Princeton Trustees in 1757, however, the projected masterworks are now the "History of the Work of Redemption" and the "Harmony of the Old and New Testament."[67] Edwards does not explain exactly why he might have abandoned the former project that once held such attraction for him, but we have some clues from his enthusiastic description of the "History of the Work of Redemption":

> This history will be carried on with regard to all three worlds, heaven, earth, and hell: considering the connected, successive events and alterations, in each so far as the Scriptures give any light; introducing all parts of divinity in that order which is most scriptural and most natural: which is a method which appears to me the most beautiful and entertaining, wherein every divine doctrine, will appear to greatest advantage in the brightest light, in the most striking manner, showing the admirable contexture and harmony of the whole.[68]

Clearly, Edwards thinks that he has found the ideal way of achieving what he is trying to accomplish theologically. Elements of the advantages afforded

[65] Not that this issue has necessarily attracted a great deal of discussion; Chamberlain's very plausible treatment of it in the introduction to *Works* 18 may have quelled further discussion for the time being.

[66] Chamberlain, "Editor's Introduction," in *Works Vol. 18*, pp. 24–25. See the discussion on the "Rational Account" above, pp. 57–58.

[67] Edwards, "Letter to the Princeton Trustees," in *Works Vol. 16*, pp. 727–28.

[68] Edwards, "Letter to the Princeton Trustees," in *Works Vol. 16*, p. 728.

include its narrative flow, its connection of events across realm and time, and the fact that it is a "scriptural and most natural" method, elements apparently lacking in more conventional approaches.

Besides these positive advantages to the historical method, Ava Chamberlain offers the following possible disadvantages of the "Rational Account":

> A purely rational defense of Christian doctrine would have required Edwards to use, as did the latitudinarians in their anti-Deist polemic, the standard of rationality advocated by his opponents. To avoid this 'tactical mistake' [Henry F. May] Edwards may have abandoned the 'Rational Account' and adopted a more historical approach to the defense of Christian doctrine.[69]

Chamberlain's analysis seems plausible, but there is perhaps more that could be said on the subject. One piece of the primary evidence that requires some further explanation is the fact that Edwards did not cease writing on topics that were earmarked for inclusion into the "Rational Account" in 1740. Why might he continue to write on many of these issues, often using the same rational apologetic approach, long after he abandoned the "Rational Account" project? Also, if Edwards found the defense of special revelation so very vital, how might this end have been served by transitioning to a historical method?

First of all, any analysis that gives the impression that Edwards made an abrupt and decisive transition to the "History" project and to an exclusively historical approach should be qualified.[70] Notice Edwards' precise words in the letter to the Princeton trustees:

> I have already published something on one of the main points in dispute between the Arminians and Calvinists: and have it in view, God willing (as I have already signified to the public), in like manner to consider all the other controverted points, and have done much towards a preparation for it. But besides these . . .[71]

Edwards does not immediately mention the "History of the Work of Redemption"; he first refers to the already published *Freedom of the Will* and

[69] Chamberlain, "Editor's Introduction," in *Works Vol. 18*, p. 29.
[70] Not that such a description was necessarily Chamberlain's intention.
[71] Edwards, "Letter to the Princeton Trustees," in *Works Vol. 16*, p. 727.

to other works in preparation on "all the other controverted points." Given the fact that Edwards' collection of data for a defense of the necessity of special revelation continued unabated until the end, it seems possible that a work making this case would have been on the list of "other controverted points." It is also possible that such a book would have made use of both rational and historical methodologies; Edwards does not say that his "entirely new" method would apply to these controversial works already in progress.

Moreover, we should consider how the necessity of special revelation material might have been incorporated into a historical methodology, whether in "History of the Work of Redemption" or in a separate work using a similar approach. Many of the conventional arguments were already predicated on the testimony of history anyhow, so the shift would only further emphasize them. What, then, of the communicative argument? Edwards' belief that God is a communicative being was for him a fundamental reality, in light of which everything else in nature and history must be understood. God seeks communion with his elect intelligent creatures, and he carries on a personal conversation with them. The problem was that Locke and the latitudinarians no less than the Deists denied the reality of this conversation at significant points. Edwards thus needed to demonstrate as convincingly as possible the reality of God's conversation. Perhaps the best way of doing this was not so much to prove its hypothetical concurrence with Enlightenment rationality but to demonstrate its reality *as a matter of historical record.* God *has* carried on this conversation with his people in human history, throughout the "History of the Work of Redemption." This conversation has continued right up until Edwards' own time, as seen in the Awakenings he personally witnessed. God is a personal, communicative being, and this is demonstrated not only in once giving a special revelation in the Scriptures but also in the prophecy of that book being fulfilled in history; in prayers being answered, in real communion being accomplished in the events of redemptive history.[72] However, we shall leave a fuller discussion of Edwards' project to the final chapter.

[72] Claude Smith noticed hints of this connection between Edwards' concerns for conversational revelation and his historical method: "[Edwards] concludes that it is wholly arbitrary and illogical to reject the general proposition that God speaks to man. Indeed, Edwards goes further. Though he could accept mystery as part of revelation, since it was God who was conversing with man, he undertook to show that the revelations of the Bible were not as mysterious as some people thought. In The History of Redemption he showed that there was a pattern and inner consistency to the various conversations which God has with his people, as these are recorded in the Bible" (Smith, "Jonathan Edwards and 'the Way of Ideas'", *Harvard Theological Review* 59, no. 2 (1966), pp. 158–59).

VI Conclusion

We have been discussing Edwards' relational apologetic for the necessity of special revelation. Over the course of this and the preceding chapters, some themes have emerged. One is that Edwards took into account a wide range of contemporary challenges, not only from the Deists but also from the definitively mainstream John Locke. Edwards thus framed his theology of revelation in the context of an intellectual milieu that was deeply hostile to the notion of a privileged, personal communication given only to a select few. Another theme is that Edwards seemed unwilling to compromise with these corrosive forces but sought rather to affirm the relevant truth in the most radical terms possible. This had the net result of a theology of revelation that was profound as well as comprehensive. Most significantly, we see the importance of Edwards' communicative model, not as a context-bound apologetic device but as an outworking of a Trinitarian theology of divine communication. We turn now to a more specific discussion of Edwards' understanding of Scripture.

Chapter 4

Scripture

"Divine Revelation is like a light that shines in a dark place."
—*Jonathan Edwards, sermon on II Peter 1:19*[1]

I Introduction

Our discussion of Edwards' doctrine of Scripture began in the previous chapter, where we observed the central place that Edwards reserved for special revelation in his theology of divine communication. The Bible was not the defective, redundant source of information the Deists made it out to be. Rather, it was God's perfect means of carrying on a privileged conversation with his chosen people. In this chapter, we explore Edwards' thought concerning this keystone of God's communicative project.

Edwards believed that Scripture shared the attributes of God, and, in his context, the most significant of these were the interrelated attributes of harmony and authority. At a time in which allegations of dissonance in Scripture were often used as a pretext to reject its authority, the demonstration of harmony was for him the obvious way to reassert it. Although Edwards' apologetic agenda was influenced primarily by the spectrum of rationalism, he also had to deal with "enthusiasts" who were damaging the credibility of the Awakenings by their claims to new supernatural revelation. Edwards responded to these stimuli with a comprehensive apologetic for Scripture centering on the demonstration of harmony.[2]

Although apologetic interests drove him to write, Edwards' own beliefs were founded on a reception of biblical authority that required no external or evidential support. The entirety of Scripture was for him the very Word of God written, attested by abundant evidence but received as such only by

[1] Edwards, sermon on II Peter 1:19, in *Works Vol. 19*, p. 710.
[2] See the discussion on the "Great Works" below, Chapter 6.

supernatural regeneration.[3] Thus, while Edwards sought to demonstrate that the Bible accords well with the best exercise of reason, he did not accept the notion that its credibility depended upon passing tests set by skeptics. In light of this, we shall begin our discussion with the authority of Scripture.

II The Authority of Scripture

The paramount question regarding Scripture in Edwards' day was one of authority. Issues such as biblical criticism and the canon, though debated independently and apparently on their own merits, were part of a larger movement working to undermine the Bible's authority.[4] Thus Edwards' efforts focused upon this subject.

a. Edwards' foundation to be distinguished from his apologetic

From the outset of our discussion, a distinction needs to be drawn between the authority structure of Edwards' own beliefs and the apologetic arguments he presented to the world. Edwards did not rest his own conviction about the Bible's absolute authority on any kind of rational proof.[5] His settled position regarding biblical authority was logically prior to other beliefs, and he would agree with Calvin that a true conviction on the matter was irreducibly of supernatural origin.[6] Moreover, the unbeliever is bereft of the only means—the "new Sense" given by the Spirit—that would allow him to "know that the Scriptures are the word of God."[7] Consider the following statement: "God gives evidences of the truth of his word by giving evidence that it is his word. God is not wont to speak to men, leaving of 'em without sufficient means to know who it is that speaks."[8] Such a statement could

[3] See the discussion below. See also Edwards, *The Distinguishing Marks of a Work of the Spirit of God*, in *Works Vol. 4*, p 227; and Edwards, "Ministers to Preach Not Their Own Wisdom but the Word of God," in Richard A. Bailey and Gregory A. Wills, *The Salvation of Souls: Nine Previously Unpublished Sermons on the Call of Ministry and the Gospel by Jonathan Edwards* (Wheaton, IL: Crossway Books, 2002), pp. 128–29.

[4] See Henning Graf Reventlow, *The Authority of the Bible and the Rise of the Modern World*, translated by John Bowden (Philadelphia: Fortress Press, 1980. Reprint, 1985).

[5] "Divine revelation in these things does not go a-begging for credit and validity by approbation and applause of our understanding" (Edwards, "Ministers to Preach Not Their Own Wisdom but the Word of God," in Richard A. Bailey and Gregory A. Wills, *The Salvation of Souls: Nine Previously Unpublished Sermons on the Call of Ministry and the Gospel by Jonathan Edwards* (Wheaton, IL: Crossway Books, 2002), p. 127).

[6] Calvin, *Institutes* II.2.18; Commentary on Acts 17:27.

[7] Edwards, "Qualifications for Full Communion," in *Works Vol. 25*, p. 438.

[8] Edwards, "Yield to God's Word, or be Broken by His Hand," in *Works Vol. 25*, p. 211.

easily be mistaken to mean that a conviction of biblical authority may be derived from evidence alone. Yet in another sermon, something very different is insisted upon: "[The unconverted] can't know that the Scriptures are the word of God . . . if he were convinced, he would be gained."[9] The reconciliation is that God gives sufficient evidence to prove the authenticity of his Word, but sinners in their depravity do not appreciate this evidence. The Spirit alone provides the requisite new sense of the heart in the regenerate.[10] So although Edwards never misses an opportunity to point to the evidence, he thought that to be truly convinced of the authority of the Bible is an irreducible mark of supernatural regeneration. His proofs were therefore made in order to answer the attacks of critics and render them inexcusable before God, not because he harbored hopes that anyone would come to full assurance of the truth through them. With this distinction noted, we shall say more on Edwards' position.

b. Scripture as the authoritative Word of God

Edwards' relationship to the Scriptures might best be characterized by the word *authority*. This relationship is further described by other concepts—such as inspiration, perspicuity, sufficiency, infallibility, and inerrancy—that explicate the ways in which this authority is manifested, but it begins with Edwards' logically prior conviction that the Scriptures were the Word of God.[11] There was a time during the mid-twentieth century when scholars tended to downplay this decidedly antimodernist aspect of Edwards,[12] prompting Carl Bogue to ask in exasperation, "What if Jonathan Edwards were first and foremost a Christian theologian willingly subjecting himself and his thoughts to the revelation of 'the King eternal, immortal, invisible, the only wise God'?"[13] Recent scholarship, however, is more willing to acknowledge Edwards' submission to biblical authority. Stephen J. Stein,

[9] Edwards, "Qualifications for Full Communion," in *Works Vol. 25*, p. 438.

[10] See, for example, Edwards' unpublished sermon no. 26 on I Cor. 2:14 given at Bolton, which teaches the doctrine, "There is a spiritual understanding of divine things which all natural and unregenerate men are destitute of" (Yale Works of Jonathan Edwards project office).

[11] See, for example, the "Natural Philosophy" Cover-Leaf Memoranda 19: "Lest I may mention a great many things, and places of Scripture, that the world will judge but frivolous reasons for the proof of what I drive at, not to mention such as I fear it of as what I depend on for proof, but to bring 'em in so that the force of reasons will naturally and unavoidably be brought to the mind of the reader" (Edwards, "Natural Philosophy," in *Works Vol. 6*, pp.194–95).

[12] With the notable exception of intellectual historian Peter Gay: "For Edwards, the authority of the Bible is absolute" (Peter Gay, *A Loss of Mastery: Puritan Historians in Colonial America* (Berkeley: University of California Press, 1966), p. 96).

[13] Carl W. Bogue, *Jonathan Edwards and the Covenant of Grace* (Cherry Hill, NJ: Mack Publishing Company, 1975), p. 5.

who has probably spent more time in Edwards' vast body of scriptural commentary than anyone else, pronounces that Edwards "never doubted the credibility, authority, unity, or sufficiency of the Bible."[14] Nathan Hatch and Harry Stout affirm that biblical exegesis held "an all-consuming hold" on Edwards.[15] Helen Westra thinks that, for Edwards, "reason must always bow to divine revelation and the authority of Scripture."[16]

There are a number of ways in which Edwards could communicate his position on biblical authority. One of the clearest statements is in a 1740 ordination sermon bearing the descriptive title, "Ministers are not to preach those things which their own wisdom or reason suggests, but the things that are already dictated to them by the superior wisdom and knowledge of God."[17] Edwards' doctrine is that ministers have no license to teach only those things that seem reasonable to them but are bound to receive and convey God's Word in Scripture:

> Sir, I would now humbly and earnestly recommend to you that Holy Book which God is about to commit into your hands, as containing that message which you are to deliver to this people in his name. God gives you this Word—which is his Word—to preach that, and not the dictates of your own reason. You are to preach the dictates of God's infinitely superior understanding, humbly submitting your reason as a learner and disciple to that, renouncing all confidence in your own wisdom and entirely relying on God's instructions.[18]

Edwards enjoins his younger brother in the ministry to ". . . renounc[e] all confidence" in his own wisdom and to rely entirely "on God's instructions," which are to be found in "that Holy Book." If one were given a hundred words or less to articulate the strongest possible endorsement of biblical

[14] Stein, "Editor's Introduction," in *Works Vol. 15*, p. 21.

[15] Nathan O. Hatch and Harry S. Stout (eds.), *Jonathan Edwards and the American Experience* (New York and Oxford: Oxford University Press, 1988), p. 9.

[16] Helen Petter Westra, "Jonathan Edwards And 'What Reason Teaches,'" *Journal of the Evangelical Theological Society* 34 (1991), p. 497.

[17] This 1740 sermon on 1 Corinthians 2:11–13 was first brought to wider attention by Westra's 1991 article and subsequently published as "Ministers Not to Preach Their Own Wisdom But the Word of God," in *Southern Baptist Journal* 3 (1999) pp. 16–33, then in Richard A. Bailey and Gregory A. Wills (eds.), *The Salvation of Souls: Nine Previously Unpublished Sermons on the Call of Ministry and the Gospel by Jonathan Edwards* (Wheaton, IL: Crossway Books, 2002), pp. 111–32.

[18] Edwards, "Ministers to Preach Not Their Own Wisdom but the Word of God," in Richard A. Bailey and Gregory A. Wills, *The Salvation of Souls: Nine Previously Unpublished Sermons on the Call of Ministry and the Gospel by Jonathan Edwards* (Wheaton, IL: Crossway Books, 2002), pp. 128–29.

authority and the most emphatic repudiation of rationalism, it would be difficult to improve upon this effort.

Edwards also supplies some logical support for this doctrine. His main argument gives us some insight into the epistemological priority he assigned to the Scriptures:

> If no doctrine is to be received but what reason teaches them, men must first see whether their reason teaches it before they receive it. And in this rule 'tis impossible that God's revelation should ever really be the ground of our receiving any one doctrine whatsoever because no doctrine is received till we have first consulted reason to know whether that teaches it. So then our receiving it is always in this way prior to our hearing the word of revelation. So then the foundation of faith is men's reason or word and not divine revelation . . .[19]

The point Edwards makes so powerfully is that "God's revelation" must be the "ground" of all that we receive as true. If we do as the rationalists insist by passing every doctrine we find in the Bible through the filter of human reason, then we have mistakenly assigned epistemic priority to reason. This would mean that "the foundation of faith is men's reason or word and not divine revelation"—a grave mistake. For, "When men come to make God's revelation to be only the handmaid or bondmaid, and to set reason over it as mistress, no wonder that it soon come to that, that the mistress casts out the bondmaid and all her progeny. . . ."[20] Subsequent Western history would seem to indicate that Edwards was prophetically correct.

c. Theology not a "science"

In another sermon given about the same time, Edwards takes sides on a debate within his immediate theological inheritance in order to pursue his radical antirationalist agenda. In the first section of what was a primary theological textbook in Edwards' day, Turretin refers to theology as a "*sciencia*" (science) dozens of times.[21] However, Edwards rejects this position

[19] Edwards, "Ministers to Preach Not Their Own Wisdom but the Word of God," in Richard A. Bailey and Gregory A. Wills, *The Salvation of Souls: Nine Previously Unpublished Sermons on the Call of Ministry and the Gospel by Jonathan Edwards* (Wheaton, IL: Crossway Books, 2002), p. 128.

[20] Edwards, "Ministers to Preach Not Their Own Wisdom but the Word of God," in Richard A. Bailey and Gregory A. Wills, *The Salvation of Souls: Nine Previously Unpublished Sermons on the Call of Ministry and the Gospel by Jonathan Edwards* (Wheaton, IL: Crossway Books, 2002), p. 128.

[21] See Turretin, *Institutes of Elenctic Theology* (ed. James T. Dennison Jr.; trans. George Musgrave Giger; 3 vols Phillipsburg, NJ: P&R Publishing 1992–97), pp. 1–4, 16–18, 22.

and instead agrees with Peter van Mastricht that theology is rather a "*doctrina*" (doctrine):[22]

> . . . this is divinity; which is not learned, as other sciences, merely by the improvement of man's natural reason, but is taught by God himself in a certain book that he hath given for that end, full of instruction. This is the rule which God hath given to the world to be their guide in searching after this kind of knowledge, and is a summary of all things of this nature needful for us to know. Upon this account divinity is rather called a doctrine, than an art or science.[23]

Science implies a human process of discovery and ratiocination to arrive at new information, and, in Edwards' view, this is not an accurate description of what happens (or should happen) in theology. Theology for him is a "doctrine" we receive from God's hand, through material already extant in "a certain book." In the 1740 ordination sermon, Edwards puts it this way: "God is now about to deliver to you a summary of doctrine already discovered and dictated to your hand, which you are to teach and zealously to maintain."[24] Considering how able a theological philosopher Edwards was, this statement is a remarkable testimony of the depth of his conviction on biblical authority.

d. Sufficiency of Scripture

We mentioned that biblical authority was manifested in various ways throughout Edwards' thought, and one of these was in his doctrine of *sufficiency*. It is one thing to say only that the Bible is the Word of God; without some further elaboration, we are free to suppose that it must be supplemented in ways that would, at least in practice, deny its authority. It is quite another to add, in the language of the Westminster divines, that the Scriptures are fully sufficient to be the only "rule for faith and life."[25] Edwards found ample occasion to write on this subject during the Awakenings:

[22] See Mastricht, *Theoretico-Practica Theologia* (Amsterdam 1715), I.1.i.
[23] Edwards, "The Importance and Advantage of a Thorough Knowledge of Divine Truth," in *Works Vol. 22*, p. 86.
[24] Edwards, "Ministers to Preach Not Their Own Wisdom but the Word of God," in Richard A. Bailey and Gregory A. Wills, *The Salvation of Souls: Nine Previously Unpublished Sermons on the Call of Ministry and the Gospel by Jonathan Edwards* (Wheaton, IL: Crossway Books, 2002), p. 129.
[25] Westminster Confession of Faith 1.2.

> Another foundation error of those that don't acknowledge the divinity of this work [the Awakenings], is not taking the Holy Scriptures as an whole, and in itself a sufficient rule to judge of such things by . . . Those that I am speaking of, will indeed make some use of Scripture, so far as they think it serves their turn; but don't make use of it alone, as a rule sufficient by itself, but make as much, and a great deal more use of other things, diverse and wide from it, to judge of this work by.[26]

Edwards' basic problem with the Old Light rationalists who opposed the Awakenings was that they were unwilling to let Scripture judge the matter. They kept on bringing experience and reason—two of the principal rivals to the authority of Scripture—into the discussion, supposing that the Bible did not deal adequately with the matter. But Edwards accuses them of using Scripture only "so far as they think it serves their turn"; but they "don't make use of it alone, *as a rule sufficient by itself*." This, he supposed, was their "foundation error."

III Conventional Arguments for Biblical Authority

With Edwards' rather definite position on biblical authority established, we turn now to examine a couple of the "conventional" arguments he used to advocate his position in the 1737 lecture "Divine Revelation is Like a Light."[27] One of these arguments was to point out that Scripture itself claimed to be the Word of God, and one must either accept this conclusion or reject the book as fraudulent: "If the Scriptures ben't the Word of God, it is the greatest cheat and falsehood that ever was in the world. For from the beginning to the end, it has that show and pretense that it is the Word of God."[28] Edwards is here, as elsewhere, assuming a complete correspondence between the Bible's divine origin and its authority. Many would say that the Bible is a "good book," though perhaps not the very Word of the living God. Edwards argues that if it is not exactly what it claims to be then it is "the greatest cheat and falsehood that ever was in the world."

Another of Edwards' "conventional" arguments is based on the effects biblical revelation has had on human society. Had not the revealed Christian religion brought the Europeans themselves from a state of tribal darkness to the height of civilization? "Our ancestors were, before the gospel came

[26] Edwards, *Some Thoughts Concerning the Present Revival*, in *Works Vol. 4*, p. 296.
[27] Edwards, "Divine Revelation is Like a Light," in *Works Vol. 19*, pp. 704–33.
[28] Edwards, "Divine Revelation is Like a Light," in *Works Vol. 19*, p. 721.

among [them], ignorant and barbarous, much like the Indians here in America. Wherever the gospel has come, it has civilized the people, and brought not only the knowledge of God, but all other useful knowledge."[29] Edwards makes the following inference from this history:

> Hence we may learn how unreasonable they are who reject or doubt of the authority of the Holy Scriptures; for 'tis most evident that this, and no other, has in fact been that revelation that has, from the beginning, been such a light in this world, as we have heard.[30]

The Bible's authority is proven by its unique power to transform people. Those who reject or doubt it are therefore, in Edwards' view, "unreasonable."

IV The Harmony of Scripture

Edwards employed a range of "conventional" arguments for the Bible's authority, but there is not much in this category that rises beyond standard eighteenth-century apologetics. The distinctive aspect of his work in this area was certainly his harmony apologetic. We have proposed that Edwards' larger project was to interpret the harmony of all reality.[31] As a subset, he sought to demonstrate that the Scriptures possessed the authenticating hallmark of harmony. Described in terms of Edwards' three unfinished "Great Works," the Scriptures exhibited harmony with itself ("The Harmony of the Old and New Testaments"), with reason ("The Rational Account"), and with history ("The History of the Work of Redemption").[32] Such perfect harmony could only mean that they were written by the "supreme harmony of all."[33]

According to Edwards, the force of the harmony apologetic came from it being a natural function of human perception. We perceive the reality of an underlying intelligence by observing harmony in phenomena. This philosophic principle is established in entry 63 of "The Mind":

> Sensible things, by virtue of the *harmony* and proportion that is seen in them, carry the appearance of perceiving and willing being. They

[29] Edwards, "Divine Revelation is Like a Light," in *Works Vol. 19*, p. 716.
[30] Edwards, "Divine Revelation is Like a Light," in *Works Vol. 19*, p. 721.
[31] See the discussion of Edwards' project below, Chapter 6.
[32] See the discussion below, Chapter 6.
[33] Edwards, "Miscellany" 182, in *Works Vol. 13*, p. 329.

> evidently show at first blush the action and governing of understanding and volition. The notes of a tune of the strokes of an acute penman, for instance, are placed in such exact order, having such mutual respect one to another, that they carry with them into the mind of him that sees or hears the conception of an understanding and will exerting itself in these appearances.[34]

Harmony is precisely the opposite of true randomness, which can never be the product of intelligent thought.[35] Harmony consists in "exact order" and "mutual respect," the appearance of which rightly leads us to believe there is a thinking agent behind the work of composition we have in view. Edwards thinks that this association is what naturally happens when any mind is exposed to harmony, and not necessarily the result of supernatural endowment. Whether the unregenerate could rightly *appreciate* the presence of harmony before them was another matter entirely.

Given this understanding of the implications of harmony, if someone believes that there is one divinely intelligent Author of Scripture and wishes to prove this to others, then one simply needs to point out the manifestations of harmony. Edwards was certain that just such a case could be made:

> The being of a God is evident by the Scriptures, and the Scriptures themselves are an evidence of their own divine authority, after the same manner as the existence of a human thinking being is evident by the motions, behavior and speech of a body of a human form and contexture, or that that body is animated by a rational mind. For we know this no otherwise than by the consistency, harmony and concurrence of the train of actions and sounds, and their agreement to all that we can suppose to be in a rational mind. [. . .] So there is that wondrous universal harmony and consent and concurrence in the aim and drift, such an universal appearance of a wonderful glorious design, such stamps everywhere of exalted and divine wisdom, majesty and holiness in matter, manner, contexture and aim; that the evidence is the same that the Scriptures are the word and work of a divine mind.[36]

[34] Edwards, "The Mind" entry 63, in *Works Vol. 6*, p. 382; emphasis mine.
[35] Indeed, it remains an open question as to whether true randomness exists anywhere in the universe. At the very least, we can be certain that people and computers are incapable of it.
[36] Edwards, "Miscellany" 333, in *Works Vol. 13*, p. 410.

The Scriptures exhibit such a "wondrous universal harmony" and "universal appearance of a wonderful glorious design" that it is clear that they must be "the word and work of a divine mind." This entry was written toward the beginning of Edwards' career, and there is no evidence that he ever changed his mind as to the potential for harmony to establish the divine origin and authority of the Bible for those who were willing to listen.[37] Rather, it seems to have been the coalescing of the main strategy he would employ throughout his lifetime to reestablish the authority of Scripture.

Toward the end of Edwards' life, we find in the 1757 "Letter to the Princeton Trustees" some summary plans for *The Harmony of the Old and New Testament.* These plans confirm the constancy of Edwards' thought on this matter and also provide mature examples of some ways he hoped would demonstrate biblical harmony:

> I have also for my own profit and entertainment, done much towards another great work, which I call *The Harmony of the Old and New Testament,* in three parts. The first considering the prophecies of the Messiah [. . .] showing the universal, precise, and admirable correspondence between predictions and events. The second part: considering the types of the Old Testament, showing the evidence of their being intended as representations of the great things of the gospel of Christ: and the agreement of the type with the antitype. The third and great part, considering the harmony of the Old and New Testament, as to doctrine and precept.[38]

Edwards thought that he had three primary avenues for pointing out the harmony he believed to be evident throughout Scripture: fulfilled prophecy, typological agreement, and doctrinal unity. Instances of Edwards finding data to populate these three categories are to be found throughout the corpus, not least in the nearly complete notebooks we have that were to have formed the bulk of the "Harmony."[39] In these, we find Edwards exerting himself to show that minute details and subtle interrelations over many centuries and through dozens of human writers demonstrate a level of prophetic, typological, and doctrinal harmony that could only be explained by divine authorship.

[37] The identity of "those who were willing to listen" is, ultimately, the regenerate.

[38] Edwards, "Letter to the Princeton Trustees," in *Works Vol. 16*, p. 728.

[39] See the transcriptions of Edwards' "Harmony" notebook and "Miscellanies" 1067 and 1068 available online at Yale University's Jonathan Edwards Center, as well as "Miscellany" 1069, in *Works Vol. 11.*

V The Inspiration of Scripture

The means by which God transmitted his verbal communication through the agency of human writers was also a topic that engaged the mind of Jonathan Edwards. Edwards was faced with the pressing apologetic task of defending the Scriptures against the skeptics' charge that the Bible was subject to all the limitations attending human authorship. The doctrine of inspiration, or something very much like it, was the only concept capable of defeating this charge. Along with this was the equally pressing polemic task of refuting the "enthusiasts" who claimed that God was still dispensing inspiration in the present day. Inspiration had to be powerful enough to explain a perfect Bible yet circumscribed relative to postcanonical (and extracanonical) claims.

Edwards' thought in this area owed much to his Puritan predecessor John Owen. Due to the doctrine of inspiration's unfashionable appeal to the supernatural as well as the authoritative privileging it necessarily lent to Scripture, this doctrine was already under increasing pressure in the later part of the seventeenth century. Owen responded with one of the most radically conservative positions on inspiration possible in his *Pneumatologia*.[40] In gauging the general bent of Edwards' position, it is useful to note that Edwards quotes with evident approval a typical statement from Owen's work in the "Blank Bible" entry for I Chronicles 28:19:

> The Spirit of God acted and guided the prophets 'as to the very organs of their bodies, whereby they expressed the revelation which they had received by inspiration from him. They spake as they were acted by the Holy Ghost. [. . .] The Spirit of God not only revealed it unto [David], but so guided him in writing of it down, as that he might understand the mind of God out of what he himself had written; or he gave it him so plainly and evidently, as if every particular had been expressed in writing by the finger of God.'[41]

God's exercise of control over the inspired prophets was "as to the very organs of their bodies," so that what they wrote was equivalent to it being "by the finger of God." As we shall see, Edwards' own statements on

[40] Owen, *Pneumatologia or A Discourse Concerning the Holy Spirit*, in *The Works of John Owen* Vol. III (Edinburgh: Banner of Truth, 2000).

[41] Edwards, "Blank Bible" entry on I Chron. 28:19, in *Works Vol. 24*, p. 410. Edwards' reference is "Owen, *On the Spirit*, Bk. 2, ch. 1, § 10," found in *The Works of John Owen* Vol. III (Edinburgh: Banner of Truth, 2000), p. 134.

inspiration will comport well with this understanding expressed by Owen. If Edwards' articulation differed at all, it was in his more extensive efforts to integrate the natural and supernatural aspects of divine revelation into a unified account of the ways in which God communicates to his creatures.[42]

First, Edwards makes the distinction that inspiration was not merely a case of God granting knowledge to someone; at least ultimately, *all* knowledge comes from God: "'Tis God that makes known all truth to men: [he] is the fountain of all light and knowledge, of those things that we know by natural means—by experience, teaching, [and] reason."[43] Since all knowledge is from God, the distinctive characteristic of inspiration must lie elsewhere. Edwards locates the defining attribute in the concept of immediacy:[44]

> But besides these ordinary ways, God has oftentimes made known truth to men in an extraordinary way, and that is by *immediately* impressing truths on their minds by suggestions of those truths then made, either by some voice or in some dream or vision, or by words or ideas *immediately* and miraculously excited, without any dependence on any notice the person to whom the truth is suggested has of that truth by way of his outward senses, or by his experience, or reason, or any preceding testimonies, or any foregoing declaration of that truth to him in any preceding revelation. This is making known truth by *immediate* revelation.[45]

God ordinarily makes use of means such as nature, Scripture, and history to communicate to his creatures, all of which entail the use of the senses. What sets inspiration apart is precisely a lack of dependence upon "outward senses" to learn the relevant information—God uses dreams, visions, or otherwise directly suggests truths. Inspiration is thus "immediate."

This understanding of inspiration does not mean, however, that the immediately revealed truth *conflicts* with the senses. On the contrary, there was often a confluence of ordinary and immediate communication in the mind of the inspired writers of Scripture:

[42] This basic concept is one that Owen emphatically endorsed (see *The Works of John Owen* Vol. III (Edinburgh: Banner of Truth, 2000), pp. 144–145), but he perhaps did not devote as much effort as did Edwards to spell out its implications.

[43] Edwards, "Extraordinary Gifts of the Spirit are Inferior to Graces of the Spirit," sermon on I Cor. 13:8–13, in *Works Vol. 25*, p. 283.

[44] See the discussion of Edwards' understanding of the supernatural in history in below, Chapter 5.

[45] Edwards, "Extraordinary Gifts of the Spirit are Inferior to Graces of the Spirit," sermon on I Cor. 13:8–13, in *Works Vol. 25*, p. 282; emphasis mine.

First, 'tis declared by a voice from heaven, which was the testimony of the Son of God, the same person spoken of in the next verse. At the same time it was inwardly revealed to John by the Holy Spirit, confirming what the voice of the Son had declared, 'Yea, saith the Spirit,' etc.[46]

This confluence is entirely consonant with Edwards' general view of the harmony of divine communication. Here also, the Trinitarian implications of this harmony are manifest, as the Son and the Spirit speak the same message in different ways.

Edwards also made abundant allowance for God to use the personalities and personal circumstances of the prophets to write what he intended them to write. This means that, although Edwards sometimes uses language that sounds like a bare dictation theory of inspiration, this was not the case. Edwards' description of Solomon is instructive:

I imagine that Solomon, when he wrote this song, being a very philosophical, musing man, and a pious man, and of a very loving temper, sees himself in his own musings to imagine and to point forth to himself a pure, virtuous, pious and entire love; and represented the musings and feelings of his mind, that in a philosophical and religious frame was carried away in a sort of transport: and in that [frame] his musings and the train of his imaginations were guided and led on by the Spirit of God.[47]

God makes a *natural* use of the personalities and life situations of those whom he superintends to write the Scriptures and does not need to force them unnaturally. This concept is again in accord with Owen's understanding of inspiration: "he that toucheth skilfully several musical instruments, variously tuned, maketh several notes of music."[48]

If God did not twist their arms in some violent fashion or put them into trances, how did the prophets *know* when they were inspired? This was of course a matter of crucial importance in the eighteenth century. In the context of a nearly full-scale epistemology found in "The Mind," Edwards writes the following:

The evidence of immediate inspiration that the prophets had when they were immediately inspired by the Spirit of God with any truth is

[46] Edwards, "Blank Bible" entry on Revelation 14:13, in *Works Vol. 24*.
[47] "Miscellany" 303, in *Works Vol. 13*, p. 389.
[48] Owen, *Pneumatologia or A Discourse Concerning the Holy Spirit*, in *The Works of John Owen* Vol. III (Edinburgh: Banner of Truth, 2000). p. 145.

> an absolute sort of certainty; and the knowledge is in a sense intuitive, much in the same manner as faith and spiritual knowledge of the truth in religion. Such bright ideas are raised, and such a clear view of a perfect agreement with the excellencies of the divine nature, that it's known to be a communication from him. All the Deity appears in the thing, and in everything pertaining to it. The prophet has so divine a sense, such a divine disposition, such a divine pleasure, and sees so divine an excellency and so divine a power in what is revealed, that he sees immediately that God is there as we perceive one another's presence when we are talking together face to face.[49]

The evidence Edwards offers for prophets knowing they were inspired might appear hopelessly subjective, consisting merely of "an absolute sort of certainty." Edwards conceives of the experience as "in a sense intuitive," similar to self-justifying experience of faith itself. Yet he also thinks that the experience to be analogous to normal sense perception, in which the inspired prophet "sees immediately that God is there as we perceive one another's presence when we are talking face to face." Here Edwards is applying in a different area the same basic conviction that fuels his harmony apologetic: given the right awareness and perspective, God's communication differs little from human conversation wherein the identity of our conversation partner is never in any doubt. He finds biblical support for his theory in I Samuel 3:7: "the prophets, after they had once had intercourse with God by immediate revelation from God, gained acquaintance with [him] so as afterwards to know him, as it were to know his voice or know what was indeed a revelation from God."[50] So both in the case of our reading the Scriptures today and in the case of the immediate inspiration of the prophets, people can know the identity of the divine author speaking to us.[51]

Edwards' most controversial opinion in relation to inspiration is no doubt his speculation that the heathen philosophers were helped by divine inspiration.[52] In order to understand why Edwards might have countenanced (privately, at least) this possibility, we would do well to recall his situation.

[49] Edwards, "The Mind," in *Works Vol. 6*, p. 346.
[50] Edwards, "Miscellany" 1144, in *Works Vol. 20*, p. 518.
[51] All of which is consonant with Edwards' notion of God having a conversation with his people, discussed above in Chapter 3.
[52] This is the subject of a controversy between Gerald R. McDermott and Greg D. Gilbert. See Greg D. Gilbert, "The Nations Will Worship: Jonathan Edwards and the Salvation of the Heathen," *Trinity Journal* 23, no. 1 (2002), pp. 53–76; and Gerald R. McDermott, "Response to Gilbert: 'The Nations Will Worship: Jonathan Edwards and the Salvation of the Heathen,'" *Trinity Journal* 23, no. 1 (2002), pp. 77–80.

Edwards was defending the necessity of special revelation before an audience increasingly convinced of the sufficiency of reason alone. As seen in his extensive use of the *prisca theologia* theory, Edwards was not about to yield all the great intellectual achievements of the pre-Christian world to the mere workings of natural reason.[53] What, then, of the ancient philosophers, for whom evidence of their dependence on *prisca theologia* was not forthcoming? Rather than concede that their reason alone could attain such truth, Edwards is willing to allow that they might have been the recipients of divine inspiration:[54]

> It may be worthy of consideration whether or no some of the HEATHEN PHILOSOPHERS had not, with regard to some things, some degree of INSPIRATION of the Spirit of God, which led 'em to say such wonderful things concerning the Trinity, the Messiah, etc. Inspiration is not so high an honor and privilege as some are ready to think. It is no peculiar privilege of God's special favorites. Many very bad men have been the subjects of it, yea, some that were idolaters. [. . .] Yea the devils themselves seem sometimes to have been immediately actuated by God and forced to speak the truth in honor to Christ and his religion. [. . .] Why might not Socrates and Plato and some others of the wise men of Greece have some degree of inspiration, as well as the wise men from the east who came to see Christ when an infant?[55]

Edwards' last reference is one of the few scriptural precedents that Edwards had to go on, that the presumably pagan Magi were granted supernatural revelation. If a case could be made that the remarkable spiritual insights of Plato and Aristotle were the result of inspiration, it would eliminate an entire class of potentially troublesome evidence for the efficacy of human reason. So the overall direction of Edwards' point is to undercut the proto-liberals, not at all to concede anything to them.

However, Edwards might have solved a minor apologetic annoyance by creating a theological headache: if these philosophers were indeed

[53] As explained by McDermott, *prisca theologia* was the theory that accounted for elements of truth in the non-Christian world by claiming that such truths came from tradition handed down from figures such as Noah or through later contact with the Jewish nation. See Edwards, "Miscellany" 953, in *Works Vol.* 20, p. 222.

[54] Interestingly, Edwards had earlier written that the reason why the heathen philosophers "affected to be thought inspired" was simply because they derived their information from "the ancient, inspired, holy fathers" (Edwards, "Miscellany" 953, in *Works Vol.* 20, p. 225). The later possibility discussed here appears to be in some tension with this earlier entry.

[55] Edwards, "Miscellany" 1162, in *Works Vol. 23*, p. 84.

inspired, why are their works not part of canonical Scripture? Edwards recognized the problem, and presumed that they were not given the "certain evidences" necessary to establish them canonically.[56] The implication is that Edwards allowed inspiration to comprise a larger circle than Scripture, meaning that there are examples of genuine inspiration that are not included in the Bible. The decisive element would appear to be the presence or absence of appropriate authenticating evidence.

Carrying on with the implications, what might have been God's purpose in granting inspiration when no Scripture would result from it? Edwards thinks, "yet a good end might be answered in giving these revelations nevertheless," and gives a list of four possibilities for how this might be true.[57] The last of these constitutes one of the more controversial statements we have in the corpus: ". . . we know not of how great benefit the truths suggested might be to their *own souls*."[58] Alerting us to the problematic possibilities, McDermott explains, "Edwards is hesitant and tentative, but he nevertheless clearly opens the possibility that these heathen could have used revelation for their own spiritual benefit—a notion that is incoherent unless it means they can be saved."[59] Whether this episode constitutes more an intriguing nod to the possibility of the salvation of the heathen or a case in which Edwards' apologetically motivated penchant for speculation exceeded his scriptural warrant depends upon one's perspective. In any case, Edwards closes the door on inspiration of any kind with the completion of John's Apocalypse; this means that even if inspired heathen could at one point be saved in this way, that possibility has long since ceased.[60]

As we conclude our discussion of Edwards' doctrine of inspiration, we turn briefly to an item pertaining to the Old Testament. Edwards addresses

[56] See Edwards, "Miscellany" 1162, in *Works Vol. 23*, pp. 84–85. Edwards elsewhere explains what these might have been: "These extraordinary gifts of the Spirit were indeed given to many others besides the apostles, to those that were not penmen of the Scriptures, but yet it will not follow but that the great end of all these gifts was to settle a standing revelation. It is to be considered that these gifts was not only to give the means of grace or impart to the church a standing rule, but to establish and confirm it: to give it with evidence. All the extraordinary gifts that were in the apostle's days were given as confirmations of the word of Christ and the apostles; they were so many seals to their mission and divine testimonies to the divinity of their gospel" (Edwards, *Extraordinary Gifts of the Spirit are Inferior to Graces of the Spirit*, sermon on I Cor 13:8–13, in *Works Vol. 25*, p. 286).

[57] Edwards, "Miscellany" 1162, in *Works Vol. 23*, p. 85.

[58] Edwards, "Miscellany" 1162, in *Works Vol. 23*, p. 85; emphasis mine.

[59] Gerald R. McDermott, *Jonathan Edwards Confronts the Gods: Christian Theology, Enlightenment Religion, and Non-Christian Faiths* (Oxford and New York: Oxford University Press, 2000), p.141.

[60] See the discussion on the closing of the canon, below in this chapter.

the problem of how the Psalmists could speak concerning their immediate situation yet communicate transcendent spiritual truths:

> There are many of the Psalms, and some other parts of Scripture, wherein the penmen immediately intended the affairs of the church of Israel. But these things being represented poetically, in those beautiful and exalted images, which a poetical genius and fire, excited and invigorated by an extraordinary exercise of grace and a holy and evangelical disposition, in which excitations there was the afflatus of God's Spirit—their minds naturally conceived such poetical images of the Jewish church, as very exactly described the affairs of the gospel and the Christian church.[61]

Though the "penmen immediately intended" only affairs of ancient Israel, an "extraordinary exercise of grace" and "the afflatus of God's Spirit" meant that they could "very exactly" describe the things of the gospel and the Christian church.

VI The Canon of Scripture

Edwards' position on the canon of Scripture is rather straightforward and is well summarized by Stein: "For Edwards, the boundaries of the Christian canon were not debatable. He accepted the prevailing view that the biblical canon had been closed long ago and that there was no need to augment it."[62] Of course this traditional position on the canon was under attack in Edwards' day, and we are not surprised to find that he was concerned to mount a sustained defense of it. His work in this area fits into three basic categories. The first category, found primarily in the notebook material, consists of scholarly apologetic material defending the canon from the attacks of skeptical critics. The second argues for the closing of the canon in the first century AD and for the cessationist position with regard to the possibility of ongoing special revelation.[63] A third category, pervasive throughout the corpus, was Edwards' demonstration of the harmony of the biblical canon.[64]

[61] Edwards, "Miscellany" 251, in *Works Vol. 13*, p. 363.
[62] Stein, "Editor's Introduction," in Edwards, *Works Vol. 15*, p. 5.
[63] See also Philip A. Craig, "'And Prophecy Shall Cease': Jonathan Edwards on the Cessation of the Gift of Prophecy," *Westminster Theological Journal* 64, no. 1 (2002), pp. 163–84.
[64] See the section on harmony, above.

Pauw notes that Edwards "was willing, as always, to borrow good arguments where he could find them," and this was certainly true of the defense of the canon.[65] Since the state of the art in this discipline involved access to ancient sources that Edwards lacked, he was largely dependent on the work of others to obtain the raw material. But this did not mean that Edwards had nothing of his own to contribute. "Miscellany" 1060 entitled "Concerning the Canon of the New Testament" is a good example of his *modus operandi*, and will form the basis of our discussion here. The entry consists primarily of extended quotations from Jeremiah Jones' *A New and Full Method of Settling the Canonical Authority of the New Testament*, a work advancing the historical thesis that "the greatest part of Christians were very early agreed, what books were canonical and to be looked upon as the rule of their faith."[66] Edwards meticulously copies Jones' scholarship at great length, but intersperses this with his own logical and theological supplements.

Edwards' approach was often to take the same data used by the skeptics and to turn it on its head. One of his favorite arguments was thus to say that the very fact that there were so many counterfeits in early church history proves not that they were all fakes but that there were some widely acknowledged genuine articles worthy of counterfeit: ". . . that there should be such a multitude of counterfeits and imitations of these Gospels shows not only that there were genuine Gospels, but also shows the great value and importance of those genuine Gospels, and the high repute they had in the Christian church."[67] Edwards reiterates this line for the Book of Acts in the same entry, and for the Book of Revelation elsewhere.[68]

Edwards tried his hand at the Synoptic Problem. He thinks that the extensive but incomplete correspondence between Matthew and Mark actually provides proof of Mark's authenticity:

> 'Tis a great argument that St. Mark's Gospel was written honestly, and that it was no knavish forgery, that 'tis so much like St. Matthew's, only shorter. For what could induce a knave to go about to forge a history of Christ's life and death having scarce anything remarkable in it, but what was in an history already extant, and very little differing from it in any respect, but only that it has not so much in it.[69]

[65] Pauw, "Editor's Introduction," in Edwards, *Works Vol. 20*, p. 13.
[66] Jeremiah Jones, *A New and Full Method of Settling the Canonical Authority of the New Testament*, (3 vols, London, 1726), quoted in Edwards, "Miscellany" 1060, in *Works Vol. 20*, p. 396.
[67] Edwards, "Miscellany" 1060, in *Works Vol. 20*, p. 416.
[68] Edwards, "Blank Bible" entry on Rev. 1, in *Works Vol. 24*, p. 1203.
[69] Edwards, "Miscellany" 1060, in *Works Vol. 20*, p. 419.

Edwards again turns on its head the objection, this time based on the *differences* between the accounts of Matthew and Mark. ". . . if St. Mark had writ with this design [of confirming Matthew's lies], he would not have said less than St. Matthew, and there should have been none of those seeming differences and inconsistencies which there are between St. Matthew's Gospel and his."[70]

Edwards also defended the inclusion of problematic books into the canon. His comments to the effect on the book of Daniel are representative:

> The matter of the first finding and receiving this remarkable book and adding it to the canon must have been a famous event among [the Jews] . . . But that all should be without the least trace or footstep in history, or that any remaining account of any such event, but that it, the whole affair, should presently sink into oblivion and so universally pass among the people as though this book had always been part of their canon and universally received as such, even from the time of the captivity, is quite incredible.[71]

Due to its remarkably precise prophetic content, Daniel has long been under suspicion as *prophecy ex eventu.* Yet as Edwards poses the question, at which point was it simply inserted into the canon without any trace of the inevitable debate? Similar defenses were employed on behalf of other books such as Job.[72]

Turning now to a stimulus arising from the other side of the theological spectrum, Edwards also took aim at those who made claims to new inspiration. Edwards strenuously reaffirmed the traditional position that the canon was completed with the Book of Revelation:

> Christ, having given this last Revelation to his church to be added to the books of Scripture, [with] which the canon was to be shut up and sealed by the instrumentality of the apostle John, who lived the longest of the apostles and wrote this book after all the rest were dead: Christ therefore orders John (v. 10) to publish this book, [. . .] and then intimates that no more revelations are to be expected, no more instruction and warnings to be added to the word of God, as the standing means of grace, any further to confirm and enforce the rest . . .[73]

[70] Edwards, "Miscellany" 1060, in *Works Vol. 20,* pp. 419–420.
[71] Edwards, "Miscellany" 1309, in *Works Vol. 23,* p. 270.
[72] Edwards, "Miscellany" 878, entitled "The Book of Job, Why Inserted into the Canon of Scripture," in *Works Vol. 20,* p. 120.
[73] Edwards. "Miscellany" 1356, in *Works Vol. 23,* pp. 577–578.

The "enthusiasts," made more numerous by the very awakenings Edwards promoted, thought that the gift of prophecy was available in their day. They did not normally presume to add to the actual canon of written Scripture, but Edwards nonetheless took their openness to fresh revelations from God as amounting to the same. His rejoinder was to say, "But since the canon of the Scripture has been completed, and the Christian church fully founded and established, those extraordinary gifts have ceased."[74]

Edwards' most extensive statement on cessation comes in the sermon on I Corinthians 13:8–13.[75] His doctrine was that "The extraordinary influences of the Spirit of God, imparting immediate revelations to men, were designed only for a temporary continuance while the church was in its minority, and never were intended to be statedly upheld in the Christian Church."[76] His first application taught that:

> Hence we may learn that it is not to be expected that any of those gifts that imply divine revelation should be bestowed in these days; because the canon of the Scripture has long since been complete, the church of God completely furnished with a standing rule of faith and practice, and the means of grace all settled and established, and therefore the great end of all these gifts is obtained.[77]

Quite simply, there is no call for ongoing special revelation, because the church already has everything she needs. Edwards' arguments for his position that follow in this sermon are remarkable perhaps only for how thoroughly they communicated the standard Reformed orthodox position on cessation.[78]

VII The Illumination of Scripture

Special revelation in Scripture begins with inspiration, but the communicative process is only completed with *illumination*. Illumination describes the action of the Holy Spirit to make Scripture accomplish its purposes within believers. One way to approach illumination is to see it as the reversal of the noetic effects of sin that inhibit the reception of God's truth. These effects are often understood in terms of the intellect. However, because

[74] Edwards, "Charity and its Fruits," in *Works Vol. 8*, p. 153.
[75] Edwards, "Graces of the Spirit," sermon on I Cor. 13:8–13, in *Works Vol. 25*, pp. 279–311.
[76] Edwards, "Graces of the Spirit," sermon on I Cor. 13:8–13, in *Works Vol. 25*, p. 281.
[77] Edwards, "Graces of the Spirit," sermon on I Cor. 13:8–13, in *Works Vol. 25*, p. 287.
[78] Edwards, "Graces of the Spirit," sermon on I Cor. 13:8–13, in *Works Vol. 25*, pp. 288–291.

Edwards located the effects of sin primarily in the *affections*, his doctrine of illumination was likewise affectional. We return to the sermon on I Corinthians 13:8–13, where Edwards contrasts illumination with inspiration:

> Observe well the difference between spiritual illumination and immediate revelation. The former consists in a person's being enabled rightly to understand and see the evidence [of the gospel preached], and this is done by enabling persons to be inwardly sensible of the divine excellency, giving a new sense, [or] a new sense of [the] heart, a new spiritual relish, and so from the discovery of this divine excellency leading a person to a right view, and apprehension of the great evidence of the truth [of the Scriptures]: of the truths that are revealed already, that were in the Bible before and would have been before [apprehended] had it not been for sinful blindness.[79]

Edwards insists that God communicates himself to people not merely in terms of knowledge but also in terms of love and joy; therefore, the human equipment needed for the reception of all these streams must be operational. The truths of Scripture were already there in the Bible for anyone to read, but because of "sinful blindness," they were not apprehended affectionally. Illumination is required to enable people to be "inwardly sensible of the divine excellency" and to give them "a new sense of the heart" so they embrace the truth set before them. Such illumination can only come from the supernatural ministry of the Holy Spirit.

This being the case, one may wonder how it could be possible that the unregenerate sometimes seem to have a fairly good grasp of revealed truth. Are these cases in which fallen, natural affections are sufficient? As we might expect, Edwards found a theological resource to cope with this problem without granting the slightest iota to fallen humanity. This was Edwards' concept of "common illumination."

> . . . the common convictions and illuminations that natural men have are in some respects the nature of the Spirit of God: for there is light and understanding and conviction of truth in these common illuminations, and so they are of the nature of the Spirit of God—that is, a discerning spirit and a spirit of truth.[80]

[79] Edwards, "Graces of the Spirit," sermon on I Cor. 13:8–13, in *Works Vol. 25*, pp. 303–304.
[80] Edwards, "Treatise on Grace," in *Works Vol. 21*, p. 180.

Edwards thought that the Holy Spirit was commonly active among unregenerate humanity and that He often granted people "light and understanding and conviction of truth." These were not *saving* graces but were part of God's overall work of providence or common grace. This concept provides another example of Edwards' determination to concede nothing significant to unaided human reason, while, on the other hand, attributing anything of value to supernatural divine agency.

As with other aspects of Edwards' doctrine of Scripture, illumination was fully integrated into his apologetic strategy to demonstrate relational harmony. Edwards thinks that the very experience a believer has of divine illumination while reading Scripture becomes its own apologetic:

> Even the being of God can be made most rationally and demonstratively evident by divine revelation and by gracious spiritual illumination [. . .] And this is every whit as rational a way of being convinced of the being of God, as it is of being convinced of the being of a man who comes from an unknown region, and shows himself to us, and converses with us for a long time.[81]

Those who have been the objects of "gracious"—not common—spiritual illumination working through Scripture were as justifiably certain of the existence of God as they would be of a man who came from afar and "converse[d] with us for a long time." Edwards once again shows the depth of his intuition that the most powerful means of demonstrating you know that some being exists is to affirm that you are engaged with him in conversation. Of course, being inaccessible to outside observers, this kind of evidence may not have been deemed admissible by secular Enlightenment canons of rationality. However, Edwards' purpose was not to create the illusion of a level playing field but to vindicate the reality of the conversation God carried on with elect humanity.[82]

VIII Locke's "Fundamentalism"

As with his defense of special revelation, the bulk of Edwards' responses to critical objections to Scripture was occasioned by Deists. However, while the Deists represented the most obvious threat, they were not the only ones on

[81] Edwards, "Miscellany" 254, in *Works Vol. 13*, p. 364.
[82] See Edwards, "Miscellany" 204, in *Works Vol. 13*, pp. 339–340.

Edwards' agenda. We again consider Edwards' relationship to John Locke, here regarding the topic of Locke's "fundamentalism." Contemporary fundamentalism usually refers to when conservatives set some minimum definition of Christianity so that those who accept *less* than these fundamentals are not legitimate Christians. However, fundamentalism can also work in the opposite direction. Early in the seventeenth century, the Socinians proposed a set of "fundamental" articles of faith that were to be the *maximum* legal definition of Christianity—the idea being that governments should not be able to require people to believe any more than a few things virtually anyone could affirm. This strategy for toleration and religious liberalization was later taken up by English Unitarians, most notably Locke.[83] Locke's monumental contribution to the project was *The Reasonableness of Christianity* (1695), which argued that the only essential doctrine of Christianity is to believe Jesus is the Messiah. This claim may sound innocuous now, but in seventeenth-century England, it was sufficiently subversive for the celebrated author of the *Essay* to write anonymously.[84] For although the Glorious Revolution had secured a considerable degree of religious liberty, toleration was specifically limited to *Trinitarian* Christianity. By making the sole fundamental that Jesus is the Messiah rather than the Son of God as in the ancient creeds, Locke implied that it was an overreach to make the doctrine of the Trinity a marker of lawful Christian faith. The subversive force of this point was not missed by Locke's critics.[85]

[83] The definition of Locke's private faith is complicated by political context, since the Toleration Act of 1689 specifically did not protect those who denied the Trinity (Act of Toleration, Ch. XXVII). We would therefore not expect Locke to be forthright had he harbored non-Trinitarian beliefs. However, the bulk of the evidence seems to point to him being a Unitarian. See Victor Nuovo, "Locke's Theology"; and John Marshall, "Locke, Socinianism, 'Socinianism,' and Unitarianism," both in M. A. Stewart (ed.), *English Philosophy in the Age of Locke* (Oxford: Oxford University Press, 2000); Dewey D. Wallace, "Socinianism, Justification by Faith, and the Sources of John Locke's *The Reasonableness of Christianity*," *Journal of the History of Ideas*, (Jan 1984) pp.49–66; and Maurice Wiles, *Archetypal Heresy: Arianism Through the Centuries* (Oxford: Oxford University Press, 1996).

[84] *The Reasonableness of Christianity as Delivered in the Scriptures* (London: A & J Churchil, 1695) was posthumously acknowledged by Locke through a provision in his will (Victor Nuovo, *John Locke and Christianity: Contemporary Response to The Reasonableness of Christianity* (Bristol: Thoemmes, 1997) p. ix), but suspicions to this effect circulated as soon as the book was published.

[85] Locke's most ardent critic on this issue was John Edwards (1637–1716; no relation to Jonathan Edwards), who wrote *Some Thoughts Concerning the Several Causes and Occasions of Atheism* (London: Robinson and Wyat, 1695); *Socinianism Unmask'd* (London: Robinson and Wyat, 1696); *A Brief Vindication of the Fundamental Articles of the Christian Faith* (London: Robinson and Wyat, 1697); *The Socinian Creed* (London: Robinson and Wyat, 1697); and *A Free but Modest Censure on the late Controversial Writings and Debates of Mr. Edwards and Mr. Locke* (London: Robinson and Wyat, 1697). See also John Milner (1628–1702), *An Account of Mr. Lock's religion* (London: Nutt, 1700).

In order to prove his point, Locke had to pare down the amount of scriptural doctrine eligible for consideration. Specifically, Locke wanted to rule out the epistles:

> . . . every Sentence of theirs [the writers of the epistles] must not be taken up, and looked on as a Fundamental Article necessary to Salvation; without an explicit belief whereof, no body could be a Member of Christ's Church here, nor be admitted into his Eternal Kingdom hereafter. [. . .] May those Truths delivered in the Epistles, which are not contained in the Preaching of our Saviour and his Apostles, and are therefore by this Account not necessary to Salvation, be believed, or disbelieved without any danger? May a Christian safely question or doubt of them?[86]

By this maneuver, Locke was proposing a radically truncated understanding of Scripture. When he asks concerning the teachings of the epistles "May a Christian safely doubt of them?" he is by implication denying the authority of Scripture. Locke operates by way of textual and theological isolation, abstracting a certain part of Scripture from the interpretive control of the rest. Shorn of this control, the gospels could appear to support his doctrinally minimalist conclusions.

Edwards takes up these issues in an early "Miscellany."[87] His strategy is to point out all the layers of truth that were necessarily bound up in the minimalist article that Jesus was the Messiah, the one sent by God:

> Then they say that [it] is necessary only to believe that Jesus Christ was a person come from God, they must be understood that it is necessary to believe that he was a person come from a true being . . . They also mean that he came from a merciful being, that did not send him to destroy mankind . . . He must also [believe] that that God he came from is wise, and that he knows how to profit mankind by sending Jesus; [. . .] So that, although they say it is only necessary to believe Jesus came from God, therein is implied that it is necessary to believe all these things: God's all-sufficiency, God's wisdom and omniscience, God's omnipotence, God's truth and faithfulness, God's mercy, God's holiness, God's justice, etc.[88]

[86] Locke, *The Reasonableness of Christianity*, p. 297.

[87] Edwards, "Miscellany" ee, in *Works Vol. 13*, pp. 182–183. *The Reasonableness of Christianity* appears in Edwards' "Catalogue of Reading," *Works Vol. 26*, p. 190. Edwards may well have been working from a critic of Locke at this point, possible Robert Jenkins, *Reasonableness and Certainty of The Christian Religion* (London: 1698). See *Works Vol. 26*, pp. 70, 158.

[88] Edwards, "Miscellany" ee, in *Works Vol. 13*, pp. 182–183.

The few words "Jesus Christ was a person come from God" are actually densely packed with doctrinal content. Belief in this fundamental requires, first of all, a robust, orthodox doctrine of God. It furthermore requires an orthodox Christology and soteriology: "'Tis also necessary to believe that what he [Jesus] did had a tendency to obtain his end; and so, in short, they say the gospel scheme is necessary to be believed."[89] Edwards does not unpack this statement but it seems that, for him, Jesus' ability to secure redemption was predicated on his identity as the incarnate second person of the Trinity. Edwards concludes "And so it will be found, that they own [affirm] almost all the articles to be necessary which good Protestants all along have said to be necessary."[90]

Having addressed the *theological* problems with "fundamentalism," Edwards then applies the same logic to the deficient doctrine of Scripture from which it arose. Just as one doctrine of Christianity implies a host of others—indeed, the whole system—so one part of the Bible is meaningless apart from the whole. This principle is epitomized by the Messiah's identity as a fulfillment of Old Testament prophecy:

> Furthermore, in this article is implied, that it is necessary to be believed [. . .] that the good that he came to do was that that he said he came to do. And in order to believing this last, it is necessary to believe, that he said he came to do that which the Scripture saith he came to do; wherefore the divine authority of the Scriptures is one of their necessary articles.[91]

Locke was content to discuss doctrine taught in the gospels as long as he was free to neglect what came before and after in the canon of Scripture. Yet, how are we to understand what Jesus meant when he said he was the Messiah, outside the context provided by the Old Testament? Edwards points out that Jesus "said he came to do that which the Scripture saith he came to do." The Old Testament had already established who the Messiah would be and what he would do. When Jesus declares that he is the fulfillment of this prophecy, Edwards thinks that we are obliged to receive the whole Scripture along with its teachings.

Likewise, what "the Scripture saith he came to do" also includes the doctrinal explanation of Christ's work provided for us in the Epistles. In a late sermon, Edwards notes "There is a connection between the various

[89] Edwards, "Miscellany" ee, in *Works Vol. 13*, p. 183.
[90] Edwards, "Miscellany" ee, in *Works Vol. 13*, p. 183.
[91] Edwards, "Miscellany" ee, in *Works Vol. 13*, p. 183.

parts of the Word of God [. . .] the word of the Apostles explains the word of the prophets . . . their word explains all and completes all."[92] The "word of the Apostles" (including the Epistles) is part of an interconnected whole, providing meaning to the rest of Scripture. Thus, as Edwards concludes in "Miscellany" ee, it is necessary to believe in "the divine authority of the Scriptures" and not merely in isolated doctrines abstracted from the canon. This episode illustrates how Edwards was alert to the full range of problems posed by Enlightenment thought to the traditional doctrine of Scripture, and not just the most obvious ones.

IX Edwards' Relation to Biblical Criticism

Closely related to the question of biblical authority was the rise of biblical criticism. The European Reformation had vested authority in Scripture, not only for doctrine and ethics but for virtually every significant aspect of public life. For those unhappy with the resulting situation, biblical criticism was a ready instrument to undermine this unwelcome authority.[93] Edwards' considerable efforts to defend Scripture by his work in this area (and indeed, his work regarding the Bible in general) have historically been underrepresented in the literature. This gap has recently been narrowed by the pioneering work of Robert E. Brown, to which I am greatly indebted.[94] In view of how Brown yet considers that his work is only the beginning of scholarship in this area, I would here take up his invitation to continue the discussion on a couple of specific points.[95]

Brown well describes the situation that Edwards faced with regard to biblical criticism:

> Deists and other skeptics were particularly keen to employ the results of the emerging field of biblical criticism in their attempts to undermine the Bible's social authority. Their popularization of the ideas of critics such as Thomas Hobbes, Benedict Spinoza, and Richard Simon helped to raise significant doubts about the historical and scientific reliability of

[92] Edwards, "Extraordinary Gifts of the Spirit are Inferior to Graces of the Spirit," sermon on I Cor. 13:8–13, in *Works Vol. 25*, pp. 288, 290.

[93] The seventeenth- and eighteenth-century freethinkers were of course preceded in this effort by Roman Catholic polemics against Protestantism.

[94] Brown, *Jonathan Edwards and the Bible* (Bloomington, IN: Indiana University Press, 2002); and "The Bible," in Sang Hyun Lee, ed. *The Princeton Companion to Jonathan Edwards* (Princeton and Oxford: Princeton University Press, 2005), pp. 87–102. Brown's PhD dissertation won the 1999 Brewer Prize for church history.

[95] See Brown, *Jonathan Edwards and the Bible*, p. 199.

> the text—and a book without intellectual cogency was a book without religious authority. It was precisely this challenge to the Bible's divine origins—and thereby its authority and relevance—to which Edwards' theological reflections on the nature of the Bible were directed.[96]

Quite simply, Edwards needed to be involved in the biblical criticism of his day because this was the central front in the war over biblical authority.

The critical approach is the logical course for those not sharing Edwards' beliefs regarding the divine authorship of Scripture. If the Bible is not the supernaturally inspired and superintended Word of God, then it must somehow be the product of ordinary human causality and the accidents of history.[97] It therefore makes sense that Spinoza would want to treat the Bible "as any other book" and would engage in criticism to explain it.[98] It also makes sense that Jonathan Edwards, believing in the harmony of all reality, would be unafraid to follow the skeptical critics in their work in order to expose their errors. What is less clear is what degree Edwards truly embraced the critical enterprise, based as it was on presuppositions that were anathema to him. It is on the issue of Edwards' *attitude* toward criticism that we have conclusions differing from Brown to report.

Let us first consider the matter of Edwards' approach to textual, or "lower," criticism. Brown states that "Edwards seems to have had little or no reservations about the fact that, for example, in their present form the received texts of the Old and New Testaments required serious emendation."[99] The evidence Brown cites for his statement are "Catalogue" entries where Edwards notes that he would like to acquire critical editions of the Hebrew and Greek texts.[100] However, the mere possession of a critical text need not imply that someone accepts the need for "serious emendation." It is moreover true that Edwards never preached nor commented on I John 5:7–8.[101] On the other hand, Edwards devoted a lengthy "Blank Bible" entry

96 Brown, "The Bible," p. 92.
97 See Brown, *Jonathan Edwards and the Bible*, pp. 33–34.
98 See Hans W. Frei, *The Eclipse of Biblical Narrative: A Study in Eighteenth and Nineteenth Century Hermeneutics* (New Haven and London: Yale University Press, 1974), pp. 42–46.
99 Brown, *Jonathan Edwards and the Bible*, p. 93.
100 Brown, *Jonathan Edwards and the Bible*, p. 93. The "Catalogue" entry which Brown quotes states ". . . where there are many Corrections of the Text," but this is Edwards' verbatim transcription from the review in the *Monthly Review*. See Edwards, "Catalogue" entry 619, in *Works Vol. 26*, p. 282. Thuesen records Samuel Johnson's quip that the *Monthly Review's* book reviewers were "Christians with as little Christianity as possible" (Thuesen, *Works Vol. 26*, p. 36 n. 5).
101 Turretin defended the long version of I John 5:7–8. See Turretin, *Institutes of Elenctic Theology*, p. 115. Brown notes that Edwards' silence on this text is "a strange silence, but perhaps not too much should be made from it . . . ." Brown, *Jonathan Edwards and the Bible*, p. 101.

to the adulterous woman passage in John 8 and preached on the long ending of Mark 16 as late as 1752.[102] Perhaps a better characterization would be that, although Edwards was aware of the relevant issues in textual criticism, there is no positive evidence to suggest that he concluded that the received text required substantial emendation.

We would also revisit Edwards' relation to higher criticism. Brown's assessment is that "... [Edwards'] approach was really a kind of hybrid traditionalism, one modified in significant ways by his accommodations to the new learning."[103] A more specific statement comes in the *Princeton Companion* essay:

> [Edwards] was completely enamored with the modern intellectual enterprise and accepted its claims to produce real knowledge about the world. In many cases this meant that he had to adjust his interpretation of the Bible. This is most clearly illustrated, perhaps, in his attempts to adjust biblical cosmology and eschatology to Newtonian astronomy and physics.[104]

Brown's contention that Edwards "had to adjust his interpretation of the Bible" in "many cases" demands a closer look.

Brown's reference to primary evidence is not made clear, but the description seems to fit a series of notebook entries in which Edwards theorizes about the physics involved in the eschatological conflagration.[105] Even if this material could be construed as a case where Edwards adjusted his interpretation of the Bible, it involves some theologically insignificant details of eschatology concerning which no settled prior interpretation existed, either in Edwards' writings or in the tradition. Such an example would seem ill-suited to support a generalized statement that runs counter to Edwards' commitment to the absolute interpretive priority of Scripture over all other data.[106]

However, the notebook entries in question actually provide rather striking counterevidence to the statement that Edwards was compelled to

[102] Edwards, "Blank Bible" entry on John 8:6, in *Works Vol. 24*; Edwards, "What is Meant by Believing in Christ," sermon on Mark 16:15–16, in McMullen (ed.), *The Blessing of God: Previously Unpublished Sermons by Jonathan Edwards* (Nashville: Broadman, 2003), pp. 237–246.

[103] Brown, *Jonathan Edwards and the Bible*, p. xvii.

[104] Brown, "The Bible," in Sang Hyun Lee (ed.), *The Princeton Companion to Jonathan Edwards* (Princeton and Oxford: Princeton University Press, 2005; pp. 87–102), p. 96.

[105] Brown's endnotes are to Stephen Stein's editorial introduction to *Works Vol. 15* and to his own book, but the exact referent in the primary works is not specified. Given the description provided, I presume he is referring to "Miscellanies" 926, 929, 930, and 931, in *Works Vol. 20.*

[106] See the discussion of Edwards' position of biblical authority, above.

alter his interpretation of the Bible to fit the findings of the modern science. Edwards' reading of Scripture informed him that the world would be destroyed in the course of six days, a supposition apparently based more on symmetry with the Genesis creation account than with any direct biblical statement. The cataclysm would involve the stars falling to earth, and humans would see this happen. Yet, Newtonian physics told him that the stars are many light years away, and it would thus take much longer than six days to traverse the distance to human observers.[107] Now, going by Brown's statement, we might have expected Edwards to conclude either that the conflagration must take longer than the creation or else the language about stars falling to the earth must be nonliteral. Neither of these possibilities would violate any received interpretation of the relevant texts, and Edwards is utterly free to make such a move were he in the least inclined to "adjust his interpretation of the Bible" in light of modern learning. Dashing any such expectations, Edwards concludes that the stars will move at speeds greater than light and that human eyes will be altered accordingly so as to be able to observe the superlight revealing their dramatic last motions.[108] So it is actually "Newtonian astronomy and physics" that are being adjusted to fit biblical eschatology, not the other way around. Edwards would rather propose something *scientifically impossible* than to alter some minor point for which he thought he had even scant biblical support.

We are not aware of any case in which critical thought or the findings of modern science compelled Edwards to adjust his interpretation of the Bible in any meaningful way. He used the findings of natural revelation to flesh out what he had in skeletal form in Scripture, but certainly not to change what he already knew. Thus, in the case of his teaching on hell, he used Newtonian physics to add some colorful detail—that hell was most likely fuelled by the fires of former stars—to the same traditional doctrine he already had.[109] This is of course precisely what we might expect of one committed to the ultimate harmony of all the media of revelation, and who believed in the interpretive priority of Scripture over reason. If we were to find a case where Edwards really did adjust his interpretation of the Bible to fit modern learning, we would have to conclude that he was acting inconsistently with his principles.

[107] Edwards, "Miscellany" 931, in *Works Vol. 20*, pp. 175–185; see also "Miscellanies" 926, 929, and 930, in *Works Vol. 20*.
[108] Edwards, "Miscellany" 931, in *Works Vol. 20*, pp. 175–185; see also "Miscellanies" 926, 929, and 930, in *Works Vol. 20*.
[109] Edwards, "Miscellany" 931, in *Works Vol. 20*, pp. 175–185.

Returning to the larger issue, we want to characterize Edwards' attitude toward biblical criticism. It is therefore relevant to notice that Edwards explicitly rejected some of the foundational assumptions of modern (critical) biblical interpretation. In his notebook "Efficacious Grace," Edwards is responding to some of the arguments the Arminians and Deists were using to support libertarian free will.[110] Edwards remarks that, "Scripture expressions are everywhere exceeding contrary to their scheme, according to all use of language in the world in these days," yet these freethinkers found in the historical–critical model a likely avenue to advance their cause:

> But then they have their refuge here: they say the ancient figures of speech are exceeding diverse from ours, and that we in this distant age can't judge at all of the true force of expression used so long ago but by a skill in antiquity, and being versed in ancient history, and critically skilled in the ancient languages—never considering that the Scriptures are written for us in these ages, on whom the ends of the world are come, yea, were designed chiefly for the later age of the world, in which they shall have their chief and, comparatively, almost all their effect; and they were written for God's people in these ages, of whom at least 99 in an hundred must be supposed incapable of such knowledge by their circumstances and education, and 999 in a thousand of God's people that hitherto have been saved by the Scriptures.[111]

Edwards is aware of those who think that, due to the vast gulf between the ancient near east and the modern world, the ability to understand Scripture demands "a skill in antiquity, and being versed in ancient history, and critically skilled in the ancient languages." This sounds like a fair summary of modern historical–critical assumptions regarding biblical interpretation. However, Edwards ascribes this position not to himself but to heretics attempting to elude clear biblical pronouncements that are ". . .exceeding contrary to their scheme." Moreover, in a rejection of the hermeneutic of original audience understanding (which would require the above-mentioned

[110] Possibly because it was being prepared for publication at the time Brown was writing and thus unavailable for his consultation, material used in Volume 21 of the Yale Edition does not appear. Brown's quote from "Efficacious Grace" on p. 94 of his book happens to be from the entry immediately preceding the one discussed here, but Brown is quoting from Minkema "The Other Unfinished 'Great Work,'" in Stephen J. Stein, ed. *Jonathan Edwards's Writings: Text, Context, Interpretation* (Bloomington, IN: Indiana University Press, 1996), p. 57.

[111] Edwards, "Efficacious Grace," in *Works Vol. 21*, p. 232.

linguistic and historical skills), Edwards' opponents are fundamentally mistaken because they do not consider that "...that the Scriptures are written for us in these ages." Taken as a whole, it would be difficult to conceive of a statement more categorically dismissive of the presuppositions of the modern, critical approach to biblical interpretation.

As we conclude this section, it should be understood that while this was a crucial correction to offer, it involves a small fraction of Brown's presentation of Edwards. The bulk is consonant with our own findings, as demonstrated in this statement:

> Despite his consuming interest in such interpretive problems, Edwards himself was not a critic, in the sense of being skeptical about the Bible's historical or religious integrity, or in the sense of employing a thoroughgoing historical analysis in his resolution of interpretive problems . . . Edwards immersed himself in modern criticism principally to head off its potentially destructive implications for the Bible's authority.[112]

We could only concur. Edwards engaged with critical issues not because he shared the critic's presuppositions but because he was fighting to vindicate the absolute authority of the Bible. He wielded the tools of modern biblical criticism while rejecting the larger project that largely gave rise to them. No doubt, Edwards thought that the results of any correctly oriented investigation would harmonize perfectly with the scriptural account, but an orientation predicated on the absolute authority of the Bible was the very point at issue. We should not be surprised if Edwards incorporated the findings of science and history into his unfinished project of demonstrating the harmony of all reality. We should, however, wonder if he really accepted the canons established by his theological adversaries.

X Conclusion

Our discussion of Edwards' doctrine of Scripture has contained at least three themes that integrate with the larger story of Edwards' theology of divine communication. One theme is Edwards' pervasive desire to demonstrate the harmony of all knowledge, a desire explained by his understanding of God's project in communicating himself multidimensionally to intelligent creatures. Another would be the use of harmony as

[112] Brown, "The Bible," p. 95.

an apologetic method, as the seal of Trinitarian character that ties together the Scriptures and proves their authority as divine revelation. The third theme would be Edwards' rejection at the deepest level the Enlightenment's critical approach toward the Bible. Fallen humanity is fully and completely dependent upon the Scriptures and the Triune God who gave them for efficacious knowledge of saving truth.

We conclude with a quotation from the "Miscellanies" that would seem to summarize Edwards' attitude toward the Scriptures as they point to the larger theological picture:

> It seems to me that God would have our whole dependence be upon the Scriptures, because the greater our dependence is on the Word of God, the more direct and immediate is our dependence on God himself. The more absolute and entire our dependence on the Word of God is, the greater respect shall we have to that Word, the more shall we esteem and honor and prize it; and this respect to the Word of God will lead us to have the greater respect to God himself.[113]

It is with this statement on the priority of Scripture that we proceed to discuss Edwards' thoughts on God's communication through history.

[113] Edwards, "Miscellany" 535, in *Works Vol. 18*, p. 80. Edwards' context was to critique a dependence upon the Fathers, an attitude that obviously predated the Enlightenment.

Chapter 5

History

"If [the setting up of Christ's kingdom] were done at once, in an instant or in a very short time, there would not be opportunity for the creature to perceive and observe all the particular steps of divine wisdom, as when the work is gradually accomplished and one effect of his wisdom is held forth to observation after another . . ."

—*Jonathan Edwards, The History of the Work of Redemption*[1]

I Introduction

In a recent book on the theology of Hans Frei, Mike Higton observes that ". . . theology as an intellectual discipline never stands far from history. It understands that history is the arena in which God works—or better, the idiom in which God speaks."[2] These words might almost have been said of an earlier American theologian whom Frei held in high esteem, one for whom history was similarly integral.[3] Jonathan Edwards understood history to be the temporal vehicle for the great work of redemption, that which above all else provides the fullest disclosure of God's character. For him, history was thus resources for knowing, loving, and enjoying God, and it occupies an appropriately prominent position in his corpus.

In this chapter, we explore what it meant for Edwards to understand history as a medium of divine communication.[4] We shall first establish some of the most important elements involved in this understanding, such as

[1] Edwards, *The History of the Work of Redemption*, in *Works Vol. 9*, p. 355.

[2] Mike Higton, *Christ, Providence and History: Hans W. Frei's Public Theology* (London and New York: T & T Clark, 2004), p. 1.

[3] See Mike Higton, *Christ, Providence and History: Hans W. Frei's Public Theology* (London and New York: T & T Clark, 2004), p. 171. Edwards was also Frei's eighteenth-century example of his favored fourth "type" of theology. See Frei, *Types of Christian Theology* (New Haven: Yale University Press, 1992), p. 4.

[4] Not that this in any way implies that Edwards saw history as special revelation, the canon of which he believed to be closed. See the discussion on the canon above, Chapter 4.

Edwards' pervasive supernaturalism and his conviction that history was harmonious with the content of Scripture. We shall then illustrate some of the ways this thinking was manifested in Edwards' work, including not only the famous "History of the Work of Redemption" project but also some lesser-known items that also demonstrate how seriously Edwards took the implications of God revealing himself through the providential workings of redemptive history. We begin with the now-familiar theme of Edwards' uncompromising opposition to problematic Enlightenment thought.

II Historiographer of Supernature

As with his treatments of nature and Scripture, Edwards' interpretation of history as the harmonious expression of God's sovereign causality was at odds with the spirit of modernity.[5] Indeed, Enlightenment-influenced models of history have so long dominated the intellectual landscape that Edwards' vision appears rather strange today. This is because Edwards was, above all, an observer and interpreter of *supernatural* agency. As we consider this feature, we must once again refer to Edwards' comprehensive campaign against the entire spectrum of rationalistic theology. Inasmuch as this theology had a core conviction lying behind its various concerns, it would seem to be a basic hostility to supernaturalism in any form. If this was the monster of the day, Edwards' enchanted weapon was a historical record alive with the supernatural workings of the living God.

The Enlightenment concept of history was perhaps epitomized by David Hume in *The Natural History of Religion* and *The History of England*.[6] Hume presupposed the purely human causes of events working without exception throughout time, seeking in his narrative to highlight these entirely natural causes in order to undermine the "prevailing systems of superstition."[7] In radical contrast to Hume's project, Edwards presupposed and sought to make manifest to his audience the *divine* causation that sometimes worked abruptly to bring about milestones in the building of Christ's kingdom.[8]

[5] See also Avihu Zakai, *Jonathan Edwards's Philosophy of History: The Reenchantment of the World in the Age of Enlightenment* (Princeton: Princeton University Press, 2003), pp. 5–13; 226–234.

[6] Hume, *The Natural History of Religion and Dialogues Concerning Natural Religion* (Oxford: Clarendon Press, 1976) and *The History of England from the Invasion of Julius Caesar to the Revolution in 1688* (Indianapolis: Liberty Fund, 1983).

[7] ". . . I have been endeavouring to open the eyes of the Public. If I live a few years longer, I may have the satisfaction of seeing the downfall of some of the prevailing systems of superstition." Hume, *Hume on Natural Religion* (ed. Stanley Tweyman; Bristol: Thoemmes Press, 1996).

[8] Edwards was familiar with Hume: "I had before read that book of essays . . . and also that book of Mr. David Hume's which you speak of. I am glad of an opportunity to read such corrupt

Take for example what was then the relatively recent case of the Glorious Revolution. Hume and Edwards both view this event as a positive development, but they explain it and understand its significance in very different terms. Hume understands the significance of 1688 entirely politically and is at pains to elucidate the human factors that render the dramatic and seemingly unlikely turn of events explicable:

> The time, when the prince [of Orange] entered on his enterprise, was well chosen; as the people were then in the highest ferment, on account of the insult, which the imprisonment and trial of the bishops had put upon the church, and indeed upon all the protestants of the nation. His method of conducting his preparations was no less wise and politic . . . . The king [James II] every moment alarmed, more and more, by these proofs of a general disaffection, not daring to repose trust in any but those who were exposed to more danger than himself, agitated by disdain towards ingratitude, by indignation against disloyalty, impelled by his own fears and those of others, precipitately embraced the resolution of escaping into France.[9]

The miraculous success of William's invasion was only apparent. When all the details of the historical record and of human motivations were examined, the outcome seems entirely explicable, if not mechanistically inevitable.

Edwards, on the other hand, understands the significance of the Glorious Revolution within the frame of redemptive history: God intervened just in time to check the reintroduction of Roman Catholicism in England. He records the main outlines of the event only to explain it simply as a sudden divine intervention:

> And just as their matters seemed to be come to an head, and their enterprise ripe for execution, God in his providence suddenly dashed all their schemes in pieces by the revolution at the coming in of King William and Queen Mary, by which all their designs were at an end.[10]

It is not that the details of providence, which very much include human instrumentation, are wholly to be ignored. Edwards in other places would go into minute detail to show the wisdom of God in his precise ordering of

books; especially when written by men of considerable genius; that I may have an idea of the notions that prevail in our nation" (Edwards, *Works Vol. 16*, p. 679).

[9] David Hume, *The History of England*, Vol. 6, part lxxi.

[10] Edwards, *History of the Work of Redemption*, in *Works Vol. 9*, p. 426.

events. However, unlike Hume, these things are not ultimately the point. For Edwards, the real protagonist in history is always God and the unified plot always the work of redemption. Good historical narrative must respect these basic parameters.

Edwards is thus a gatherer and interpreter of supernatural workings amidst the ordinary events of history. This point is basic enough, but it has not always been easy to maintain in practice. Take for example a typically arresting yet incomplete statement from Perry Miller. He writes that, for Edwards, "Nature—or history, which is nature in time—was not a disjointed series of phenomena; it was a living system of theology, it was a complete, intelligible whole."[11] Nature and history are indeed part of a "living system" in Edwards' theology of revelation, and at this level, Miller's observation is correct. If the whole of reality at any moment is the self-communication of the divine mind in the act of continual creation, history is the series of such ontologically real communications over time. However, Edwards also maintained this crucial distinction between the natural and the supernatural, such that although history includes "nature in time," more to Edwards' point, it features *super*nature in time. And it is the intelligent appreciation of God's supernatural actions in redemptive history that is the glorious purpose of everything else.

One might ask what is the basis of Edwards' distinction between nature and supernature; a distinction that would appear rather arbitrary in light of Edwards' radically theocentric doctrine of "continuous creation" wherein all phenomena have an immediate and momentary supernatural cause.[12] For our purposes, let us just say that Edwards predicated his distinction upon secondary causation, such that "supernatural" means whatever God accomplishes without the usual layer of intermediate means.[13] We can see this concept at work in Edwards' famous sermon "A Divine and Supernatural Light," here applied to the problem of theological epistemology:

> God is the author of all knowledge and understanding whatsoever . . . . Mortal men are capable of imparting the knowledge of human arts and sciences, and skill in temporal affairs. God is the author of such

[11] Perry Miller, *Images or Shadows of Divine Things* (New Haven, CT: Yale University Press, 1948), pp. 28–29.

[12] See the discussion on Edwards' doctrine of continuous creation in Stephen R. Holmes, *God of Grace & God of Glory* (Edinburgh: T&T Clark, 2000), pp. 92–94. It is possible that Edwards did not in fact achieve a fully satisfactory philosophical resolution of this tension, but the requisite discussion is beyond our scope.

[13] Edwards was not always precise in his use of "immediate"; he sometimes intended to indicate some level of *relative* immediacy rather than to assert *absolute* immediacy.

knowledge by those means: flesh and blood is made use of by God as the mediate or second cause of it; he conveys it by the power and influence of natural means. But this *spiritual* knowledge, spoken of in the text, is what God is the author of, and none else: he reveals it, and flesh and blood reveal it not. He imparts this knowledge *immediately*, not making use of any intermediate natural causes, as he does in other knowledge.[14]

God stands ultimately behind all kinds of knowledge, as he stands behind every aspect of reality. What distinguishes the "spiritual" or supernatural is the omission of the usual "intermediate natural causes."[15]

Theologically, we might have expected that the work of the *Holy Spirit* in a given situation would be for Edwards the essential element of the specifically supernatural. But this does not seem to be the case. Edwards' sermon teaches that the Spirit's involvement does not require that the accompanying phenomenon will in fact be supernatural:

. . . this light and conviction [in natural men] may be from the Spirit of God; the Spirit convinces men of sin: but yet nature is much more concerned in it than in the communication of that spiritual and divine light, that is spoken of in the doctrine; 'tis from the Spirit of God only as assisting natural principles, and not as infusing any new principles.[16]

Flowing from Edwards' very robust doctrine of common grace in which the Spirit is involved in a whole host of activities in natural humanity—including certain forms of conviction of sin—there is no simple correlation between the Spirit's involvement and what turns out to be "spiritual" or supernatural.[17] The Spirit is always involved when and where God is, but for a given work to be properly spiritual, it must involve the "communication" of "new principles" having no natural antecedent.[18]

Having outlined Edwards' nuanced but critical distinction between natural and supernatural, we consider how this distinction applies to his reading of history. Edwards explores the topic in the context of defending the old Puritan concern of special providence:

[14] Edwards, "A Divine and Supernatural Light," in *Works Vol. 17*, p. 409; emphasis mine.
[15] Given the title of Edwards' sermon, "A Divine and *Supernatural* Light," as well as its content, it is legitimate to assume a functional equivalence between "spiritual" and "supernatural" here.
[16] Edwards, "A Divine and Supernatural Light," in *Works Vol. 17*, p. 410.
[17] See Edwards, "A Divine and Supernatural Light," in *Works Vol. 17*, p. 409.
[18] My thanks to Gerald R. McDermott for providing additional clarity on this issue.

> Seeing that God is certainly an intelligent and voluntary being, it is rational to suppose that in his government of the world there should not only be a series of events that he brings to pass in a constant uninterrupted series, by certain fixed unvaried laws, such as the laws of nature; but that he should manifest himself in his dealings with his intelligent and voluntary creatures in a series of more arbitrary acts and dispensations, not confined to certain unalterable rules and laws in all circumstances, but acts done more in the manner of intelligent voluntary creatures, and more directly showing the will and arbitrament of the governor, as it is in God's dispensations towards his church from the beginning of the world, both in the extraordinary dispensations of his providence in miracles, and the arbitrary influences of his Spirit on their hearts, in the course of his ordinary dispensations in his church and kingdom.[19]

Edwards will not let us forget that—contra the Deists—God is personal and communicative and that his ultimate purposes in history are communicative. Just as he thought that it was only reasonable that God would converse with his intelligent creatures through special revelation, Edwards here thinks "it is rational to suppose" that an intelligent God "should manifest himself in his dealings with his intelligent and voluntary creatures in a series of more arbitrary acts and dispensations."[20] Thus Edwards defines supernatural events such as miracles not so much by the voluntary divine causation that lies behind every event but in the voluntary or arbitrary *appearance* of the event as we observe it, precisely as it is a deviation from the ordinary course of God's routine providence. In other words, God communicates to his creatures through the medium of history most clearly in those happenings that are least explicable in Humean terms.

Edwards' supernaturalism as it relates to history is therefore semiotic: the relatively arbitrary appearance of events provides the basis for our observation of God's intentional communicative activity. Edwards thus observed history and current events expecting to find such intentionally arbitrary or supernatural events. Not, however, that this history stood alone as self-intelligible data. As with nature, history accomplishes its full revelatory purposes only within a hermeneutical nexus built from special revelation and only within regenerate minds supernaturally enabled to

[19] Edwards, "Miscellany" 749, in *Works Vol. 18*, pp. 397–398.

[20] See above, Chapter 3. Modern theologians have recently begun to think in similar categories to Edwards on this point. See, for example, Kevin J. Vanhoozer, *The Drama of Doctrine: A Canonical-Linguistic Approach to Christian Theology* (Louisville and London: Westminster John Knox, 2005).

appreciate the complex Trinitarian harmony that is the mark of God's authorship.[21] We now consider the spectrum of ways in which Edwards thinks God is able to communicate through his arbitrary hand in history, along with some relevant implications.

III Typology, Harmony, and Prophecy

Thus far, we have discussed Edwards' approach to history as a revelatory medium in terms of its sheer apparent deviation from natural causation. However, the "arbitrariness" marking God's intentionality could take a range of forms, some of which are more subtle and intricate. Edwards therefore relied upon an interconnected hermeneutical web to ascertain communicative content, as he did with nature. The primary framework for this web came from Scripture, comprising both the relevant points of its unified theology and, more specifically in the context of history, its prophecy. It was this inspired intimation of God's plan for the general flow of redemptive history—and at points, even its details—that enabled Edwards to derive valid revelatory content from uninspired sources. Secondary to this framework was the use of a typological hermeneutic, a recurring feature of Edwards' interpretation of revelation, in which events are related typologically to fixed theological features of the perspicuous inspired framework. Underlying the entire enterprise was the concept of Trinitarian harmony, enabling Edwards to recognize in history an incredibly complex yet beautiful pattern of God's self-communication.

The framework provided by Edwards' systematic theology must be largely passed over, but we are mindful that he did not turn to history to find any new doctrines. To invoke a metaphor of the stage, Scripture provides the inspired program to help us understand God's performance in redemptive history.[22] Thus, although in Edwards' perspective it was preferable to view firsthand the great show in its final dramatic acts, one would still be able to know what was needful simply by reading the biblical program. Furthermore, any observation of the show that seemed to be at odds with the program was necessarily a failure of harmonization; for the show's omnipotent director was also the program's omniscient author.

[21] See above, Chapters 2 and 4.

[22] See above, Chapters 3 and 4. Some contemporary theologians have recently been thinking in similar categories. See, for example, Kevin J. Vanhoozer, *The Drama of Doctrine: A Canonical-Linguistic Approach to Christian Theology* (Louisville and London: Westminster John Knox, 2005).

Typology has already occupied a fair amount of attention in this book, but suffice it to say that Edwards approached fine details of history in much the same way he did those of nature. He assumed that the virtuoso behind these media of revelation packed a layer of spiritual meaning into virtually everything— "I am not afraid to own that I believe the whole universe, heaven and earth, air and seas, and the divine constitution and history of the holy Scriptures, be full of the images of divine things, as full as a language is of words."[23] There are many examples of the application of Edwards' typological theory to history in the "Types" notebook, but entry 81 provides the most succinct: "The Roman triumph was a remarkable type of Christ's ascension."[24] The ritual of the Roman triumph, which Edwards learned of from noninspired historical sources, was not merely a suitable *illustration* of Christ's ascension but a historical type intentionally instituted by God much as the sun was "designed on purpose" as a natural type of the Trinity.[25]

The status Edwards gives to noninspired historical sources deserves some discussion at this point. One simply cannot lose sight of Edwards' voluminous work arguing for the necessity and uniquely privileged status of inspired Scripture.[26] However, in accordance with Edwards' expansive understanding of general revelation, he yet allocated a spacious provision for the use of extra-biblical history. Edwards discloses some of his thoughts on the matter in the following statement, made within the very context of an argument for the necessity of Scripture: "And in general, it was necessary that we should have a history of God's church till such times as come within our view and reach, that we might have some tolerable account of it without revelation."[27] Edwards' implication seems to be that, in God's providence, human culture after the close of the Canon *was* sufficiently advanced as to be able to provide a "tolerable account" of church history for our use. If so, Edwards would seem to be able to make use of this imperfect yet serviceable historical record at least in some ways akin to the faultless history in Scripture. Edwards' practice of typologizing extra-biblical historical events and of interpreting some of them as specific fulfillments of prophecy in a manner paralleling his use of biblical history would appear to support this understanding.[28]

[23] Edwards, "Types," in *Works Vol. 11*, p. 152. See also "Miscellany" 362, in *Works Vol. 13*, pp. 434–435.
[24] Edwards, "Types" entry 81, in *Works Vol. 11*, p. 82.
[25] Edwards, 'Miscellany" 362, in *Works Vol. 13*, p. 434.
[26] See above, Chapter 3.
[27] Edwards, "Miscellany" 359, in *Works Vol. 13*, p. 432.
[28] See Stein, "Editor's Introduction," in *Works Vol. 15*, pp. 2–3.

As "Miscellany" 777 is in many ways vital to Edwards' larger theology of revelation, so "Types" entry 77 is important for understanding his approach to discerning the hand of God in the oft perplexing contours of history. Edwards explains by expositing typologically the familiar New England example of a river basin comprised of a bewildering network of streams:

> There is a wonderful analogy between what is seen in RIVERS: their gathering from innumerable small branches beginning at a great distance on from another in different regions, some on the sides or tops of mountains, others in valleys, and all conspiring to one common issue . . . The innumerable streams, of which great rivers are constituted, running in such infinitely various and contrary courses, livelily represent the various dispensations of divine providence . . . . I need not run the parallel between this and the course of God's providence through all ages, from the beginning to the end of the world, when all things shall have their final issue in God . . . .[29]

Edwards acknowledges that the reading of history is in no easy matter. From a close perspective, it can appear as if streams of events are running utterly counter to God's purposes made known in the program of Scripture. But even these apparent reversals eventually have a "common issue" in the work of redemption. What was called for was some interpretive account of history that would map out the sometime confusing turns of providence to its human observer, a *desideratum* Edwards wanted to address in the "History of the Work of Redemption." This reconciliation of history would be a key component of his attempt to demonstrate the harmony of all reality as reflective of the complex harmony inherent in the Trinity.[30]

Another element of Edwards' understanding of history as it relates to revelation was his explanation of the drawn-out nature of the building of Christ's kingdom. Edwards poses the question as to why "the setting up of Christ's kingdom after his humiliation should be so gradual, by so many steps that are so long in accomplishment, when God could easily have finished it at once." [31] Edwards here expresses the principle that God's project of self-revelation to finite creatures can be accomplished only in time:

> In this way the glory of God's wisdom in the manner of doing this is more visible to the creature's observation. If it were done at once, in an

[29] Edwards, 'Types" entry 77, in *Works Vol. 11*, pp. 77–79.
[30] Edwards, 'Miscellany" 182, in *Works Vol. 13*, p. 329.
[31] Edwards, *History of the Work of Redemption*, in *Works Vol. 9*, p. 355.

> instant or in a very short time, there would not be opportunity for the creature to perceive and observe all the particular steps of divine wisdom, as when the work is gradually accomplished and one effect of his wisdom is held forth to observation after another. 'Tis wisely determined of God to accomplish his great design by a wonderful and long series of events, that the glory of his wisdom may be displayed in the whole series and that the glory of his perfections may be seen as appearing, as it were, by parts and in particular successive manifestations. For if all that glory that appears in all these events should be manifested at once, it would be too much for us and more than we at once could take notice of; it would dazzle our eyes and be too much for our sight.[32]

We already know that God's purpose in creation was to communicate himself to finite intelligent creatures. Edwards thus does not hesitate to say that Christ prolongs his warfare in this world just so that God's wisdom might be "more visible to the creature's observation." As we shall see in the case of the redemptive-historical beatific vision, the temporal implications of God's revelatory project were something Edwards took with utmost seriousness throughout his work.

Providing more detailed control to the observation and interpretation of redemptive history—perhaps, in our stage metaphor, furnishing the scene titles—was biblical prophecy. Prophecy was the preeminent means of God publicly exercising lordship over his creation, and Edwards held the usual Reformed orthodox position that the ability to accurately foretell future events was a component of divine identity. "Miscellany" 1193 makes this point:

> Great changes in kingdoms and nations coming to pass according to God's prediction is often spoken of by God himself in the Old Testament as a great evidence of his being the only true God, vastly distinguished from all other gods and infinitely above 'em . . .[33]

This principle has particular application to Jesus' claim to being God. Edwards later cites Christ's prediction of the destruction of Jerusalem in AD 70 as apologetic evidence. Edwards finds the mini-apocalypse in the synoptic Gospels a potent apologetic argument precisely because the events foretold were in themselves so unlikely when spoken.[34]

[32] Edwards, *History of the Work of Redemption*, in *Works Vol. 9*, pp. 355–356.
[33] Edwards, "Miscellany" 1193, in *Works Vol. 23*, p. 114.
[34] Edwards, "Miscellany" 1316, in *Works Vol. 23*, pp. 279–280.

Such views of the apologetic value of fulfilled prophecy were standard among Edwards' tradition. Slightly less standard, but certainly not unprecedented among colonial Puritans, was Edwards' consuming interest in the detailed interpretation of biblical prophecy as it was being fulfilled in more recent history and contemporary events.[35] A large volume of manuscript material, much of which can be sampled in *Volume 5: Apocalyptic Writings*, is taken up with Edwards' lifelong efforts along these lines. Edwards' private interest in correlating the pages of Revelation with the newspapers occasionally spilled over into published writings, as when he suggested that the revivals in America might be "the dawning, or at least a prelude, of that glorious work of God, so often foretold in Scripture, which in the progress and issue of it, shall renew the world of mankind."[36] But Edwards was not alone in such interests. Large tracts of the notebooks are in fact devoted to gleaning from other similarly minded authors, such as lengthy extracts from Moses Lowman's *Paraphrase and Notes.*[37] The concurrence Edwards found in Lowman[38] in particular seems to have emboldened Edwards in a more public direction.[39]

Understanding how specific prophecies were fulfilled in history was a demanding and possibly dubious enterprise, yet it was requisite in Edwards' theology of revelation. Indeed, God revealed his plans prophetically just so that his intelligent creatures would recognize their outworking in reality and participate in their further advancement:

> It is an argument of the truth of the Christian revelation; for there is nothing else that informs what God's design [is in] that series of revolutions and events that are brought to pass in the [world], what end he seeks, and what scheme he has laid out.... 'Tis most fit that the intelligent

35 See Stein, 'Editor's Introduction,' in *Works Vol 5*, p. 8; see also C. C. Goen, 'Jonathan Edwards: A New Departure in Eschatology,' *Church History 28* (1959): 25–40.

36 'Tis not unlikely that this work of God's Spirit, that is so extraordinary and wonderful, is the dawning, or at least a prelude, of that glorious work of God, so often foretold in Scripture, which in the progress and issue of it, shall renew the world of mankind. [. . .] And there are many things that make it probable that this work will begin in America' (*Some Thoughts Concerning the Present Revival*, in *Works Vol. 4*, p. 353).

37 Edwards, *Works Vol. 5*, pp. 219–250.

38 With the notable exception of the interpretation of the 6th vial in Revelation 16:12, which, *contra* Lowman, Edwards believed was being fulfilled in his own day in the financial ruination of Roman Catholic nations. See 'An Account of Events Probably Fulfilling the Sixth Vial on the River Euphrates, The News of Which was Received Since October 16, 1747,' in *Works Vol. 5*, pp. 253–284.

39 'One public measure of the impact of Lowman upon Edwards was the series of sermons he preached between March and August of 1739, published posthumously as *A History of the Work of Redemption* (1774)' (Stein, 'Editor's Introduction,' in Edwards, *Works Vol. 5*, p. 22).

> beings of the world should be made acquainted with it; they are the beings that are principally concerned in it . . . And then 'tis rational to suppose, that God should reveal the design he has [been] carrying on to his rational creatures: that as God has made them capable of it, they may [be] actively falling in with it and promoting it, and acting herein as the subjects and friends of God.[40]

We see again Edwards' insistence that the elucidation of God's plans for human history sets Christianity apart from other false religions and authenticates the Scriptures apologetically. More to the present point, however, is the larger, positive purpose that he posits for prophecy. God reveals his "design" to intelligent creatures (angels and humans) so that they might be equipped for "actively falling in with it and promoting it." God's project of self-communication in Edwards' view was that it was intended not merely to provide information but to enable them to re-emanate actively the revelation they receive. Edwards' construction of a detailed eschatological account incorporating the events of his day thereby takes on a new meaning when we consider how his theology demanded that his readership *act* as well as reflect upon their situation in history.

IV The Development of Edwards' Use of History

In our discussion thus far, it has become plain that Edwards' theology was conceived in a way that would give history great prominence. However, although the relevant theoretical fundamentals were in place from the outset, the fuller realization of the theological potential for history grew over the course of Edwards' career. This is seen particularly in Edwards' shift of apologetic/polemic master project from the "Rational Account" to the "History of the Work of Redemption." As discussed in Chapter 3, much of the earlier notebook material was intended for inclusion into Edwards' planned great work "A Rational Account of the Main Doctrines of the Christian Religion Attempted."[41] However, although some probable spin-offs are mentioned, we find no mention of this project in the 1757 letter to the Princeton Trustees, and in its place we find the "History of the Work of Redemption" project.[42] How can this shift be accounted for? In the context of Chapter 3, our discussion focused on how the "History" project might

[40] Edwards, "Miscellany" 547, in *Works Vol. 18*, p. 95.
[41] Edwards, "Outline of A Rational Account," in *Works Vol. 6*, p. 396. See above, Chapter 3.
[42] Edwards, "Letter to the Princeton Trustees" of 19 October, 1757, in *Works Vol. 16*, pp. 727–729.

have been better suited to pursue Edwards' relational/communicative argument for the necessity of special revelation. Here we consider Ava Chamberlain's suggestion that Edwards' own experience of redemptive history might have persuaded him to make this transition:

> 'The Miscellanies' confirm what Edwards' failure to write the 'Rational Account' and his plan to revise 'A History of the Work of Redemption' only suggest, that over time he concluded that the argument from history was more persuasive than the argument from reason . . . That this shift occurred after the Connecticut Valley awakening may give some indication of its cause. Having witnessed a decisive moment in salvation history, Edwards turned to history to pursue his debate with the deists.[43]

To put the matter in other terms, why should Edwards bother casting about for logical proofs for the Christian faith when God has providentially supplied irrefutable proof through current events? If he wished to show that the God of the Bible and the doctrine of his religion were true, there could hardly be a better method of demonstration than the supernatural in-breaking evidenced by the revivals, as well as their precedents and parallels throughout recorded history. However, it should also be kept in mind that Edwards does not repudiate his former approach or delete his source material based upon it; beyond the shift in large-scale method, the two projects seem to have shared much in terms of goals and probably even in content.

Edwards' appreciation for the apologetic/polemic value of history is actually to be seen in one of his earliest published works, the 1738 *Discourses on Various Important Subjects*. Looking back on the Connecticut Valley awakening of 1734–36, Edwards wrote:

> The beginning of the late work of God in this place was so circumstanced, that I could not but look upon it as a remarkable testimony of God's approbation of the doctrine of *justification by faith alone*, here asserted and vindicated . . . . The following discourse of justification, that was preached . . . at two public lectures, seemed to be remarkably blessed, not only to establish the judgments of many in this truth, but to engage their hearts in a more earnest pursuit of justification, in that way that had been explained and defended; and *at that time*, while I was greatly reproached for defending this doctrine in the pulpit, and just upon my suffering a very open abuse for it, God's work wonderfully brake forth amongst us,

[43] Ava Chamberlain, 'Editor's Introduction,' in *Works Vol. 18*, p. 34.

> and souls began to flock to Christ, as the Savior in whose righteousness alone they hoped to be justified.[44]

The doctrine of justification by faith was the first of many orthodox teachings imperiled by Enlightenment rationalism that Edwards would defend publicly. In this case, Edwards' lectures on the subject convinced some but elicited "great reproach" from others. His scriptural and logical discourse falling on deaf ears among this latter group, it appeared to Edwards that God himself took up the cause when he "wonderfully brake forth amongst us" in the Connecticut Valley revival, using as his instrument the very doctrine in question.[45] This was to Edwards' mind, a "remarkable testimony of God's approbation" of biblical doctrine. This was all said in the context of a specific instance, but the larger principle to which Edwards seemed to be warming was that God is able to supply his own apologetic in the workings of providential history.

In the final explicit mention we have of the intact "Rational Account" project in the corpus, the "Preface to Rational Account" found in "Miscellany" 832, Edwards applies this principle in a negative direction:

> And besides, the Scripture teaches that 'tis God's manner to bless his truth, and to cause that the pure doctrines of the gospel should be accompanied with the power of his Spirit, and with a powerful effect on the hearts and lives of men. Since this fashionable divinity has been growing and getting ground, han't vice and deadness and a decay of vital Christianity kept pace with it? . . . . They see, as they imagine, the errors and impertinence of the tenets of their fathers; but han't unsuccessfulness in their ministry kept pace with their refinings? Has there ever been any instance, in any age, of any great reformation of manners wrought in any society whatever, by proceeding on the foot of those principles that are now so fashionable? Incontestable and plentiful instances can be produced of this effect of other principles.[46]

Just as God provided a supernatural historical apologetic for orthodoxy through the spiritual vitality seen in the revivals, so God gives a sort of negative apologetic in the withholding of such conditions where false doctrine prevails. Edwards notices that those who hold "fashionable divinity"

[44] Edwards, preface to *Discourses on Various Important Subjects*, in *Works in Two Volumes*, Vol. 1, p. 621; emphasis original. See also Goen, 'Editor's Introduction,' in *Works Vol. 4*, p. 19.
[45] See also Goen, 'Editor's Introduction,' in *Works Vol. 4*, p. 19.
[46] Edwards, "Miscellany" 832, in *Works Vol. 18*, pp. 546–547.

(rationalist theology) are rewarded with a commensurate level of "unsuccessfulness in their ministry." We might even see this as a point of transition, the moment in which Edwards began to shift the emphasis of his polemic/apologetic theology from fighting rationalist fire with fire toward the apparently "incontestable" evidence provided in supernatural history.

V The "History of the Work of Redemption"

With this theological and historical context in place, the fact that Edwards would eventually focus his efforts on a project such as the "History of the Work of Redemption" becomes more explicable. We shall now discuss the contours of this project in terms of what Edwards himself intended for this unfinished work. For this purpose, it is preferable to exegete afresh the prospectus he detailed for the project in the letter to the Princeton Trustees rather than to draw conclusions from the 1739 sermon series of that name.[47] The "History" was to be:

> . . . a body of divinity in an entire new method, being thrown into the form of an history, considering the affair of Christian theology, as the whole of it, in each part, stands in reference to the great work of redemption by Jesus Christ [. . .] particularly considering all parts of the grand scheme in their historical order.[48]

Edwards considered such a method to be "entirely new" because Edwards was proposing a radical shift in the way works of systematic theology were done. Instead of the time-tested format found in say, Turretin's *Institutio Theologiae Elencticae*, in which the *loci* of theology are introduced in logical order and discussed by answering potted questions with "we affirm" or "we deny," Edwards planned to teach theology "in the form of an history." Edwards was at the very least proposing a new pedagogical and apologetic strategy—it would be "a method which appears to me the most beautiful and entertaining, wherein every divine doctrine, will appear to greatest advantage in the brightest light."[49] In a way not unlike his modification of

[47] As is frequently noted, it is important to recognize that the "History of the Work of Redemption" *project* was never finished and may not have been identical with the 1739 sermon series of that name found in anthologies.

[48] Edwards, "Letter to the Princeton Trustees" of 19 October, 1757, in *Works Vol. 16*, pp. 727–729.

[49] Edwards, "Letter to the Princeton Trustees" of 19 October, 1757, in *Works Vol. 16*, pp. 727–729. For Edwards, who thought that beauty was fundamentally reflective of the Trinity, a valuation of 'most beautiful' represented something stronger than a mere personal preference.

Puritan homiletics in a direction that better brought together a sermon's noetic content with the affections that were appropriate to it, Edwards wanted to renovate systematic theology to make this discipline "beautiful and entertaining" in better keeping with its glorious subject matter.[50]

It is likely, however, that Edwards thought such a methodological shift also had deeper implications for the resulting content of theology. He says that it would be a means of "introducing all parts of divinity in that order which is *most scriptural and most natural* [. . .] showing the admirable contexture and *harmony* of the whole."[51] Since "harmony"—harmony between the testaments, harmony between theology and reason, harmony between history and Scripture—was the very thing Edwards wished to demonstrate in all his work,[52] it would seem that Edwards considered the historical presentation of theology to be significant for its content, not to mention that it was "most scriptural."[53]

Another aspect of Edwards' project that is highly relevant here is the nature of the material that was to be taken into account. All of the aspects of redemptive history would be

> . . . brought forth to view, in the course of divine dispensations, or the wonderful series of successive acts and events; beginning from eternity and descending from thence to the great work and successive dispensations of the infinitely wise God in time, considering the chief events coming to pass in the church of God, and revolutions in the world of mankind, affecting the state of the church and the affair of redemption, which we have an account of in history and prophecy; [. . .] This history will be carried on with regard to all three worlds, heaven, earth, and hell: considering the connected, successive events and alterations, in each so far as the Scriptures give any light . . .[54]

[50] See Edwards, 'Miscellany' 539, in *Works Vol. 18*, p. 86.
[51] Edwards, 'Letter to the Princeton Trustees' of 19 October, 1757, in *Works Vol. 16*, p. 728.
[52] At least this is my contention; see below, Chap. 6. See also E. Brooks Holifield, 'Edwards as Theologian,' in Stephen J. Stein (ed.), *The Cambridge Companion to Jonathan Edwards* (Cambridge: Cambridge University Press, 2007), pp. 145–146, 154.
[53] Edwards' proposal sounds very much like the Biblical Theology popularized by Vos in the twentieth century. In a 1994 article, Stephen M. Clark makes this point of how Edwards long anticipates Vos: 'His 1739 History of the Work of Redemption sermons articulate a historical principle of treatment that appears fifty years before Johann Philip Gabler, and a full two centuries before Geerhardus Vos' classical Reformed treatment' (Stephen M. Clark, 'Jonathan Edwards: The History of the Work of Redemption,' *Westminster Theological Journal 56*, no. 1 (1994), p. 56).
[54] Edwards, 'Letter to the Princeton Trustees,' in *Works Vol. 16*, p. 728.

Edwards' narrative would include "revolutions in the world of mankind" no less that significant events in ecclesiastical history, and would use as its sources accounts in both "history and prophecy." This suggests a seamless integration of postbiblical historical records with the biblical account, though still controlled by the contents of Scripture: "so far as the Scriptures give any light." The critical phrase "give any light" perhaps needs some clarification provided by the context of the preceding section of the letter, where he explains that his method was ". . . to improve every important hint; pursuing the clue to my utmost, when any thing in reading, meditation, or conversation, has been suggested to my mind, that seemed to promise light in any weighty point . . . ."[55] With this context suggesting Edwards' habitual extrapolation in mind, it seems that he wanted to include in his account not only the contents of Scripture but also the portions of postbiblical history that were predicted or explained by them. This is of course precisely what we find even in the 1739 sermon series *A History of the Work of Redemption* that would provide the core of Edwards' larger project.[56]

Yet again, it is important to see that such integration of historical material did not imply that Edwards considered church history to be fully on a par with Scripture. Scripture was necessary and sufficient, whereas history was not:

> . . . the Scriptures should sufficiently explain themselves; so that we should have no need of joining unto them the writings of the fathers or church historians, and being acquainted with them, in order to our being directed and determined in any important matter . . .[57]

Thanks to the sufficiency of Scripture, we simply do not need the "fathers or church historians" to determine "any important matter" such as church doctrine. However, Edwards' purpose for using church history in the "History" project was not to acquire new doctrine but to enhance what was already believed by adding to it a record of divine affirmation and colorful reiteration in history.

Returning now to Edwards' statement that he planned to show ". . . the admirable contexture and *harmony* of the whole," it is worth repeating that the demonstration of harmony was for Edwards the key to the entire apologetic and polemic enterprise. This subject is treated at length above, but notice that Edwards' alternate title for the "Rational Account" apologetic

[55] Edwards, "Letter to the Princeton Trustees," in *Works Vol. 16*, p. 727.
[56] See Edwards, *A History of the Work of Redemption*, in *Works Vol. 9*, p. 111–528.
[57] Edwards, "Miscellany" 535, in *Works Vol. 18*, p. 79.

project—of which the "History" project was far more a development rather than a discontinuation—was in fact "The Perfect *Harmony* between the Doctrines of the Christian Religion and Human Reason Manifested."[58] Moreover, the apologetic/polemic enterprise was itself an engine for the progression of redemptive history. Edwards believed that one day God was going to accomplish his own "Enlightenment," ". . . when he will himself by his own immediate influence enlighten men's minds; [. . .] when human learning shall be subservient to understanding the Scriptures and a clear explaining and glorious defending the doctrines of Christianity."[59] Until then, however, ministers like Edwards were to set forth to unbelievers the doctrines of Christianity in as clear and convincing a manner as possible to accomplish similar effects, though on a smaller scale.[60]

Harmony was, if you like, God's calling card, examples of which were to be found throughout a seemingly bewildering phenomenological reality. Edwards thus thought that, properly narrated and interpreted, history brought us face-to-face with the harmonious actions of an intelligent agent directing the seemingly disparate parts of history. Of course the Deists and other rationalists did not share this view. Just as they looked at the Bible and saw 66 books written by dozens of human authors each expressing varying theological viewpoints, so they saw in history millions of human actors all advancing their own individual or cultural causes in the absence of transcendent direction. Moreover, they saw orthodox theology as wildly out of step with the pronouncements of human reason, the "candle of the Lord."[61] Edwards, enlightened by a regenerate understanding of God's transcendent ways, looked at all these things and saw perfect harmony. Edwards' ambitious goal in the "History" was thus to get his readers to recognize that harmony, enabling them to realize their own purpose in God's own project of self-communication.

We have seen that Edwards states explicitly and publicly his opinion that the Awakening of the 1730's was God's vindication of orthodox doctrine. And it is well known that the bulk of Edwards' early work was taken up with the defense of the Awakenings as the supernatural work of God.[62] Was, then, the "History" project a further attempt to vindicate the pro-revival perspective? Avihu Zakai adopts this position, pointing out that Edwards joins a long line

[58] Chamberlain, "Editor's Introduction," in *Works Vol. 18*, p. 25; emphasis mine.

[59] Edwards "Sermon 24" of *History of the Work of Redemption*, in *Works Vol. 9*. See also "Exposition of the Apocalypse," in *Works Vol. 5*, p. 118.

[60] See Edwards, "Miscellany" 539, in *Works Vol. 18*, p. 86; see also below, Chapter 6.

[61] Locke, *Essay*, IV.3.20.

[62] See the contents of Edwards, *Works Vol. 4*.

of other theologians-turned historians who sought to justify the present situation of the church via the construction of a historical account:

> Attempting to provide historical justification for the revival, he refashioned himself more and more as an historian, one who constantly sought to unveil the sacred historical background for this New England movement . . . . In consciously assuming the task of situating the revival within ecclesiastical history, Edwards resembled other figures in the history of the church who wrote their narratives in response to some decisive historical changes in order to explain the changing circumstances of the Christian church in the world. [cites Eusebius, Augustine and Foxe][63]

Zakai's comparisons with figures such as Augustine are apt, reminding us that Edwards' theological and apologetic use of history has significant precedent. And it seems likely that the "History" project was at least partially occasioned by the recent experience of exceptional events that called for a defense. In Edwards' view, God was revealing himself in the Awakenings even if the antirevival "Old Lights" refused to see it. Just as most of this group resisted God's Word as it taught justification by faith, they were now resisting his works that confirmed the same. Edwards therefore needed to show that periodic revivals were God's method of advancing his kingdom in Scripture and throughout history. Yet in terms of Edwards' larger goals it would perhaps be a mistake to focus too much on this issue of simply vindicating the revivals, since it is clear that the "History" sought to defend the entirety of orthodox Christian doctrine.

VI Current Events and *The Christian History* Periodicals

The "History of the Work of Redemption" project is one of the best-known aspects of Edwards' work. Far less known, but perhaps equally indicative of his attitude toward God's works in providence as a revelatory medium was the short-lived American periodical called *The Christian History* and its Scottish counterpart *The Christian Monthly History*. To get there, we first consider the remarkable attitude toward the current events Edwards presents in the "Personal Narrative":

> If I heard the least hint of anything that happened in any part of the world, that appeared to me, in some respect or other, to have a favorable

[63] Zakai, *Reenchantment*, p. 279.

aspect on the interest of Christ's kingdom, my soul eagerly catched at it; and it would much animate and refresh me. I used to be earnest to read public news-letters, mainly for that end; to see if I could not find some news favorable to the interests of religion in the world.[64]

What is interesting about this quote is the apparent symmetry between Edwards' portrayal of the role played by current events and similar portrayals regarding Scripture and nature he expresses elsewhere in the "Personal Narrative." In all three cases, supernatural regeneration allows him to receive God's several streams of revelation with zeal and joy. These parallel affective experiences are consistent with Edwards' reality-sized theology of revelation.

Edwards did not want to see God's revelation in history go to waste either by neglect or by distortion, certainly not in times of revival where the sheer density and pace of events made conventional secular outlets unsuitable. Thus, the very last measure he proposed in the 1742 *Some Thoughts Concerning the Present Revival* to promote God's work was to call for a periodical dedicated to revival news:

One thing more I would mention, which if God should still carry on this work, would tend much to promote it, and that is that an history should be published once a month, or once a fort-night, of the progress of it, by one of the ministers of Boston, who are near the press and are most conveniently situated to receive accounts from all parts. It has been found by experience that the tidings of remarkable effects of the power and grace of God in any place, tend greatly to awaken and engage the minds of persons in other places. 'Tis great pity therefore, but that some means should be used for the most speedy, most extensive and certain giving information of such things, and that the country ben't left only to the slow, partial and doubtful information and false representations of common report.[65]

Notice the activist tone seen in this proposal, as with the numerous others that preceded it: the history newsletter would "tend very much to promote" the ongoing revival. Edwards provides as support for his case the observation that "the tidings of remarkable effects of the power and grace of God in any place, tend greatly to awaken and engage the minds of persons in other

[64] Edwards, "Personal Narrative," in *Works Vol. 16*, p. 797.
[65] Edwards, *Some Thoughts Concerning the Present Revival*, in *Works Vol. 4*, p. 529.

places," comporting with his remarks in the "Personal Narrative" and with his theology generally.

Edwards states in a letter to a Scottish minister of May 1743 that the proposed project was being undertaken by Thomas Prince, Jr. in Boston.[66] Prince indeed began the weekly publication of *The Christian History* in March 1743, and Robe himself undertook the Scottish equivalent.[67] Goen describes the brief course of these publications in a footnote:

> The periodical [*The Christian History*] published two annual volumes before expiring in 1744. A Scottish counterpart, *The Christian Monthly History*, was issued at Edinburgh under the editorship of James Robe, friend and correspondent of [Edwards]; appearing irregularly in sixteen numbers between November 1743 and January 1746, it printed many items of American intelligence.[68]

The periodicals eventually dried upon along with the Awakenings they chronicled. What does this episode tell us about Edwards? Perhaps it shows how seriously he took the mandate for intelligent creatures to observe, understand and re-emanate God's self-communication in time. As we shall soon see, Edwards had been proving in his private notebooks that the work of redemption is by far the greatest of God's works and that even the glorified saints in heaven will gain in their knowledge and love of God by carefully watching the events of redemptive history on earth. It makes sense that he would want to promulgate among the earthly saints such a significant episode of this great work through the use of these short-lived news periodicals.

VII The Redemptive-Historical Beatific Vision

Many of Edwards' distinctive contributions as a theologian can be identified simply by observing the recurrent themes we find in the "Miscellanies." Certain problems or possibilities interested him more than others, and would thus become the subject of multiple revisions in his attempts to come to the truth of the matter and to state the resulting doctrine most precisely. One such recurring theme was Edwards' preoccupation with something we might call the redemptive-historical beatific vision. Traditionally, the beatific vision describes the blessed state of the saints in heaven as those who are in

[66] Edwards, "Letter to the Rev. James Robe," in *Works Vol. 4*, p. 538.
[67] Goen, "Editor's Introduction," in Edwards, *Works Vol. 4*, p. 59.
[68] Goen, editorial note in Edwards, *Works Vol. 4*, pp. 78–79, note 7.

some manner enabled to see God. Edwards certainly affirms this basic doctrine. But he also expends a great amount of effort in the "Miscellanies" to prove something rather unexpected: in addition to their enjoyment of the immediate divine presence, one of the great privileges and joyful occupations of the saints in heaven will be to witness the progress of redemptive history on earth. This thesis, one that appears to have no clear precedent among Edwards' inheritance, is somewhat underrepresented in the secondary literature.[69] More importantly for our purpose here, an understanding of the redemptive-historical beatific vision will serve to underscore the enormous place history had in Edwards' theology of revelation and his overall project.

The first record we have of Edwards' thoughts on this subject comes in "Miscellany" 105, written in early 1724:[70] "That the glorified spirits shall grow in holiness and happiness to eternity, I argue from this foundation, that their number of ideas shall increase to eternity."[71] This doctrine of the progressive nature of heavenly joy is consonant with the theological underpinnings of Edwards' doctrine of revelation discussed above.[72] To review, Edwards thought that intelligent creatures were created to know God, love the God they knew (with this love being the essence of holiness), and enjoy the God they loved (the foundation of their happiness). It seemed intuitively clear to Edwards that "glorified spirits" would endlessly have new input into this process in the form of new ideas. Edwards does not need to say "ideas *about God*" here because his all-encompassing doctrine of revelation makes this unnecessary: any real information is ultimately valuable for, and is in fact intended expressly for, knowing God. Thus, the saints and angels would forever know him more, love him more, and enjoy him more in an eternally upward spiral. At this point, Edwards does not seem to be propelled to this conclusion by any explicit exegetical data, but rather out of systematic considerations.[73]

Edwards would soon go on to find scriptural support for his concept, however, as shown in "Miscellany" 372:

> It seems to be quite a wrong notion of the happiness of heaven, that it is in that manner unchangeable, that it admits not of new joys upon

[69] The topic was taken up by Paul Ramsey in Appendix II to Edwards, *Works Vol. 8*, written in 1989, but it does not seem to have figured since.

[70] Schaefer, "Editor's Introduction," in *Works Vol. 13*, p. 94.

[71] Edwards, "Miscellany" 105, in *Works Vol. 13*, p. 275.

[72] See above, Chapter 1.

[73] Edwards later appended to "Miscellany" 105 a reference to his notes on Psalm 89:1–2.

> new occasions. The Scripture tells us that there is joy in heaven and amongst [the angels] upon the conversion of one sinner; and why not among the saints? . . . . Their joy is continually increased, as they see the purposes of God's grace unfolded in his wondrous providences towards his church . . . . I believe also that it greatly contributed to the happiness of the saints in heaven, to see the success of the gospel after Christ's ascension, and its conquering the Roman empire; and that they greatly rejoiced at the reformation from popery, and will exceedingly rejoice at the fall of Antichrist and the conversion of the world to Christianity (these things seem clear to me by many passages in the Revelation); and that their joy is increasing and will be increasing, as God gradually in his providence unveils his glory till the last day.[74]

Edwards begins by informing us of the polemic agenda lying behind his interest in the topic: he is convinced that the traditional understanding of the heavenly state as a static condition is wrongheaded and inadequate. He then moves quickly to scriptural exegesis in support of his position, most importantly Luke 15:7's teaching that human repentance on earth brings joy in heaven. Edwards then concludes with a more general reference to the Book of Revelation whereby such "things seem clear to me." Edwards also makes a fairly seamless transition from biblical material to examples taken from history, such as the conversion of the Roman state to Christianity and the Reformation.

The basic parameters of Edwards' theory—that the heavenly beatific state is progressive and that the revelation funding this progression comes at least partially from witnessing redemptive history—are now in place. But one loose end remains. Edwards has not yet answered the fundamental objection of why anything would *need* to be added to the traditional beatific vision, or why would anyone *want* to look at earthly events if they could see God directly. This question is answered in the mature statement of the doctrine completed many years later in "Miscellany" 777, an essay that is no doubt one of the most significant sources for Edwards' doctrine of revelation generally. This lengthy entry begins thus:

> HAPPINESS OF HEAVEN IS PROGRESSIVE, and has various periods in which it has a new and glorious advancement, and consists very much in BEHOLDING the manifestations that God makes of himself in the WORK OF REDEMPTION. There can be no view or knowledge that one

[74] Edwards, 'Miscellany' 372, in *Works Vol. 13*, pp. 444–445.

> spiritual being can have of another, but it must be either immediate and intuitive, or mediate, or [by] some manifestations or signs.[75]

The points that Edwards wants to prove are two. The happiness of heaven is progressive rather than static, and it consists "very much" in beholding the work of redemption. Immediately following this thesis statement, Edwards begins to explain his response to the question of why the beatific vision cannot consist simply of beholding God directly: God cannot simply be gazed upon in this way because he is a spiritual being and thus requires a mediated sighting even by other spiritual beings.

From there, Edwards might have moved straight on to his specific point about the revelatory role of redemptive history. But in this theologically rich statement, Edwards continues to probe the implications of God's invisibility in order to introduce the unique situation of the Son of God: ". . . there is no creature can thus have an immediate sight of God, but only Jesus Christ, who is in the bosom of God."[76] Here at what would seem to be the core of Edwards' doctrine of revelation is a restatement of the Reformed orthodox view of Christ as *the* medium of revelation. Edwards explains that "Jesus Christ, who alone sees immediately, [is] the grand medium of the knowledge of all others; they know no otherwise than by the exhibitions held forth in and by him, as the Scripture is express."[77]

With this crucial element established, Edwards puts all the pieces together to make a full statement on one of his most characteristic doctrines:

> And they see and know God in heaven by his Word or speech, for there the saints are with God, and converse with God, and God converses with them by voluntary manifestations and significations of his mind, either by external signs or by impulses of his Spirit; and this also is by Christ. They converse with God by conversing with Christ, who speaketh the words of God . . . 'Tis God's pleasure that Christ should be the light, the Sun of heaven, by which God should be seen and known there, for it pleases the Father that in him all fullness should dwell. And again they see and know God in heaven by his works, which are the effects of the glorious perfections there are in him; and this also is in Christ, for all the works of God are wrought in him by whom all things are made . . . And especially do they see his glory as it is manifested in the work of redemption . . .[78]

[75] Edwards, "Miscellany" 777, in *Works Vol. 18*, p. 427.
[76] Edwards, "Miscellany" 777, in *Works Vol. 18*, p. 428.
[77] Edwards, "Miscellany" 777, in *Works Vol. 18*, p. 428.
[78] Edwards, "Miscellany" 777, in *Works Vol. 18*, pp. 429–430; emphasis mine.

Certainly the saints do see God in heaven, because they see Jesus Christ. And they "converse with God" by conversing with Christ. But they also know God by his glorious works, which indeed are done by God through the agency of Christ. And the greatest of these works is the work of redemption, wherein by viewing the ongoing events on earth the saints continually learn more of God's glory.

Edwards sometimes theorized in the "Miscellanies" or other notebooks on speculative topics that never made an appearance in his sermons. Edwards was, after all, a pastor, and he did not consider each and every such item important or certain enough to preach on. But he apparently felt free enough to preach on his doctrine of the redemptive-historical beatific vision. This is seen in a sermon preached for the funeral of his friend David Brainerd, who had spent his final days in the Edwards' home. Here we find Edwards pushing the limits of human language to convey the blessedness of heaven, where the great reward will be our intimate conversation with Christ. And one of the main topics of this conversation will be, astonishingly, *the state of affairs on earth*:

> That part of the family that is in heaven, are surely not unacquainted with the affairs of that part of the same family that is on earth. They that are with the king, and are next to him, the royal family, that dwell in his palace, are not kept in ignorance of the affairs of his kingdom. [. . .] And that which gives them much greater advantage for such an acquaintance, than the things already mentioned, in their being constantly in the immediate presence of Christ, and in the enjoyment of the most perfect intercourse with him, who is the King who manages all these affairs, and has an absolutely perfect knowledge of them.[79]

Edwards is not beyond proving his case to his auditors, but no more so than what he would customarily do as a homiletic strategy for any number of uncontroversial doctrines. It would thus appear that by the time of Brainerd's death, Edwards had satisfied himself that his understanding of the beatific vision was essentially beyond doubt. The sermon also develops a contextually important nuance—the title being "True Saints are Present with the Lord"—regarding Christ's central role in even the media of the redemptive-historical beatific vision. It is not that saints merely witness the progress of the work of redemption on their own recognizance, which could presumably be done on earth. The great advantage of the saints in heaven is their "enjoyment of

[79] Edwards, "True Saints are Present with the Lord," in *Works Vol. 25*, p. 237.

the most perfect intercourse with him, who is the King who manages all these affairs, and has an absolutely perfect knowledge of them." In other words, *Christ narrates and interprets* the course of events on earth for the benefit of the saints in heaven so they might enter into a perfect understanding of their revelatory, doxological content. Such a statement might also describe Edwards' own theological project—more on this in the concluding chapter.

VIII Zakai on "Miscellany" 777

Considering the prominence history held in Jonathan Edwards' thought, Avihu Zakai's recent book-length study devoted to the subject, *Jonathan Edwards's Philosophy of History: The Reenchantment of the World in the Age of Enlightenment*, is a most welcome contribution to the literature.[80] Zakai, however, takes a debatable position on a subject that is most relevant to our study: did Edwards' enthusiasm for the possibilities of nonscriptural revelation really outstrip his allegiance to traditional Calvinist assumptions about the supremacy of Scripture?[81] Michael J. McClymond asked this question in his review of Zakai, noting ". . . Zakai's claim that Edwards showed "an exaltation of nature to a level of authority co-equal with revelation" . . . overlooks Edwards's criticisms of the Deists and their reliance on natural theology."[82] Indeed, we have devoted an entire chapter to Edwards' unambiguous assertion of the necessity of special revelation.[83] How, then, could Zakai think that Edwards posited "an exaltation of nature to a level of authority co-equal with revelation"? Moreover, he is apparently not alone in so thinking; Zakai was in fact quoting Perry Miller, the original General Editor of Yale's *Works of Jonathan Edwards*.[84] Furthermore, both the original statement in Miller and Zakai's approving quotation are linked to assertions by their respective authors that Edwards broke with Calvin on the value of natural revelation.[85] It would seem, then, that either there is some complexity in the issue that could so lead them astray, or else there is some inconsistency in Edwards. In either case, the issue is worth some further investigation.

[80] Avihu Zakai, *Jonathan Edwards's Philosophy of History: The Reenchantment of the World in the Age of Enlightenment* (Princeton, NJ: Princeton University Press, 2003). This book has already been referred to above.
[81] Zakai, *Reenchantment*, p. 74.
[82] Michael J. McClymond, 'Review of Avihu Zakai, Jonathan Edwards's Philosophy of History,' *The Journal of Religion 85*, no. 1 (2005), p. 122.
[83] See above, Chapter 3.
[84] Zakai, *Reenchantment*, p. 74; quoting Perry Miller, *Images or Shadows of Divine Things* (New Haven: Yale University Press, 1948), p. 28.
[85] See Zakai, *Reenchantment*, pp. 72–74.

When we examine Zakai's relevant reference to the primary material, it seems at first glance that not only does he have support for Miller's statement but actually has license to say even more than he does. This apparent warrant comes from the aforementioned "Miscellany" 777, which Zakai quotes at length just before making his controversial statement:

> So far as they see God and know him in his works (which is *the principal way in which God manifests himself, and to which the manifestation of himself in his Word is subordinate*: [Zakai begins his quote here] the manifestations God makes of himself in his works are the principal manifestations of his perfections, and the declarations and teaching of his Word are to lead to those . . . .[86]

Recall that Zakai said only that Edwards assigns nature/history a "co-equal" status with Scripture. Edwards himself, it seems, does not shrink from saying that "the manifestation of himself in his Word is *subordinate*" to that in his "works" (meaning nature and redemptive history). This portion of "Miscellany" 777 has, either understandably or oddly depending on one's perspective, rarely seen the light of day in the secondary literature. The leading clause containing the "subordinate" dynamite is in fact elided from Zakai's own quotation, no doubt saying too much even for a purpose he judged to be sufficiently controversial to oblige an appeal to Miller's authority.[87]

The possibility of inconsistency in Edwards now becomes problematically real, for McClymond is surely right to point to Edwards' strident arguments for the necessity of special revelation in his anti-Deist polemic documented above.[88] We need turn only to such statements as "Miscellany" 350 to see that Edwards utterly denies the possibility of natural theology: "If there never had been any revelation, I believe the world would be full of endless dispute about the very being of a God, whether the world was from eternity or not, and whether the form and order of the world don't result from the mere nature of matter . . . ."[89] Yet, it hardly seems likely that the unremittingly logical author of *Freedom of the Will* could allow himself to fall into such a blatant inconsistency on such an important issue.

[86] Edwards, "Miscellany" 777, in *Works Vol. 18*, p. 430; emphasis mine. Although Zakai also cites the *Works* edition, his symbol-laden quotation in *Reenchantment*, p. 73, seems to be from the manuscript or an early transcription.
[87] Zakai, *Reenchantment*, p. 73.
[88] See above, Chapter 3.
[89] Edwards, "Miscellany" 350, in *Works Vol. 13*, pp. 421–422.

The resolution to this problem comes at least partially when attention is paid to the tri-world (consisting of heaven, this world, and hell; in past, present, and future time) contexts that Edwards flits between in his notebook entries. We notice that "Miscellany" 777 is entitled "HAPPINESS OF HEAVEN IS PROGRESSIVE" and that Edwards is speaking in the third person about the condition of *perfected saints in heaven*, not on earth. Edwards' statements here and in similar places are not directly relevant to the human situation in this world, where our condition absolutely necessitates special revelation in the form of Scripture. Zakai seems not to have given sufficient weight to the fact that Edwards was, as so often, speculating about another world.

The fuller resolution of this issue, however, turns on what Edwards meant when he spoke of God's works being "principal" and his Word "subordinate." Here is the quotation again, down to the end of the section:

> So far as they see God and know him in his works (which is the principal way in which God manifests himself, and to which the manifestation of himself in his Word is subordinate: the manifestations God makes of himself in his works are the principal manifestations of his perfections, and the declarations and teaching of his Word are to lead to those; . . .) they see and know [him] as he manifests himself in the work of redemption, which [is] the greatest and most glorious of all God's works, the work of works to which all God's works are reduced. And [this] is the end, and as it were the sum of all God's works, to the purposes and ends of which work heaven and all its angels were created; and which is a work that the redeemed saints in heaven are concerned [with] far above all other works of God, in which the glory of the divine perfections, and especially the glory of his love, appears as much more brightly than in any other work, as the light of the sun is above that of the stars, and of which work all their glory and blessedness in heaven is a fruit and a part. And this work by way of eminency is THE WORK of Jesus Christ, the image of the invisible [God], by whom alone God is seen and known by the saints.[90]

Edwards' comparison between God's Word and his works has nothing whatever to do with the relative *authority* of natural and special revelation, which is what Miller and Zakai seemed to have thought. The purpose of this part of "Miscellany" 777 is to provide the foundation for Edwards' doctrine of the redemptive-historical beatific vision, and the issue is about *logical*

[90] Edwards, "Miscellany" 777, in *Works Vol. 18*, pp. 430–431.

priority. Considered absolutely, God's Word is indeed "subordinate" to his works, but not because it is somehow of less authority or otherwise deficient. It is simply because God's Word is necessarily secondary to the works it describes to us, logically speaking. Without God's works there would not be much for the Word to say to us. To return again to the metaphor of the theater, the inspired program of Scripture does not exist in isolation from the play (the work of redemption) it describes.

Notice also that this logical priority does not, at least to Edwards' mind, end up disparaging the second person of the Trinity. As the image of the Father he is the Word of God; but no less is the great work of redemption "THE WORK of Jesus Christ, the image of the invisible [God]." All of God's works and all of God's words come through him. It is all by Christ, "by whom alone God is seen and known by the saints," whatever side of the coin we chose to look at.

IX Conclusion

Edwards was both a historian and a theologian of history. His use of history was not that of his godless Enlightenment contemporaries venerating human machinations but that of a preacher glorifying God as the true protagonist of history. Through the interpretive guide of Scripture, history became for him a hugely important media of divine revelation. In both the construction of his theology and the production of his corpus, he took God's purposes in providence with the utmost seriousness. In his earnest speculations about heaven, he looked forward to hearing Christ's perfect explanation of the oft-confusing course of events on earth. In his works such as the *History of the Work of Redemption*, he sought to provide his own generation with as best an approximation as he could muster. He did so not only to help people to appreciate the God who carried out his glorious purposes in history but also to enable them to fall in actively with those purposes.

In the course of this chapter, the story of Edwards' lifelong project has been building. It is to a fuller discussion of this subject that we now turn in the final chapter.

Chapter 6

Edwards' Project

"His works are various and manifold, but the end ultimately aimed at in all is the same. He han't different and separate designs that have no relation one to another in his various works, but has one great design in all."

—*Jonathan Edwards, "Approaching the End of God's Grand Design"*

I Introduction

Jonathan Edwards lived in an age of purposefulness, and this was surely one aspect of the *zeitgeist* he embraced unconditionally. Edwards' sense of purpose is famously evident in his "Resolutions," where he resolves things like ". . . no other end but religion, shall have any influence at all on any of my actions; and that no action shall be, in the least circumstance, any otherwise than the religious end will carry it."[1] It is hardly incredible to suppose that such a man, living at such a time, would have an overarching project in mind for his work.[2] The difficulty, however, lies in describing the project. We began our attempt to do so in Chapter 1 with Edwards' theology proper, where we focused on the concept of divine communicativeness. God is a "communicative being," and his communicativeness provided the answer to one of the most important and original questions, if not *the* question, of Edwards' theological career: why did God create the universe? God created the universe in order to communicate himself to angels and men so they would know him, love him, and partake of his joy. Since the Trinity is defined by perfect harmony *ad intra*, any communication *ad extra*

[1] Edwards, "Resolutions" 44, in *Works Vol. 16*, p. 756.

[2] For instance, we have noted above that Edwards' contemporary Hume maintained throughout his diverse works the tacit purpose of disabusing his generation of what he regarded to be their superstitious religious beliefs: " . . .I have been endeavouring to open the eyes of the Public. If I live a few years longer, I may have the satisfaction of seeing the downfall of some of the prevailing systems of superstition" (Hume, quoted in Stanley Tweyman (ed.), *Hume on Natural Religion* (Bristol: Thoemmes Press, 1996), p. 13).

must be marked indelibly by harmony. And in Edwards' radically theocentric metaphysics, all of reality is precisely the ongoing communication of the divine mind.[3] The purpose of human beings in this universe is to receive and re-emanate this harmonious communication. This objective can be realized only through supernatural regeneration, which bestows upon fallen humanity the taste that enables them to know, love, and enjoy the God who communicates to them.[4]

Even with this regenerate capacity in place, there yet remains the actual task of appropriating the content of revelation. And this is no trivial matter. Not only is the sheer quantity of God's communication in nature, Scripture, and history vast beyond imagination, the harmony that unites it all is complex. Even twice-born humanity needs help to appreciate it all. This is why, as we saw in the previous chapter, Edwards thought that Christ *interprets* the ongoing work of redemption on earth for the benefit of the saints in heaven. Likewise, Edwards did not think that God had left his elect entirely to their own devices in this present world but gave them a special class of beings—angels, apostles, and ministers—who shared in Christ's work of conveying and interpreting divine communication. Edwards undoubtedly saw himself as a member of this class, and it would have been strange had he *not* somehow integrated the functions of conveying communication and interpreting harmony in his own project.

Edwards' communicative/interpretive project is manifested in his corpus in various ways. The harmony concept runs like a golden thread throughout the chapters on Edwards' thought on nature, Scripture, and history. As we shall now discuss in this chapter, Edwards' retelling of his own regenerate experience in the "Personal Narrative" was the story of one who was enabled to perceive the exquisite harmony found in all aspects of divine communication. Perhaps the single most important piece of evidence pointing us to the nature of his larger project, however, is the common purpose of his three "Great Works." These unfinished works do not seem at first glance to have all that much in common, yet in each case, Edwards tells us that his underlying purpose is to demonstrate the *harmony* to be found in and among the media of revelation.

Such a project is entirely explicable in terms of Edwards' Enlightenment context. At a time when the Deists were pronouncing the *discord* of nature with Scripture, history with Scripture, and Scripture with itself, Edwards'

[3] Michael J. McClymond maintains that theocentricity is indeed the central motif of Edwards' work. See McClymond, *Encounters with God: An Approach to the Theology of Jonathan Edwards* (Oxford: Oxford University Press, 1998).

[4] See Edwards, "Miscellany" 123, in *Works Vol. 13*, p. 287.

life work was to argue the opposite: nature, Scripture, and history are all in perfect, though highly complex, harmony within themselves and with one another, and this very harmony points to the underlying reality of the beautiful divine mind. At the cognitive level, all aspects of reality awaited reasoned demonstration that they were in perfect accord—it could not be otherwise. Conversely, harmony was itself the authenticating hallmark engraved on every part of God's communicative project. Yet this was not rationalism by another name. Edwards believed that harmony endowed phenomena with a meaning well beyond the mere information it conveyed, that is, for those who had the supernaturally regenerate eyes to see it.

Of course, the project of interpreting harmony could conceivably have included everything under the sun. This is in fact exactly what Edwards had in mind when he first put pen to paper on this project.[5] Yet, in light of the real limitations of his life, we must consider what could have influenced this intensely purposeful minister to prioritize certain topics above others. Much of the answer comes in terms of the larger intellectual currents we have just mentioned and which have made appearances throughout this book. Yet, Edwards did not get around to every problematic aspect of contemporary Enlightenment thought, while he did get around to some things that do not seem to have all that much direct connection. It is here that the Awakenings seem to have some role in the setting of Edwards' specific agenda. Almost all of the issues that actually saw some measure of completion during his lifetime were the items that, in his opinion, played crucial roles in the revivals. The doctrines that he chose to defend, such as in *The Freedom of the Will* and *Original Sin*, were the ones he believed to be especially used by God in this work. The projects that he pursued, such as "The History of the Work of Redemption" series and the revival news periodicals, were those he considered to be useful to fan revival flames. Thus, it seems that the agenda of the Awakenings provides the final factor to explain the actual form of Edwards' project.

Having laid out the broad outlines of Edwards' project and what seems to have led him to pursue it as he did, we turn to an examination of some supporting evidence. This examination will consist of a brief recap of relevant aspects of Edwards' theology, a discussion of his understanding of the minister's communicative purpose and interpretive function, the message of the "Personal Narrative," the common purpose of harmony in the three

[5] "PREFACE: To shew how all arts and sciences, the more they are perfected, the more they issue in divinity, and coincide with it, and appear to be as parts of it. And to shew how absurd for Christians to write treatises of ethics distinctly from divinity as revealed in the Gospel" (Edwards, "Preface to the Rational Account," in *Works Vol. 6*, p. 397).

unfinished "Great Works," and, finally, the agenda of the Awakenings. We shall conclude with some thoughts on how this theory relates to previous theories on Edwards.

II Relevant Highlights of Edwards' Theology

We saw in the first chapter that Edwards believed all created reality was the manifestation of God's self-communicative activity, and this concept need not be rehearsed in detail. The point here is simply to recall that Edwards thought God had a "project" in creation and redemption, and that project was to communicate himself to intelligent beings in knowledge, love, and joy. The Christian's corresponding project is to "[a]ct as a creator with God in the pursuit of that good design God has in view and not as an opposer of it."[6] The implications for Edwards' theological project are fairly straightforward. We might expect that he would align his own work with this carefully developed teleology, posthumously recommended to the world in *The End for Which God Created the World.*[7] We might expect Edwards to spend his life conveying to his fellow human beings the abundant knowledge, love, and joy he had been given for this purpose, and we are not disappointed. This communicativeness was the foundation of his project and, in a general way, informed his method—he would teach people God's truth using words and ideas that would tend to stir the appropriate affections.[8]

Edwards' theology also had more specific methodological implications for his project. Edwards thought that the salvific reception of God's communication, though dependent upon the prior work of the Holy Spirit, was characterized by the *apprehension of harmony.*[9] The Triune God is the ". . . supreme harmony of all"; and when God communicates himself, he communicates harmoniously.[10] This harmony permeates all aspects of reality, so if we are experiencing the universe rightly, this harmony will be perceived. Indeed, intelligent beings were created with the very purpose of perceiving and taking delight in it.[11] And since harmony can be created

[6] Edwards, "Approaching the End of God's Grand Design," in *Works Vol. 25*, p. 125.
[7] Edwards, The End for Which God Created the World, in Works Vol. 8, pp. 405–536.
[8] See Edwards, "Subjects to be Handled in the Treatise on the Mind," in *Works Vol. 6*, p. 388. On the counterbalancing point that the preacher can only do so much under God, see "Miscellany" 123, in *Works Vol. 13*, p. 287.
[9] See Edwards, "Miscellany" 123, in *Works Vol. 13*, p. 287.
[10] Edwards, "Miscellany" 182, in *Works Vol. 13*, p. 329.
[11] Edwards, "Miscellany" 108, in *Works Vol. 13*, pp. 278–279.

only by intelligence, logically, the perception of harmony leads one to know the intelligent being that lies behind it: "Sensible things, by virtue of the *harmony* and proportion that is seen in them, carry the appearance of perceiving and willing being."[12] All of the media of revelation carry this divine stamp of harmony pointing toward their author, as in the example of Scripture:

> . . . there is that wondrous universal harmony and consent and concurrence . . . that the evidence is the same that the Scriptures are the word and work of a divine mind, to one that is thoroughly acquainted with them, as 'tis that the words and actions of an understanding man are from a rational mind, to one that has of a long time been his familiar acquaintance.[13]

When one apprehends the harmony manifested in God's Word and works, one is drawn to the reality of its author; when one knows the author, one can better recognize and enjoy his handiwork. This insight determined the distinctive methodology of Edwards' project: to demonstrate harmony.

The twin concepts of God's Trinitarian communicativeness and divine harmony are fairly central to Edwards' core theology. At a level removed from this foundation, yet equally important for understanding Edwards' project, is a peculiar aspect of his Christology. This is the idea that Christ *interprets* redemptive history for the benefit of the saints in heaven, a teaching discussed in the previous chapter under the heading of the redemptive-historical beatific vision.[14] We saw how Edwards believed that the saints are better off in heaven, not simply because they have a better vantage point for witnessing the ongoing affairs of God's great work of redemption but because Christ, who "has an absolutely perfect knowledge" of these events, is there to *explain* it all to them.[15] This original twist to the usual handling of Christ's prophetic role is indicative of the stress Edwards put on the need for interpretation of the revelatory content always available in reality around us, even for the regenerate and sinless inhabitants of heaven. Now, as we shall see, Edwards thought that there was a correspondence between Christ's prophetic role and the minister's role. If Christ had an ongoing ministry of interpreting communicative reality for the benefit of the saints, and if ministers emulated this function, then the interpretive project we

[12] Edwards, "The Mind" entry 63, in *Works Vol. 6*, p. 382; emphasis mine.
[13] Edwards, "Miscellany" 333, in *Works Vol. 13*, p. 410.
[14] See above, Chapter 5.
[15] Edwards, "True Saints are Present with the Lord," in *Works Vol. 25*, p. 237.

have been describing was simply part of what Edwards thought every good minister should do. In any case, it is almost certain that there would be some overlap between his theology of the ministry and his personal application of that theology, so we turn to consider some of his thoughts on the subject.

III The Minister's Project

Edwards was many things, but above all, he understood himself as a minister.[16] With the exception of a couple early years serving as a tutor at Yale and the final months of his life presiding over The College of New Jersey (Princeton), Edwards spent his entire career in the pastoral ministry. Edwards applied his theological mind to understand the nature of his calling, and he left us a fair amount of his thoughts on the subject. Indeed, scholars are at long last taking this vocational self-understanding nearly as seriously as Edwards himself did, and good books on the subject have recently appeared.[17] If we wish to describe Edwards' larger project, then we must at least consider some aspects of his carefully thought-out theology of the ministry.

It might first be useful to locate Edwards' view of the ministry in relation to the larger Reformed tradition, taking Calvin as our point of reference. Calvin held a high doctrine of the ministry, in the sense that he maintained a significant functional distinction between minister and flock. This distinction issues in an ecclesiology that is more clerical than might superficially be supposed of the antipriest, antipapacy Reformer:[18]

> For, as he did not commit his ancient people to angels, but raised up teachers on the earth to perform a truly angelical office . . . . he [God] by

[16] It is true that Edwards said "So far as I myself am able to judge of what talents I have, for benefiting my fellow creatures by word, I think I can write better than I can speak" (Edwards, "Letter to the Princeton Trustees," in *Works Vol 16*, p. 729). However, the writing that Edwards spoke of was all done while serving as a minister, and, as we shall see, he explicitly understood the work of writing theology to be part of the ministerial office.

[17] See John Carrick, *The Preaching of Jonathan Edwards* (Edinburgh: Banner of Truth, 2008), and Douglas A. Sweeney, *Jonathan Edwards and the Ministry of the Word: A Model of Faith and Thought* (Downers Grove, IL: IVP Academic, 2009). Previous works on the subject would include Ralph Gale Turnbull, *Jonathan Edwards the Preacher* (Grand Rapids, MI: Baker Book House, 1958); Harry S. Stout, *The New England Soul: Preaching and Religious Culture in Colonial New England* (New York: Oxford University Press, 1986); Helen Petter Westra, "'Above All Others': Jonathan Edwards and the Gospel Ministry," *American Presbyterians* 67 (1989), pp. 209–19; and Kenneth P. Minkema and Richard A. Bailey, "Reason, Revelation, and Preaching: An Unpublished Ordination Sermon by Jonathan Edwards," *Southern Baptist Journal of Theology* 3.2 (1999), pp. 16–33.

[18] See Calvin, *Institutes* IV.ii; IV.vi; and IV.vii.

> an admirable test proves our obedience when we listen to his ministers just as we would to himself . . . . he deigns to consecrate the mouths and tongues of men to his service, making his own voice to be heard in them . . . . he in this (as we have said) uses the ministry of men, by making them, as it were his substitutes . . .[19]

Calvin taught that God commits to men "a truly angelical" office, making "his own voice to be heard" in them. He enjoins the faithful to listen to ministers, who are as it were God's "substitutes," just as we would to God himself. This authority has nothing to do with Roman Catholic claims regarding the Pope's *personal* teaching or ruling authority.[20] Rather, ministers are to act as conduits through which God, "as it were," speaks.

Edwards' thought on this issue is in continuity with the direction set by Calvin, though with some typical Edwardsean touches.[21] To wit, Edwards spoke as though he thought of ministers as in some respects a distinct order of intelligent being, closer to angels than to ordinary men with regard to their special function in the work of redemption: "There are two kinds of persons that are given to Christ, and appointed and devoted of God to be his servants, to be employed with Christ, and under him, in his great work of the salvation of the souls of men; and they are *angels* and *ministers.*"[22] Angels and ministers are thus in the same category as "persons that are . . . to be employed with Christ" in the work of redemption, set apart to be the instruments of salvation for ordinary people. Edwards even likens the work of ministers to the prophetic aspects of Christ's salvific work: "The work of ministers is in many respects like the work that Christ himself was appointed to, as the Savior of men; and especially the same with the work which Christ does in his prophetical office."[23] The similarity is not one of personal merit or ontological parity but of prophetic function in communicating God's revelation. In this vein, Edwards went as far as to say in another sermon ". . . whereby as Christ himself is the author of eternal salvation, so ministers become a kind of subordinate saviors."[24] "*Subordinate saviors*"—the fact that Edwards would use such language is testimony to his conviction that

[19] Calvin, *Institutes* IV.i.5 and IV.iii.1.

[20] See Calvin, *Institutes* IV.vi; IV.vii; IV.xv.6; and IV.iixx.

[21] Wilson H. Kimnach does note that Edwards places " . . .a new stress upon the heroic personal dimensions of ministers as true ambassadors of Christ" (Kimnach, "Editor"s Introduction," in *Works Vol. 25*, pp. 14–15). See also Helen Petter Westra, "'Above All Others': Jonathan Edwards and the Gospel Ministry," *American Presbyterians* 67 (1989), pp. 209–19.

[22] Edwards, "Christ the Example of Gospel Ministers," in *Works Vol. 25*, p. 344; emphasis original.

[23] Edwards, "Christ the Example of Gospel Ministers," in *Works Vol. 25*, p. 341.

[24] Edwards, "Sons of Oil, Heavenly Lights," in *Works Vol. 25*, p. 271.

ministers are an integral component, and a functional microcosm, of God's own work of communicating himself to humanity.[25]

The minister's prophetic function includes not only the proclamation of received truths, but also the work of theology: "'Tis God's design to make use of ministers thus: to correct the mistakes of his people and gradually introduce an increase of light."[26] Ministers have been correcting the church's errors and gradually increasing the purity of the church's message by engaging in polemic discourse. This work of theological clarification has been at work over the history of the church, and Edwards thinks it will comprise part of the means by which God ushers in more glorious times yet to come:

> And this increase of light shall be very much by means of ministers; God will make use of his own institution and bless them in order to bring about this increase of light . . . . he will make use of them at that day to clear divine truths and to refute errors, and to reclaim and correct God's people wherein in any respect they have been mistaken and have been going out of the way of duty.[27]

It has long been recognized that Edwards' promotion of the Awakenings was an effort to advance things spiritually toward the glorious eschatological age. Much less has been said of how he thought that ministers doing polemic theology were just as much a divinely appointed means to this end. In this frame of reference, *Freedom of the Will* was every bit as important a contribution as was the transatlantic concert of prayer.

In a similar way, notice how Edwards thought that ministers engage in *apologetics* to forward God's work.[28] In his commentary on Revelation 16:21, Edwards depicts apologetic theology as God's lethal instrument to destroy Satan: "For we know that Antichrist is to be destroyed by clear light, by the breath of Christ's mouth, [by the] brightness of his coming, that is, by plain

[25] This very high view of the ministry is reflected in Edwards' typology: "The different glory of the sun, moon and stars represents the different glory of Christ and the glorified saints. The sun represents Christ. The moon well represents the glory of the prophets and apostles and other ministers of Christ that have been improved as great lights of his church and instruments of promoting and establishing his kingdom and glory, and so have been luminaries to enlighten the world by reflecting the light of the sun, that is, of Christ, and conveying his beams to them . . ." (Edwards, "Types" entry 53, in *Works Vol. 11*, pp. 65–66).

[26] Edwards, "One End in God's Appointing the Ministry," in *Works Vol. 25*, pp. 445–46.

[27] Edwards, "Christ the Example of Gospel Ministers," in *Works Vol. 25*, p. 444.

[28] Polemics and apologetics are sometimes similar exercises. I distinguish them here in this way: polemics are intramural discussions between Christians, whereas apologetics are, at least ostensibly, directed toward those outside the pale of the faith.

reason and demonstration, deduced from the Word of God."[29] Edwards has in mind the work of theologians like himself, who would bring to bear "invincible arguments" against the atheistical and antichristian enemy.[30] Thus when Edwards was refuting the philosophical errors of his day, he likely saw himself doing work that was of material contribution to the advent of the Kingdom no less than world missions and evangelism.[31]

Returning to the larger picture, all that remains is for Edwards himself to make the connection between his theology of divine communication and the interpretive role of ministers. We hear this rather clearly in a sermon entitled "The Great Concern of a Watchman of Souls." In it, Edwards explains that ministers participate in God's program of communicating himself in order to enable the people to fulfill their own purpose of re-emanating divine revelation:

> He [God] commits men's souls to ministers . . . that by their means they may answer their end in glorifying him. God has made all things for himself, he has created them for his glory; but more especially those creatures that he has endued with understanding; as he has done the souls of men. It is by them that God has his glory from all his creatures, as they are the eye of the creation to behold the glory of God manifested in the other creatures, and the mouth of the creation to praise him and ascribe to him the glory that is displayed in them. [. . .] God glorifies himself in his works that are manifest in the irrational and inanimate creation, in the view of his rational creatures that he has made capable of beholding and admiring them, and adoring, loving and praising him for them.[32]

Human beings are created to observe intelligently all the streams of divine communication flowing from every aspect of created reality; they are the "eye of the creation to behold the glory of God." Moreover, it is given to

[29] Edwards, "Exposition of the Apocalypse" entry for Revelation 16:21, in *Works Vol. 5*, p. 118.

[30] "They shall be dreadfully confounded, by those invincible arguments that shall be used against them. They shall be full of unsettledness, of self-contradiction and contradiction on of another, and shall be exceedingly divided in their schemes and the answers they shall give to the arguments, which shall be brought against them, as men stumble and run one against another in the dark" (Edwards, "Exposition of the Apocalypse," in *Works Vol. 5*, pp. 137–38).

[31] This should not be taken to mean that ministers were able to do more than Edwards' supernaturalist epistemology would allow: "From hence it necessarily follows, that the best and most able men in the world, with their greatest diligence and laboriousness, most eloquent speaking, clearest illustrations and convincing arguments, can do nothing towards the causing of knowledge of the things of the gospel; for the disposition, as we have shown, must necessarily be changed first" (Edwards, "Miscellany" 123, in *Works Vol. 13*, p. 287).

[32] Edwards, "The Great Concern of a Watchman for Souls," in *Works Vol. 25*, p. 66.

them to re-emanate this knowledge actively as "the mouth of the creation to praise him." Noetic understanding is the foundation, but this leads to the appropriate affectional response; so that they are "capable of beholding and admiring them, and adoring, loving and praising him." Thus far the now-familiar Edwardsean theology of divine communication. However, Edwards begins by asserting that ministers, as God's representatives, were the *means* by which people were enabled to achieve their communicative purpose: "He commits men's souls to ministers . . . that by their means they may answer their end in glorifying him." In God's plan, ministers serve as the instruments by which people are enabled to realize their doxological purpose for existence.

In his "Farwell Sermon" to the Northampton congregation that ousted him, Edwards remarks that "Ministers are his [God's] messengers, sent forth by him; and in their office and administrations among their people, represent his person, stand in his stead, as those that are sent to declare his mind, to do his work, and to speak and act in his name."[33] This representation of God often involves the work of *interpretation*, as in the case of those who "don't understand God's language, and they therefore need the help and advice of ministers under that conviction as *interpreters* for them."[34] In wider terms, God is in fact "pleased to convey his light to men by means and instruments; and has sent forth his messengers, and appointed ministers in his church to be subordinate lights, and to shine with the communications of his light, and to reflect the beams of his glory on the souls of men."[35] The "light" that ministers convey to men is multidimensional divine communication, consisting of affectional as well as notional elements.[36] As a general principle, just as God himself is a communicative being, so "ministers ought to be *communicative* of spiritual good."[37] Ministers in this respect act very much as God himself acts, as they take part in the great work of communicating God's goodness to men.

The most distinctive of all of Edwards' teachings on the nature of the ministerial calling, and one that most clearly shows the extent to which he envisioned his vocation as functionally set apart from ordinary saints, is surely his belief that human ministers would have an ongoing role in heaven. In contrast to other aspects of his doctrine of the ministry, here Edwards was knowingly departing from his direct inheritance. Turretin,

[33] Edwards, "A Farewell Sermon," in *Works Vol. 25*, p. 473.
[34] Edwards, "Blank Bible" entry on Genesis 42:23, in *Works Vol. 24*, p. 191; emphasis mine.
[35] Edwards, "True Excellency of a Minister of the Gospel," in *Works Vol. 25*, p. 89.
[36] Edwards, "True Excellency of a Minister of the Gospel," in *Works Vol. 25*, p. 90.
[37] Edwards, "Sons of Oil, Heavenly Lights," in *Works Vol. 25*, p. 267; emphasis mine.

representing the acme of Reformed orthodoxy in Edwards' day, put it bluntly: ". . . there will be no more need of the ministry of the Scriptures or of pastors [in heaven.]"[38] Edwards would beg to differ, as he did in the "Exposition on the Apocalypse":

> And the place of a servant or minister is at the door; and they will there be employed in promoting and ministering to the happiness of the saints, leading and conducting them to the fountains of knowledge and blessedness . . . . Gospel ministers sit at the gates as judges and as servants or doorkeepers who have the keys of the gates which Christ has given to them, whose office it is to bring in and admit persons into the church, and to conduct souls to heaven. And in the triumphant state of the church after the resurrection, they may still be represented as being at the gates in the same manner, as they may still be said to be the foundations . . . . And I believe that those who have [been] thus eminently instrumental of carrying the blessed work of the gospel in this world, will be employed in still assisting and promoting the happiness of the saints in a glorified state, and so may as well as the angels be represented at the gates, introducing and conducting the inhabitants of the new earth to the pleasures of Jerusalem.[39]

Ministers—or at least those that have been "eminently instrumental" in the work of the gospel—will continue to serve in very much the same spiritual capacity in heaven as they did on earth. It seems Edwards could not imagine a heaven lacking the services of the human conduits that he believed were so crucial to the work of divine communication in this world. It was noted early on that a characteristic feature of Edwards' theology is continuity between the ontological and economic Trinity.[40] Perhaps it could just as well be said that Edwards imagined the fullest possible continuity between this world and the next for God's church. In both worlds, the work of God's communication to his elect creatures went on in analogous ways, and thus the need for the agency of ministers to "assist and promote the happiness of the saints in a glorified state."[41]

[38] Francis Turretin, *Institutes of Elenctic Theology*, translated by George Musgrave Giger, edited by James T. Dennison Jr. 3 vols. (Phillipsburg, NJ: P&R Publishing, 1992), vol. 1 p. 59.
[39] Edwards, "Exposition of the Apocalypse" entry for Revelation 21:12, in *Works Vol. 5*, pp. 154–155.
[40] See above, Chapter 1.
[41] "The church in heaven and the church on earth are more one people, one city, and one family than generally is imagined." Edwards, "Miscellany" 421, in *Works Vol. 13*, p. 478.

Edwards also gave voice to this teaching in "Miscellany" 681, where the close correlation between his theology of Trinitarian communication, his doctrine of the earthly ministry, and his concept of heavenly ministry is made plain. "What has been said above confirms that some in heaven will be a kind of ministers in that society [of heaven]—teachers, ministers to their knowledge and love, and helpers of their joy, as ministers of the gospel are here."[42] Edwards' depiction of the minister's function, heavenly as well as earthly, exactly parallels his multidimensional theology of communication—it encompasses "knowledge and love" as well as "joy." Assisting God to communicate these things to the elect creatures is what ministers do on earth, and this is what they will continue to do in heaven.

To conclude this section, we see how Edwards conceived of the ministerial task: to emulate and participate in God's own project of imparting multidimensional divine communication to human beings. This task, which they will carry on in heaven as God's appointed means of increasing the knowledge, love, and joy of his saints, involved the work of interpretation, polemics, and apologetics. Edwards' personal application of his theology of the ministry was the communicative and interpretive project we have been describing, carried out over a lifetime of preaching and writing.

IV The "Personal Narrative"

Any plausible theory on Edwards' larger project needs to be able to integrate the "Personal Narrative." This is because, while one could argue as to what extent the "Narrative" is idealized, all would agree that it represents an important statement about Edwards' idea of true religion. George Claghorn, editor of the *Works* volume containing the "Narrative," writes, "Edwards edited his own experience to fit his prescription of the model saint."[43] This statement, while moving us in the right direction, requires some qualification. It is true that the "Narrative" was no casual reminiscence jotted down in a fully private letter; as Daniel Shea points out (and Claghorn seems to agree), it shows signs of careful composition and expectation of at least some readership beyond the immediate correspondent.[44] However, neither was it a work of fiction.[45] If the revival writings and the *Diary of David Brainerd*

[42] Edwards, "Miscellany" 681, in *Works Vol. 18*, p. 243.

[43] George S. Claghorn, introduction to the "Personal Narrative," in *Works Vol. 16*, p. 748.

[44] See Daniel B. Shea Jr., "The Art and Instruction of Jonathan Edwards's Personal Narrative." *American Literature 37* (1965) pp. 17–34; quoted in *Works Vol. 16*, p. 748.

[45] Perry Miller's assessment of the "Personal Narrative" was that " . . .it cannot be taken as an altogether factual record of his earliest years" (Miller, *Jonathan Edwards*, p. 39).

provide patterns for this kind of work, Edwards was scrupulously accurate in the matters he reported, even if he was also capable of leaving out other things he considered extraneous or distracting from the point he wished to make. So, regardless of how much or how little editorial liberty we wish to ascribe to Edwards, Claghorn's basic point remains: the "Narrative" offers an important glimpse into what he thought true religion *ought* to look like.[46]

In terms of understanding Edwards' project, perhaps we can understand the "Narrative" as a subjective paradigm for what he was trying to achieve. It depicts an example of someone for whom the goals of the project were being met, someone for whom the media of nature, history, and Scripture were harmoniously integrated and whose regenerate soul was joyfully re-emanating all the divine communication it had taken in. In other words, the "Narrative" is a success story for God's communicative/interpretive project that Edwards sought to promote.

Consider, for instance, the elements of his experience that Edwards selected to include in the "Narrative." First of all, he records the discord that previously prevailed in his mind between the scriptural teaching of divine sovereignty and his own human reason:

> From my childhood up, my mind had been wont to be full of objections against the doctrine of God's sovereignty, in choosing whom he would to eternal life, and rejecting whom he pleased; leaving them eternally to perish, and be everlastingly tormented in hell. It used to appear like a horrible doctrine to me.[47]

Perhaps Edwards could identify at some level with the Deists and Arminians he fought with over the sovereignty of God, since it seems he knew something of the aversion to this doctrine they expressed. Thanks to the work of God, however, Edwards' reason became perfectly reconciled to this doctrine: "[T]here has been a wonderful alteration in my mind, with respect to the doctrine of God's sovereignty, from that day to this; so that I scarce ever have found so much as the rising of an objection against God's sovereignty."[48] Edwards was enabled to see the *harmony* between what Scripture taught

[46] "With Edwards, the purpose of the Personal Narrative was didactic—to instruct others. . . .In this sense, the depiction may be a particular construction, a partial version, of his private self." Kenneth P. Minkema, "Personal Writings," in *The Cambridge Companion to Jonathan Edwards*, edited by Stephen J. Stein, pp. 39–60 (Cambridge: Cambridge University Press, 2007), p. 51.

[47] Edwards, "Personal Narrative," in *Works Vol. 16*, pp. 791–792.

[48] Edwards, "Personal Narrative," in *Works Vol. 16*, p. 792.

regarding the doctrine of election and true reason. This is just the sort of theological and philosophical harmony Edwards wanted to help his readers to attain in his theological treatises.

But it was not that Edwards had merely achieved a correct *notional* understanding of the truth. Trinitarian communication requires love and joy as well, and we see that Edwards is careful to add that his rational reconciliation was accompanied by the appropriate *affectional* response: "I have often since, not only had a conviction, but a *delightful* conviction. The doctrine of God's sovereignty has very often appeared, an exceeding pleasant, bright and sweet doctrine to me: and absolute sovereignty is what I *love* to ascribe to God."[49] Edwards' paradigmatic spiritual state is one that apprehends the beautiful harmony between scriptural doctrine and reason, a state of joyous affectional response as well as noetic integration.

Another item that Edwards includes in the "Narrative" is the related shift in his attitude toward natural manifestations of God's power, such as thunderstorms:[50]

> I used to be a person uncommonly terrified with thunder: and it used to strike me with terror, when I saw a thunderstorm rising. But now, on the contrary, it rejoiced me. I felt God at the first appearance of a thunderstorm. And used to take the opportunity at such times, to fix myself to view the clouds, and see the lightnings play, and hear the majestic and awful voice of God's thunder: which often times was exceeding entertaining, leading me to sweet contemplations of my great and glorious God.[51]

The unregenerate Edwards recoiled from God's absolute power manifested theologically in predestination, and likewise shrank from this attribute as it was displayed in natural phenomena such as lightning. However, the regenerate Edwards found that he took delight in "the awful voice of God's thunder," just as he had grown to love the truth of God's sovereignty taught in Scripture. The sensory input is exactly the same before and after, but the supernaturally regenerate heart is able to *appreciate* the beauty of which it was previously insensible or where it had

[49] Edwards, "Personal Narrative," in *Works Vol. 16*, p. 792; emphasis mine.

[50] Edwards thought that God's majesty can be known by immediate intuition as well as by reasoned reflection. Thunder is given as an example of the former: "The manifestations of God's majesty in heaven, and at the day of judgment, and in many of his works, as thunder and earthquakes, etc., tend immediately to impress the mind with a sense of majesty, without any reasoning or reflection." Edwards, "Miscellany" 493, in *Works Vol. 13*, p. 537.

[51] Edwards, "Personal Narrative," in *Works Vol. 16*, p. 794.

previously perceived dissonance. This is at the heart of so much of Edwards' unpublished scientific writings—many of which were intended for inclusion in the "Rational Account"—which are meant to incite our wondrous contemplation of the "great and glorious God."[52]

Edwards then describes his regenerate response to the clearest medium of God's communication, the Scriptures:

> I had then, and at other times, the greatest delight in the holy Scriptures, of any book whatsoever. Oftentimes in reading it, every word seemed to touch my heart. I felt an *harmony* between something in my heart, and those sweet and powerful words. I seemed often to see so much light, exhibited by every sentence, and such refreshing ravishing food communicated, that I could not get along in reading. Used oftentimes to dwell long on one sentence, to see the wonders contained in it; and yet almost every sentence seemed to be full of wonders.[53]

As we might expect, the vocabulary of divine communicativeness flowed from Edwards' pen when he was describing the centerpiece of God's communicative project. He saw "such refreshing ravishing food *communicated* . . ." in the fresh knowledge of God it conveyed to him. Notice also the words "I felt an *harmony* between something in my heart, and those sweet and powerful words." Rather than the dissonance or disaffection the Deists usually expressed, regenerate minds experience the real harmony that exists between their Spirit-indwelt souls and the Spirit-inspired Scriptures. And of course, Edwards does not neglect the affectional dimension; his main point was to say that reading the Bible gave him the "greatest *delight*."

Finally, Edwards explains how history and current events were grist for his apprehension of the harmony of reality. "The histories of the past advancement of Christ's kingdom, have been sweet to me. When I have read histories of past ages, the pleasantest thought in all my reading has been, to read of the kingdom of Christ being promoted."[54] Given those sentiments, we can see why Edwards would have been so enthusiastic about his "History of the Work of Redemption" project.[55] The pages of history have become such rich fuel for Edwards' joy that it is natural he would want to help others to join in this delightful appropriation of God's revelation throughout time. But there is perhaps an even brighter note sounded when

[52] See above, Chapter 2.
[53] Edwards, "Personal Narrative," in *Works Vol. 16*, p. 797; emphasis mine.
[54] Edwards, "Personal Narrative," in *Works Vol. 16*, p. 800.
[55] Edwards, "Letter to the Princeton Trustees," in *Works Vol. 16*, pp. 727–728.

Edwards talks about his attitude toward *current* events of redemptive history:

> I had great longings for the advancement of Christ's kingdom in the world. My secret prayer used to be in great part taken up in praying for it. If I heard the least hint of anything that happened in any part of the world, that appeared to me, in some respect or other, to have a favorable aspect on the interest of Christ's kingdom, my soul eagerly catched at it; and it would much animate and refresh me. I used to be earnest to read public news-letters, mainly for that end; to see if I could not find some news favorable to the interests of religion in the world.[56]

Edwards' reception of God's communicative project in redemptive history was not confined to the past. Rather, he turned his expectant eye to the events of his own day to detect how Christ was advancing his kingdom, an activity he was convinced the saints in heaven were simultaneously occupied with. This is why Edwards wanted the world to know about the Awakenings of his day, whether through his own revival writings or in the news periodicals he promoted.[57]

To summarize the message of the "Personal Narrative," the believing soul is enabled to integrate all aspects of reality in a delightful experience of divine harmony. Doctrines such as absolute sovereignty that are so repugnant to unregenerate human reason seem gloriously true. Frightful natural phenomena like thunderstorms become a welcome token of God's majestic power. History comes alive with the delightful details of God's redemptive work. The Scriptures make perfect sense and are imbibed with relish. All the media of divine revelation are in perfect accord in a balanced exercise of head and heart—knowledge, love, and joy—which is then expressed back to God and to humanity. One more "mouth of creation" is fulfilling his or her teleological purpose. In other words, the "Personal Narrative" was Edwards' portrait of what it looks like when one has been the beneficiary of God's gracious work of communicating himself to intelligent beings. Edwards' lifelong project was to bring others into this saving, beatific condition by conveying and interpreting the harmony he saw throughout reality.

[56] Edwards, "Personal Narrative," in *Works Vol. 16*, p. 797.
[57] See above, Chapter 5.

V The Three "Great Works"

If Edwards' project is exemplified subjectively in the "Personal Narrative," it is expressed programmatically in his unfinished "Great Works." Edwards proposed a total of three major projects in his lifetime: the "Rational Account," "The History of the Work of Redemption" and "The Harmony of the Old and New Testament." Treatments of these projects in the secondary literature sometimes give the impression that there were only two main projects, and largely tend to ignore the "Harmony of the Old and New Testament." This tendency explains the title of the recent exception to this trend, Kenneth Minkema's "The *Other* Unfinished 'Great Work.'"[58] Furthermore, discussion of Edwards' unfinished works tends to focus on the momentous change in approach between the philosophical "Rational Account" and the redemptive-historical "History of the Work of Redemption." Indeed, the obvious and significant discontinuity between these two projects was discussed somewhat along these lines earlier in this study.[59] However, let us now ask an entirely different question in relation to these projects (and their neglected sibling): what might they have in *common*? The answer, when we look at Edwards' own titles and descriptions for these projects, is rather clear: they all seek to demonstrate the harmony found in and among the media of revelation. The reason *why* they exhibit this common purpose is, I suggest, because the demonstration of harmony was the characteristic method of Edwards' project.

Edwards' brief outline for his first "Great Work" bears the title "A Rational Account of the Main Doctrines of the Christian Religion Attempted."[60] The draft preface found in this outline explains Edwards' goals for the work: "To shew how all arts and sciences, the more they are perfected, the more they issue in divinity, and coincide with it, and appear to be as parts of it."[61] To paraphrase, Edwards planned to demonstrate the coincidence or harmony of natural revelation with revealed religion. This reading is validated by the alternative title for this project that appears in Edwards' "Catalogue": "A Rational Account of Christianity, or, The Perfect *Harmony* between the Doctrines of the Christian Religion and Human Reason Manifested."[62]

[58] A notable exception to this trend would be Kenneth P. Minkema, "The Other Unfinished "Great Work": Jonathan Edwards, Messianic Prophecy, and "The Harmony of the Old and New Testament," in Stephen J. Stein (ed.), *Jonathan Edwards's Writings: Text, Context, Interpretation* (Bloomington, IN: Indiana University Press, 1996), pp. 52–65.

[59] See above, Chapters 3 and 5.

[60] Edwards, "Outline of a Rational Account," in *Works Vol. 6*, p. 396.

[61] Edwards, "Outline of a Rational Account," in *Works Vol. 6*, p. 397.

[62] Edwards, "Catalogue" unnumbered letter leaf, in *Works Vol. 26*; emphasis mine.

Everything else we know of this project simply confirms that Edwards was consistent with this stated intent. Some of the proposed items that were likely intended for inclusion in the project bear this out: "To shew how all nature consists in things being precisely according to strict rules of justice and *harmony*,"[63] and "Remember to place all about motion under the head of the manner or *harmony* of existence."[64] Edwards' first unfinished "Great Work," conceived at the very start of his career, was explicitly intended to demonstrate the harmony between nature—a category that included human reason as well as science—and special revelation.

In like manner, "The History of the Work of Redemption" was a demonstration of the harmony to be found between history and special revelation. This project, particularly the marked contrast between Edwards' use of history predicated upon divine harmony and contemporary Enlightenment approaches, was discussed in the previous chapter. Here we simply recall the crucial point that Edwards describes this project as one in which ". . . every divine doctrine, will appear to greatest advantage in the brightest light, in the most striking manner, showing the admirable contexture and *harmony* of the whole."[65] Edwards' second "Great Work," though it took definitive shape toward the end of his career, carried the very same overall objective as the first in terms of interpreting harmony. The apparently radical shift in method can be explained simply as a shift in object within a common overall methodology. Both works sought to show the harmony between scriptural doctrine and some other media of revelation. By its very nature, doing this for natural revelation and reason lent itself to a rational mode of discourse. When Edwards turned his attention to history, no doubt influenced by factors we have discussed, the task naturally led him to a redemptive-historical mode. Even if one object (history rather than reason) appeared more attractive than others at different parts of his career, it is clear that Edwards never lost confidence in the basic methodology of interpreting the harmony of reality.

The "Harmony of the Old and New Testament" material actually seems to have been the most complete of the three "Great Works" at the time of Edwards' death but has since been limited to specialist interest and was not included in the letterpress portion of the Yale edition of his works.[66] It was,

[63] Edwards, "Things to be Considered an[d] Written fully about" [Long Series] entry 15, in *Works Vol. 6*, p. 231; emphasis mine.

[64] Edwards, "Things to be Considered an[d] Written fully about" [Long Series] entry 31, in *Works Vol. 6*, p. 236; emphasis mine.

[65] Edwards, "Letter to the Princeton Trustees," in *Works Vol. 16*, p. 728; emphasis mine.

[66] As previously noted, the 26 letterpress volumes comprise only a sizeable fraction of Edwards' extant writings; the remainder are available in the Jonathan Edwards Center's online volumes beginning with "volume" 27.

however, apparently the project conceived latest in Edwards' career, and its title most explicitly pronounces its purpose in terms of harmony: "I have also for my own profit and entertainment, done much towards another great work, which I call The Harmony of the Old and New Testament, in three parts."[67] Another, fuller title was "The Harmony of the Genius, Spirit, Doctrines and Rules of the Old Testament and the New."[68] Sweeney describes the first two parts of the project thus:

> For part one, on biblical prophecy, he penned four entries in his 'Miscellanies' notebooks, all treating what he labeled either 'Prophecies of the Messiah' (mainly in the Old Testament) or 'Fulfillment of the Prophecies of the Messiah' (in the New). Two of these entries proved to be so large that they consumed a whole book. For part two, on the wealth of biblical types of the Messiah, Edwards drafted another entry in a 'Miscellanies' notebook: 'That the Things of the Old Testament Are Types Appertaining to the Messiah and His Kingdom and Salvation, Made Manifest from the Old Testament Itself.'[69]

Edwards first intended to show the perfect agreement between the Old Testament *prophecies* of the Messiah and their fulfillment in the New, secondly to do this for the biblical *types* of the Messiah, and finally to demonstrate the agreement between the *doctrine* of the Old and New Testaments. One need not belabor the point that Edwards himself made so patently clear—"The Harmony" project was to be a systematic demonstration of the comprehensive harmony found within the pages of Scripture itself.

So then, all three of Edwards' unfinished "Great Works" sought to demonstrate the harmony resident in and among the media of revelation. This is a significant feature, one that would seem to demand the attention of any attempt to describe Edwards' larger project. At the very least, Edwards is telling us that the projects that he considered of greatest importance and the ones that expressed his systematic intentions in their abstract purity all had this highly distinctive attribute in common. However, we know that none of these projects ever saw published completion during his lifetime. To what extent, then, can we say that these "Great Works" are truly representative of the man? Is it a matter of unrealized ideals entirely

[67] Edwards, "Letter to the Princeton Trustees," in *Works Vol. 16*, p. 728.
[68] See Minkema's note on transcribed "Miscellany" 1068.2 at the Jonathan Edwards Center, Yale.
[69] Douglas A. Sweeney, *Jonathan Edwards and the Ministry of the Word: A Model of Faith and Thought* (Downers Grove, IL: IVP Academic, 2009), pp. 88–89.

disconnected from Edwards' pedestrian reality as a task theologian, or is there something more?

The "Great Works" and their common purpose of interpreting harmony indeed represent Edwards' ideal program, but I want to suggest that he pursued the basic ideas of this program throughout his corpus. Take, for example, the published works from which Edwards' reputation as a philosopher and theologian largely derive, *Freedom of the Will* and *Original Sin*. Much of the core material for these works was accumulated in the "Miscellany" notebooks under headings that indicate earmarking for the planned "Rational Account." By the time of their publication, Edwards was apparently no longer pursuing this project as a single work, but that does not mean that they were not in absolute continuity with his goal to demonstrate the "Perfect Harmony between the Doctrines of the Christian Religion and Human Reason." The same holds for the *Two Dissertations*, which were also major elements of the "Miscellany" material probably intended for inclusion in the "Rational Account."[70] Also, as suggested earlier, all the revival writings might be seen as fully compatible with the overall vision cast by the "History of the Work of Redemption" project. Even though the "Harmony of the Old and New Testaments" seemed only to have solidified as a discrete project later on, his basic purpose to demonstrate the harmony among the various parts of Scripture runs throughout his "Notes on Scripture" and "Blank Bible."[71] So while it is true that none of Edwards' three intended "Great Works" saw published completion during his lifetime, it is at least possible to say that the entirety of his theological output was in some way a fulfillment of their stated purpose to demonstrate the harmony of divinely communicated reality.

VI The Agenda of the Awakenings

Having examined some of the main evidence for the nature of Edwards' larger project, we return now to the problem of why he might have focused on some topics and not others within his impossibly open-ended assignment. We have discussed the role of Enlightenment thought throughout. Let us now focus on the ways in which Edwards' specific agenda may have been determined by his observation of the Awakenings.

[70] The *Two Dissertations* are an integral work consisting of two volumes, *The End for Which God Created the World*, and *The Nature of True Virtue*, found in *Works Vol. 16*.

[71] See Edwards, *Works Vols. 15* and *24*.

Edwards' believed that the success of the Awakenings was connected instrumentally to the preaching of Calvinist orthodoxy.[72] To Edwards, God seemed to have been making a point by using to greatest effect the specific doctrines then under strongest attack by the rationalists. An obvious example of this was justification by faith alone: "The beginning of the late work of God in this place was so circumstanced that I could not but look upon it as a remarkable testimony of God's approbation of the doctrine of justification by faith alone."[73] In another place, Edwards recalls "There were then some things said publicly on that occasion concerning justification by faith alone," for which the young minister received criticism. Yet this doctrine was ". . . most evidently attended with a very remarkable blessing of heaven to the souls of the people in this town."[74] Given such a seemingly direct correlation between unadulterated Reformed doctrine and revival success, it is little wonder that "Justification by Faith Alone" was among the very first of Edwards' publications.[75] Edwards promoted the revivals by defending the doctrines that were of most use for them.

Today, Edwards is associated with his preaching on an even less fashionable doctrine—hell.[76] This aspect of his preaching was not unreflective traditionalism but a kind of orthodox pragmatism. In *The Distinguishing Marks* (1741), delivered at Yale only two months after "Sinners in the Hands of an Angry God," Edwards explains that he saw this doctrine as rightly instrumental in bringing careless sinners to an awakened condition:

> 'Tis no argument that a work is not from the Spirit of God, that is seems to be promoted by ministers insisting very much on the terrors of God's holy law, and that with a great deal of pathos and earnestness. If there be really a hell of such dreadful, and never-ending torments, as is generally supposed, that multitudes are in great danger of, and that the bigger part of men in Christian countries do actually from generation to generation fall into, for want of a sense of the terribleness of it, and their danger of it, and so for want of taking due care to avoid it; then why is it nor proper for those that have the care of souls, to take great pains to make men sensible of it?[77]

[72] This topic is discussed above, Chapter 5.

[73] Edwards, preface to *Discourses on Various Important Subjects*, in *Works in Two Volumes*, Vol. 1, p. 621; emphasis original. See also Goen, "Editor's Introduction," in *Works Vol. 4*, p. 19.

[74] Edwards, *A Faithful Narrative*, in *Works Vol. 4*, pp. 148–149.

[75] Edwards, *Discourses on Various Important Subjects*, in *Works Vol. 19*, pp. 143–242.

[76] "Sinners in the Hands of an Angry God" perennially represents Edwards in anthologies of American literature and is often the only contact with the great American theologian people have.

[77] Edwards, *The Distinguishing Marks*, in *Works Vol. 4*, p. 246–247.

There was no question as to *whether* preaching on hell led to awakened souls; this correlation was precisely the basis of the Old Light critique to which Edwards was responding. The question is whether or not this was legitimate. Edwards answers that it only makes sense that teaching on the true depth of the human problem would help people turn their attention to spiritual matters. Indeed, ". . . the preaching of the Gospel is like to be in vain without it."[78] If one really wants to help sinners and to advance Christ's kingdom, then one should be sure to preach on such things.

Edwards also pointed out the instrumentality of certain Reformed doctrines in the lives of awakened individuals. One example was in the "Personal Narrative," where Edwards shows us how God used the much-maligned doctrine of divine sovereignty in his own personal history. In the case of Abigail Hutchinson, one of but two extended personal examples in the *Faithful Narrative,* he implies a similarly important role for the doctrine of original sin:

> . . . it had been an opinion, which till now she had entertained, that she was not guilty of Adam's sin, nor any way concerned in it, because she was not active in it; but that now she saw she was guilty of that sin, and all over defiled by it; and that the sin which she brought into the world with her, was alone sufficient to condemn her.[79]

Given that Edwards highlights the instrumentality of these doctrines in the lives of two of his main examples of true spirituality, it is perhaps significant that *Freedom of the Will* and *Original Sin* feature among the fairly short list of systematic loci to which he devoted full-length attention.

In addition to how God seemed to use particular doctrines in the Awakenings, Edwards saw the Awakenings *themselves* as a fitting refutation of Deism's polite, "underdeveloped cousin," Arminianism:[80]

> . . . and whether any good medium can be found, where a man can rest with any stability, between owning this work and being a Deist; and also to consider whether or no, if it be indeed so that this be the work of God, it don't entirely overthrow their scheme of religion; and therefore whether it don't infinitely concern 'em, as they would be partakers of eternal salvation, to relinquish their scheme. Now is a good time for Arminians to change their principles.[81]

[78] Edwards, *The Distinguishing Marks,* in *Works Vol. 4,* p. 248.
[79] Edwards, "A Faithful Narrative," in *Works Vol. 4,* p. 193.
[80] McDermott, *Jonathan Edwards Confronts the Gods,* p. 46.
[81] Edwards, *Some Thoughts Concerning the Present Revival,* in *Works Vol. 4,* p. 503.

God's sudden interjection of sovereign, supernatural agency simply overpowered the rationalists' vaunted theories about God's passivity in human destiny. Recent scholarship by McDermott has revealed how much of Edwards' theological activity was animated against Deism, an insight we would build upon by incorporating the influence of revival history.[82] Edwards thought that the revivals were God's own irrefutable apologetic against rationalist religion. In this frame of reference, the best way to defeat Deism is simply to promote the revivals, which is exactly what Edwards in fact did.

Edwards is well known for his interest in the religious affections, and we have said more than once that the affections are integral to his concept of Trinitarian divine communication. It would seem that his interest in this area was also encouraged by the revivals. The Old Lights were complaining that the Awakening preachers were illegitimately playing on people's emotions. Edwards responded that the affections were necessarily part and parcel of true Christianity: "[it is] false divinity to suppose that religious affections don't appertain to the substance and essence of Christianity: on the contrary, it seems to me that *the very life and soul of all true religion consists in them.*"[83] Edwards' ongoing interest in this subject, which was partly fostered by the connection between affectional preaching and revival success, culminated in *The Religious Affections.*

It was not, incidentally, just any show of emotion that impressed Edwards. In the case of Abigail Hutchinson, what really caught his attention was the universal character of her love: "She told one of her sisters that day that she loved all mankind, but especially the people of God. Her sister asked her why she loved all mankind. She replied because God had made them."[84] To Edwards' mind, this kind of disinterested, universal love characteristic of the awakened could only be the result of gracious regeneration. This thesis he would explain at great length in *The Nature of True Virtue.*

Besides the affections as seen in isolation, Edwards' descriptions of awakened saints very often reflect his theology of *multidimensional* divine communication. He always notices the collocation of knowledge, love, and joy, as how Abigail Hutchinson's ". . . *mind* was led into such contemplations

[82] See Gerald R. McDermott, *Edwards Confronts the Gods: Christian Theology, Enlightenment Religion, and Non-Christian Faiths* (Oxford and New York: Oxford University Press, 2000); "The Deist Connection: Jonathan Edwards and Islam," in Stephen J. Stein, *Jonathan Edwards's Writings: Text, Context, Interpretation* (Bloomington, IN: Indiana University Press, 1996), pp. 39–51; and "Jonathan Edwards, Deism, and the Mystery of Revelation," *Journal of Presbyterian History* 77, no. 4 (1999), pp. 211–24.

[83] Edwards, *Some Thoughts*, in *Works Vol. 4*, p. 297; emphasis mine.

[84] Edwards, *A Faithful Narrative*, in *Works Vol. 4*, p. 194.

and views of Christ, as filled her exceeding full of *joy*."[85] Many others spoke of ". . . being drawn out in *love* to God and Christ; and their *minds* being wrapped up in *delightful* contemplation of the glory and wonderful grace of God."[86] The people desired ". . . to have their hearts filled with *love* to God and Christ, and a disposition to lie in the dust before him. They seem to have given [to] them a lively conviction of the *truth of the Gospel* . . . ." Indeed, powerful evidence that God had in fact visited Northampton was that "This town never was so *full of love, nor so full of joy*, nor so full of distress as it has lately been."[87] Of course, such observations are only convincing if you believed that God communicates himself with more than mere rational knowledge; this is one of the main ideas Edwards advanced in *The End for Which God Created the World.*

As with the "Personal Narrative," Edwards noted the involvement of the three media of communication—nature, Scripture, and history—in his portrayal of the Awakenings. For instance, in *A Faithful Narrative*, Edwards describes the awakened appreciation of nature:

> The light and comfort which some of them enjoy, gives a new relish to their common blessings, and causes all things about 'em to appear as it were beautiful, sweet and pleasant to them: all things abroad, the sun, moon and stars, the clouds and sky, the heavens and earth, appear as it were with a cast of divine glory and sweetness upon them.[88]

The sensory input from the natural world remained the same, but the awakened, regenerate heart has "a new relish" for creation and is able to see the "cast of divine glory" upon them. It was the same with Abigail Hutchinson, who ". . . often expressed a sense of the glory of God appearing in the trees, and growth of the fields, and other works of God's hands."[89] And so it was for the zenith of all his examples—his wife, Sarah, who expressed ". . . a continual rejoicing in all the works of God's hands, the works of nature, and God's daily works of providence, all appearing with a sweet smile upon them . . . ."[90] Keeping in mind that the point of Edwards' reportage is to establish the fact that an extraordinary work of God had occurred, Edwards

[85] Edwards, *A Faithful Narrative*, in *Works Vol. 4*, p. 193.
[86] Edwards, *A Faithful Narrative*, in *Works Vol. 4*, p. 181.
[87] Edwards, "Unpublished Letter to Benjamin Coleman," in *Works Vol. 4*, p. 104; emphasis mine.
[88] Edwards, *A Faithful Narrative*, p. 183.
[89] Edwards, *A Faithful Narrative*, p. 195.
[90] Edwards, *Some Thoughts*, in *Works Vol. 4*, p. 340.

evidently thought that the ability to truly rejoice in the works of creation was a significant marker of valid spiritual activity.

Naturally, Edwards also noted his subjects' changed attitude toward Holy Scripture. "While God as so remarkably present amongst us by his Spirit, there was no book so delighted in as the Bible . . . ."[91] He takes it as axiomatic that any ". . . spirit that operates in such a manner, as to cause in men a greater regard to the Holy Scriptures, and establishes them more in their truth and divinity, is certainly the Spirit of God."[92] The very fact that the revivals gave the people a greater reverence for Scriptures was good evidence for them being from God.

History, particularly in the form of current events, was a hugely important issue connected with Edwards' revival writings. This is because news of someone being awakening was known to have contagious effects on their neighbors, and reports of an awakening in one town would often spark a fresh outbreak elsewhere. This phenomenon was readily acknowledged by the friends of the Awakening, as seen in the four Boston ministers who reiterate Edwards' own hope for "A Faithful Narrative" in this regard:

> Yea, as the author observes, 'There is no one thing I know of, that God has made such a means of promoting his work among us as the news of others' conversions'; we hope that the further spreading of this narrative may, by the divine blessing, still promote the conversion of souls, and quicken God's children to labor after the clearer evidences of their adoption . . .'[93]

This effect was, however, noted with disapproval by the movement's detractors. If the Awakenings were from God, why would he use such devices rather than his usual means? Edwards replied that the good example of others *is* in fact one of God's means established in Scripture: "'Tis agreeable to Scripture that persons should be influenced by one another's good example . . . By which it appears that *example is one of God's means . . . .*"[94]

Perhaps then, example might be theoretically permissible, but why might it be so pervasive as to appear to be a main engine of the Awakenings? Edwards' response to this objection is quite important because it explains his understanding of the Word of God as primary among all of God's other means of communication, the "principal means" by which "the other means operate":

[91] Edwards, *A Faithful Narrative*, in *Works Vol. 4*, p. 184.
[92] Edwards, *The Distinguishing Marks*, in *Works Vol. 4*, p. 253.
[93] "Preface" to the Third Edition of *A Faithful Narrative*, in *Works Vol. 4*, p. 140–141.
[94] Edwards, *The Distinguishing Marks*, in *Works Vol.* 4, pp. 238; emphasis mine.

> 'Tis no valid objection against examples being made so much use of, that the Scriptures speaks of the Word of God as the principal means of carrying on God's work; for the Word of God is the principal means nevertheless, as that is the means by which other means operate, and are made effectual: the sacraments have no effect but by the Word. And so it is that *example becomes effectual*; for all that is visible to the eye is unintelligible and vain, without the Word of God to instruct and guide the mind. 'Tis the Word of God that is indeed held forth and applied by example, as the Word of the Lord sounded forth to other towns in Macedonia and Achaia, by the example of those that believed in Thessalonica.[95]

God uses the medium of history (in this case, news of the revivals), but this does not at all stand apart from the Word of God. In a manner akin to the way the sacraments are invested with beneficial meaning through the Word, so "example become effectual" only by the Word of God. Indeed, it is precisely the Word that is "held forth and applied by example."

The requirement for such apologetic work meant that Edwards had to develop a theology of history. This in addition to the need to fuel further revivals with examples throughout history virtually ensured that Edwards would devote a significant work to the subject— "The History of the Work of Redemption." The other two "Great Works," of course, were given to the remaining media of communication that likewise featured in Edwards' revival narratives. Thus, as with numerous other cases, Edwards' observation of the role of these elements in the Awakenings can be linked with his devoting significant writings to them.

Lest we neglect a topic that loomed so large for him, Edwards thought that ministers played a crucial role in the Awakenings. He observed an unfailing correlation between the revival work and people's reception of their ministers: "This work of God had also a good effect to unite the people's affections much to their minister."[96] This is the case for settled ministers and visiting preachers alike, "They have a greater respect to ministers than they used to have; there is scarcely a minister preachers here but gets their esteem and affection."[97] Even little Phoebe Bartlett exhibited this trait: "She has manifested great love to her minister . . . ."[98] Such sentiments are entirely in line with the larger contours of God's project,

[95] Edwards, *The Distinguishing Marks*, in *Works Vol. 4*, p. 240.
[96] Edwards, *A Faithful Narrative*, in *Works Vol. 4*, p. 184.
[97] Edwards, "Unpublished Letter to Benjamin Coleman," in *Works Vol. 4*, p. 105; emphasis mine.
[98] Edwards, *A Faithful Narrative*, in *Works Vol. 4*, p. 205.

which was carried on through the mediation of ministers. Small wonder that Edwards had no sympathy for the enthusiasts' denigration of the ordained ministry.[99]

The fact that Edwards noticed these things as being useful in the revivals and the fact that he chose to pursue them in his work are not related by mere accident. In many cases, they were included in Edwards' explicit manifesto to encourage the revivals.[100] In this regard, he was simply advancing the agenda he had advocated publicly for the entire church. In his own words, "Let us all be hence warned, by no means to oppose, or do anything in the least to clog or hinder that work that has lately been carried on in the land, but on the contrary, to do our utmost to promote it."[101] And in Edwards' thought, doing what one could to encourage the revivals cannot be separated from doing what one could to bring in the millennial reign; the former was in full continuity with the later. So we could just as well explain Edwards' agenda in terms of his desire to advance the millennium.

VII This Theory in Relation to Some Others

We come now to discuss this theory in relation to a brief sampling of the existing large-scale perspectives on Edwards. In a manner something like the process of "bracketing" in field artillery practice, in which the first shell might fall well short, the second long, and thereafter increasingly close to the target, scholarly descriptions of Edwards have been gradually converging. The best way to land the next volley even closer is to make corrections taking into account previous efforts as well as the target itself. Likewise, although our main focus has been on the primary source material, our study has benefited greatly from the increasingly accurate rendering the secondary literature provides.

For a rather straightforward example of this function, we refer to a recent shot that lands in territory nearby our own. E. Brooks Holifield argues in the *Cambridge Companion* that "Edwards's attraction to the theme of 'excellency' reflected an angle of vision that found expression in almost everything he wrote."[102] "Excellency" is of course a term closely related to "harmony" in Edwards, and we could only concur that these interrelated

[99] See Edwards, "Blank Bible" note on Heb 10:25, in *Works Vol. 24*.
[100] See Edwards, *Some Thoughts*, in *Works Vol. 4*, pp. 496–530.
[101] Edwards, *Works Vol. 4*, p. 270.
[102] E. Brooks Holifield, "Edwards as Theologian," in Stephen J. Stein (ed.), *The Cambridge Companion to Jonathan Edwards* (Cambridge: Cambridge University Press, 2007), p. 145.

themes indeed pervade the corpus. Moreover, Holifield goes on to say things like "Edwards attempted to discern patterns of harmony in divine activity, 'fit' congruities among doctrines, correspondences within the diverse books of Scripture, and symmetries between the natural and the supernatural."[103] As to *why* this harmonizing activity should be so ubiquitous in such a wide spectrum of contexts, Holifield only hints. Our theory concludes that it is because Edwards believed that demonstrating the divine hallmark of harmony in all the media of revelation was fundamental to his task of forwarding God's self-communication to intelligent beings.

Another example comes with reference to Michael J. McClymond's *Encounters with God: An Approach to the Theology of Jonathan Edwards.*[104] McClymond very rightly seeks to uncover the connections across Edwards' corpus and comes away with insight into Edwards' core theology.[105] Similar to the way in which our study discusses a key doctrine—revelation—and makes a closely linked statement about Edwards' larger project in light of it—interpretive harmonization—McClymond focuses on the interrelated issues of spiritual perception and apologetics. Perhaps, however, the perspective we have presented can provide a higher-level understanding of these themes. The theme of spiritual perception could be seen simply as an important implication of Edwards' multidimensional doctrine of revelation, in which the crucial affectional dimension of revelation demands a highly developed understanding of, and emphasis upon, spiritual perception.[106] It is only in those who are supernaturally enabled to apprehend divine beauty that God's project of self-communication to intelligent beings can be consummated, so Edwards needed to work in this area. On the other hand, apologetics could be understood as Edwards' great project of demonstrating the harmony to be found in all reality, *with specific respect to unbelievers.*[107] Edwards was as concerned with interpreting the media of revelation for the sake of those who were already regenerate as for those who were not—all were alike designed to actively re-emanate revelation as the "mouth of the

[103] E. Brooks Holifield, "Edwards as Theologian," in Stephen J. Stein (ed.), *The Cambridge Companion to Jonathan Edwards* (Cambridge: Cambridge University Press, 2007), p. 159.

[104] Michael J. McClymond, *Encounters with God: An Approach to the Theology of Jonathan Edwards* (Oxford and New York: Oxford University Press, 1998).

[105] Michael J. McClymond, *Encounters with God: An Approach to the Theology of Jonathan Edwards* (Oxford and New York: Oxford University Press, 1998), p. v.

[106] The other two main implications would be an emphasis on the dissemination of knowledge and the use of reason with regard to the noetic dimension and an emphasis on sanctification and holiness with regard to the ontological dimension.

[107] A similar observation could be made with reference to Stephen J. Nichols' explanation of Edwards in terms of apologetics expressed in *An Absolute Sort of Certainty: The Holy Spirit and the Apologetics of Jonathan Edwards* (Phillipsburg, NJ: P & R, 2003).

creation."[108] Our theory would therefore include preaching and polemic theology along with apologetics among the various ways in which Edwards carried out his single work of interpretive harmonization.[109]

An earlier study that also deals with some similar territory is Roland A. Delattre's 1968 *Beauty and Sensibility in the Thought of Jonathan Edwards: An Essay in Aesthetics and Theological Ethics.*[110] Delattre's thesis is that ". . . the aesthetic aspect of Jonathan Edwards' thought and vision, which finds its definitive formulation in his concepts of beauty and sensibility, provides a larger purchase upon the essential and distinctive features of his thought than does any other aspect."[111] He insists that if we want to understand Edwards' vision, ". . . we must dare to take seriously his frequent suggestion that beauty is the central clue to the nature of reality."[112] Again, it is important to recognize that "beauty" is interrelated and functionally synonymous with "harmony" in Edwards, so we are not quibbling about terminology.[113] We concur that this aesthetic concept, call it what you wish, is indeed the distinctive feature of Edwards' work.[114] What the present study adds is that it explains what Edwards was attempting to *do* with it. As a good minister sent to reflect the light of the Son, he was pointing out harmony to assist intelligent beings in fulfilling their purposes and to forward God's purpose in creating them.

Stephen R. Holmes' *God of Grace and God of Glory* is perhaps the nearest volley to our own.[115] Both accounts take Edwards' attempts at understanding the meaning of God's self-enlargement in creation as the basic foundation to understanding his distinctive theology.[116] Holmes would emphasize

[108] Edwards, "The Great Concern of a Watchman for Souls," in *Works Vol. 25*, p. 66.

[109] I readily concede that Edwards' Enlightenment context made the apologetic piece more prominent, and that his ostensibly apologetic literature was perhaps done with believers in mind, to better equip Christian minds so endangered by the pernicious intellectual currents of his day.

[110] Roland A. *Delattre, Beauty and Sensibility in the Thought of Jonathan Edwards: An Essay in Aesthetics and Theological Ethics* (New Haven and London: Yale University Press, 1968).

[111] Roland A. *Delattre, Beauty and Sensibility in the Thought of Jonathan Edwards: An Essay in Aesthetics and Theological Ethics* (New Haven and London: Yale University Press, 1968), p. vii.

[112] Roland A. Delattre, *Beauty and Sensibility in the Thought of Jonathan Edwards: An Essay in Aesthetics and Theological Ethics* (New Haven and London: Yale University Press, 1968), p. 1.

[113] See Edwards, *Works Vol. 6*, p. 305.

[114] We would, however, agree with William J. Danaher's point that Edwards' doctrine of the Trinity was the foundation for his aesthetics and ethics, and not the other way around as Delattre suggests. See Danaher, *The Trinitarian Ethics of Jonathan Edwards* (Louisville and London: Westminster John Knox Press, 2004), p. 4.

[115] Stephen R. Holmes, *God of Grace and God of Glory: An Account of the Theology of Jonathan Edwards* (Edinburgh: T&T Clark, 2000).

[116] See Stephen R. Holmes, *God of Grace and God of Glory: An Account of the Theology of Jonathan Edwards* (Edinburgh: T&T Clark, 2000), Chapter 2.

"glory" whereas we would emphasize "communicativeness," but these are two sides of one coin reflective of the different doctrinal foci—theology proper and revelation, respectively—of these studies. Holmes notices how Edwards sought to incorporate all the disciplines of learning into his account and to use typology as a means of "finding meaning and coherence" in nature and history.[117] Our theory would just add that this and other aspects of Edwards' work were specifically about the demonstration of Trinitarian harmony. However, the primary additional layer of interpretation that our theory offers would again be to state the purpose to which Edwards put the distinctive insights that Holmes rightly identifies.

VIII Conclusion

Jonathan Edwards was a purposeful man who believed in a purposeful God. Edwards believed he knew what God's project in creation and redemption was, and he sought to forward this project in as many ways as he knew how. Very often, this took the form of responding to aspects of the Enlightenment he found corrosive to the true faith, particularly British Deism. As we noted, the Deists argued that there was no harmony between reason and the claims of revelation, no harmony between Scripture and history, no harmony between the Old Testament and the New, and certainly no harmony among the supposed persons of the monstrous Trinity. Their version of reality was as ugly as it was mistaken. Edwards responded with a radically opposite vision of the beautiful harmony of the entire cosmos. God is harmonious in himself as Trinity, and he communicates his harmony in nature, Scripture, and history. The perception of this harmony led Edwards to the condition he described in his "Personal Narrative" and which he saw in others during the Awakenings. Through his method of interpreting the harmony of reality, Edwards did what he could to bring others into this state eternally. He did this as a minister, whose job it was to "communicate" God's knowledge, love, and joy to his people.

[117] See Stephen R. Holmes, *God of Grace and God of Glory: An Account of the Theology of Jonathan Edwards* (Edinburgh: T&T Clark, 2000), pp. 12–14, 100.

Bibliography

I Primary Works by Jonathan Edwards

Edwards, Jonathan, *The Blessing of God: Previously Unpublished Sermons by Jonathan Edwards* (ed. Michael McMullen; Nashville, TN: Broadman 2003).

—, *The Salvation of Souls: Nine Previously Unpublished Sermons on the Call of Ministry and the Gospel by Jonathan Edwards* (eds. Richard A. Bailey, and Gregory A. Wills; Wheaton, IL: Crossway Books 2002).

—, *Selections from the Unpublished Writings of Jonathan Edwards, of America* (ed. Alexander B. Grosart; Edinburgh: Ballantyne (for private distribution) 1865).

—, "Transcriptions of Unpublished 'Harmony' Notebooks," The Works of Jonathan Edwards Project, Yale University, 2007.

—, "Transcriptions of Unpublished 'Miscellanies' Nos. 1067 and 1068," The Works of Jonathan Edwards Project, Yale University, 2007.

—, "Transcriptions of Unpublished Sermons Nos. 50, 72, 156, 196, 253, 449, 866, 883, 921, 928, 945, and 952," The Works of Jonathan Edwards Project, Yale University, 2006.

—, *Treatise on Grace and Other Posthumously Published Writings* (ed. Paul Helm; London: James Clark 1971).

—, *The Works of Jonathan Edwards* (2 vols, Peabody, MA: Hendrickson, Reprint 2000, 1834).

—, *The Works of Jonathan Edwards, Vol. 1: Freedom of the Will* (ed. Paul Ramsey; New Haven: Yale University Press 1957).

—, *The Works of Jonathan Edwards, Vol. 2: Religious Affections* (ed. John E. Smith; New Haven: Yale University Press 1959).

—, *The Works of Jonathan Edwards, Vol. 3: Original Sin* (ed. Clyde A. Holbrook; New Haven, CT and London: Yale University Press 1970).

—, *The Works of Jonathan Edwards, Vol. 4: The Great Awakening* (ed. Clarence Curtis Goen; New Haven, CT and London: Yale University Press 1972).

—, *The Works of Jonathan Edwards, Vol. 5: Apocalyptic Writings* (ed. Stephen J. Stein; New Haven, CT and London: Yale University Press 1977).

—, *The Works of Jonathan Edwards, Vol. 6: Scientific and Philosophical Writings* (ed. Wallace E. Anderson; New Haven, CT and London: Yale University Press 1980).

—, *The Works of Jonathan Edwards, Vol. 7: The Life of David Brainerd* (ed. Norman Pettit; New Haven, CT and London: Yale University Press 1985).

—, *The Works of Jonathan Edwards, Vol. 8: Ethical Writings* (ed. Paul Ramsey; New Haven, CT and London: Yale University Press 1989).

—, *The Works of Jonathan Edwards, Vol. 9: A History of the Work of Redemption* (ed. John F. Wilson; New Haven, CT and London: Yale University Press 1989).

—, *The Works of Jonathan Edwards, Vol. 10: Sermons and Discourses, 1720–1723* (ed. Wilson H. Kimnach; New Haven, CT and London: Yale University Press 1992).

—, *The Works of Jonathan Edwards, Vol. 11: Typological Writings* (eds. Wallace E. Anderson, and Mason I. Lowance with David H. Watters; New Haven, CT and London: Yale University Press 1993).

—, *The Works of Jonathan Edwards, Vol. 12: Ecclesiastical Writings* (ed. David D. Hall; New Haven, CT and London: Yale University Press 1994).

—, *The Works of Jonathan Edwards, Vol. 13: The 'Miscellanies,' A-500* (ed. Thomas A. Schafer; New Haven, CT and London: Yale University Press 1994).

—, *The Works of Jonathan Edwards, Vol. 14: Sermons and Discourses, 1723–1729* (ed. Kenneth P. Minkema; New Haven, CT and London: Yale University Press 1997).

—, *The Works of Jonathan Edwards, Vol. 15: Notes on Scripture* (ed. Stephen J. Stein; Vol. 15, New Haven, CT and London: Yale University Press 1998).

—, *The Works of Jonathan Edwards, Vol. 16: Letters and Personal Writings* (ed. George S. Claghorn; New Haven, CT and London: Yale University Press 1998).

—, *The Works of Jonathan Edwards, Vol. 17: Sermons and Discourses, 1730–1733* (ed. Mark Valeri; New Haven, CT and London: Yale University Press 1999).

—, *The Works of Jonathan Edwards, Vol. 18: The 'Miscellanies,' 501–832* (ed. Ava Chamberlain; New Haven, CT and London: Yale University Press 2000).

—, *The Works of Jonathan Edwards, Vol. 19: Sermons and Discourses, 1734–1738* (ed. M. X. Lesser; New Haven, CT and London: Yale University Press 2001).

—, *The Works of Jonathan Edwards, Vol. 20: The 'Miscellanies,' 833–1152* (ed. Amy Plantinga Pauw; New Haven, CT and London: Yale University Press 2002).

—, *The Works of Jonathan Edwards, Vol. 21: Writings on the Trinity, Grace, and Faith* (ed. Sang Hyun Lee; New Haven, CT and London: Yale University Press 2003).

—, *The Works of Jonathan Edwards, Vol. 22: Sermons and Discourses, 1739–1742* (eds. Harry S. Stout, and Nathan O. Hatch; New Haven, CT and London: Yale University Press 2003).

—, *The Works of Jonathan Edwards, Vol. 23: The 'Miscellanies,' 1153–1360* (ed. Douglas A. Sweeney; New Haven, CT and London: Yale University Press 2004).

—, *The Works of Jonathan Edwards, Vol. 24: The 'Blank Bible'* (ed. Stephen J. Stein; 2 vols, New Haven, CT and London: Yale University Press 2006).

—, *The Works of Jonathan Edwards, Vol. 25: Sermons and Discourses, 1743–1758* (ed. Wilson H. Kimnach; New Haven, CT and London: Yale University Press 2006).

—, *The Works of Jonathan Edwards, Vol. 26: Catalogues of Books* (ed. Peter J. Thuesen; New Haven, CT and London: Yale University Press 2008).

II Other Primary Sources

Aquinas, St. Thomas, *Summa Theologica* (trans. Fathers of the English Dominican Province; Second and Revised edn; 5 vols, London: Burns, Oates & Washborne 1921–1929).

Augustine of Hippo, St., *On the Trinity* (ed. Philip Schaff; trans. Authur West Haddan; 14 vols; Vol. 3, *The Nicene and Post-Nicene Fathers*, Grand Rapids, MI: Eerdmans 1957).

Baillie, John, *Church Dogmatics, Vol. I, Part II: The Doctrine of the Word of God* (trans. G. T. Thomson; 1978 edn, Edinburgh: T&T Clark 1956).
—, *The Idea of Revelation in Recent Thought* (New York: Columbia University Press 1957).
—, *Our Knowledge of God* (Oxford: Oxford University Press 1939).
Barth, Karl, *Church Dogmatics, Vol. I, Part I: The Doctrine of the Word of God* (trans. G. T. Thomson; 1963 edn, Edinburgh: T&T Clark 1936).
Bavinck, Herman, *The Philosophy of Revelation: The Stone Lectures for 1908–1909, Princeton Theological Seminary* (London: Longmans, Green, and Co. 1909).
—, *Reformed Dogmatics, Vol. 1: Prolegomena* (ed. John Bolt; trans. John Vriend; Grand Rapids, MI: Baker Academic 2003).
Bennet, Benjamin, *The Truth, Inspiration, and Usefulness of the Scriptures Asserted and Proved. In Several Discourses on 2. Tim. Iii. Xv* (London: L. Latham 1730).
Brine, John, *A Treatise on Various Subjects: Viz. . . . Defects Which Attended the Morality of All Other Philosophers . . .* (London: John Ward 1750).
Brunner, Emil, and Karl Barth, *Natural Theology* (trans. Peter Fraenkel; Eugene, OR: Wipf and Stock Publishers 2002).
Burr, Esther Edwards, *The Journal of Esther Edwards Burr* (eds. Carol F. Karlsen, and Laurie Crumpacker; New Haven, CT and London: Yale University Press 1984).
Butler, Joseph, *The Analogy of Religion, Natural and Revealed, to the Constitution and Course of Nature* (ed. F. A. Malleson; London: Ward, Lock, Bowden, and Co. 1736).
Calvin, John, *Calvin's Commentaries* (trans. John King; London: The Calvin Society 1847).
—, *Institutes of the Christian Religion* (ed. John T. McNeill; trans. Ford Lewis Battles; 2 vols, *The Library of Christian Classics*, Philadelphia, PA: Westminster Press 1960).
Chambers, Ephraim, *Cyclopedia; or, an Universal Dictionary of Arts and Sciences* (5th edn, London 1741).
Chubb, Thomas, *A Collection of Tracts, on Various Subjects* (London 1730).
—, *A Discourse Concerning Reason with Regard to Religion and Divine Revelation: Wherein It Is Shown That Reason Is, or Else That It Ought to Be, a Sufficient Guide in Matters of Religion* (London: T. Cox 1733).
—, *The True Gospel of Jesus Christ Asserted: Wherein Is Shown What Is, and What Is Not That Gospel; What Was the Great and Good End It Was Intended to Serve; How It Is Excellently Suited to Answer That Purpose; and How, or by What Means That End Has Been in a Great Measure Been Frustrated* (London: T. Cox 1738).
Clarke, Samuel, *A Demonstration of the Being and Attributes of God and Other Writings* (Cambridge: Cambridge University Press, 1998).
Cudworth, Ralph, *The True Intellectual System of the Universe* (London 1678).
Emerson, Ralph Waldo, Divinity School Address, in, http://www.emersoncentral.com/divaddr.htm. (accessed March 9, 2010).
Goodwin, Thomas, *The Works of Thomas Goodwin, D.D., Sometime President of Magdalene College, Oxford* (Edinburgh: James Nichol 1861–66).
Grotius, Hugo, *De Veritate Religionis Christianae* (London 1632).
Hume, David, *The History of England from the Invasion of Julius Caesar to the Revolution in 1688* (Indianapolis, IN: Liberty Fund 1983).

—, *The Natural History of Religion and Dialogues Concerning Natural Religion* (Oxford: Clarendon Press 1976).

Hutcheson, Francis, *An Essay on the Nature and Conduct of the Passions and Affections* (3rd edn, London: Ward and Knapton, 1742).

Jones, Jeremiah, *A New and Full Method of Settling the Canonical Authority of the New Testament* (3 vols, London 1726).

Lardner, Nathaniel, *The Credibility of the Gospel History . . .* (17 vols, London 1727–57).

Leibniz, Gotfried, *Philosophical Papers and Letters* (trans. Leroy E. Loemaker; 2 vols, Chicago, IL: University of Chicago Press 1956).

Leland, John, *An Answer to a Late Book Intituled Christianity as Old as the Creation* (2 vols, London 1733).

Locke, John, *An Essay Concerning Human Understanding* (ed. John W. Yolton; London: J. M. Dent 1961).

—, *The Reasonableness of Christianity* (London 1695).

—, *Writings on Religion* (ed. Victor Nuovo; Oxford: Oxford University Press 2002).

Mastricht, Peter van, *Theoretico-Practica Theologia* (Amsterdam 1715).

—, *Treatise on Regeneration: Extracted from His System of Divinity, Called Theologia Theorectico-Practica and Faithfully Translated into English* (New Haven, CT: Thomas and Samuel Green 1770).

Mather, Cotton, *The Christian Philosopher* (Boston, MA 1721).

—, *Magnalia Christi Americana* (Boston, MA 1702).

Mather, Samuel, *The Figures or Types of the Old Testament, by Samuel Mather* (ed. Mason I. Lowance; New York: Johnson Reprint Corp. 1969).

Noll, Mark A. (ed.), *Confessions and Catechisms of the Reformation* (Vancouver, BC: Regent College Publishing 1997).

Norris, John, *Cursory Reflections Upon a Book Call'd, an Essay Concerning Human Understanding* (4th edn, London: S. Manship 1699).

—, *Theory of the Ideal World* (London 1701).

Nye, Stephen, *An Historical Account and Defence of the Canon of the New Testament: In Answer to Amyntor* (London 1700).

Owen, John, *Pneumatologia or a Discourse Concerning the Holy Spirit* (Vol. 2, Edinburgh: Banner of Truth 2000).

—, *The Reason of Faith, or the Grounds Whereon the Scripture Is Believed to Be the Word of God* (Vol. 3, *The Works of John Owen*, Edinburgh: Banner of Truth 2000).

Poole, Matthew, *Annotations Upon the Holy Bible* (4th edn, London 1700).

Prideaux, Humphery, *The Old and New Testament Connected in the History of the Jews and Neighbouring Nations* (Glasgow, Reprint 1763, 1729).

Ramsay, Andrew Michael, *Philosophical Principles of Natural and Revealed Religion* (London 1748–49).

Reynolds, John, *The Religion of Jesus Delineated* (London 1726).

Shaftesbury, Anthony Ashley Cooper, *Characteristics of Men, Manners, Opinions, Times Etc.* (ed. John M. Robertson; 2 vols, London 1900).

Skelton, Philip, *Deism Revealed. Or, the Attack on Christianity Candidly Reviewed in Its Real Merits, as They Stand in the Celebrated Writings of Lord Herbert, Lord Shaftesbury, Hobbes, Toland, Tindal, Collins, Manderville, Dodwell, Woolston, Morgan, Chubb, and Others* (2nd edn, Vol. 2, London 1751).

Spinoza, Benedict de, *A Theologico-Political Treatise* (trans. R. H. M. Elwes; 1951 edn, New York 1670).

Stapfer, Johann Friedrich, *Institutiones Theologicæ Polemicæ Universæ* (5 vols, Tiguri [Zurich]: Heideggerum and Company, 1743–47).

Stebbing, Henry, *A Treatise Concerning the Operations of the Holy Spirit: Being the Substance of the Late Reverend and Learned Dr. William Clagett's Discourse Upon That Subject* (London 1719).

Stillingfleet, Edward, *Origines Sacrae: Or a Rational Account of the Grounds of Natural and Revealed Religion: Wherein the Foundations of Religion and the Authority of the Scriptures, Are Asserted and Clear'd with an Answer to the Modern Objections of Atheists and Deists* (London 1662).

Tindal, Matthew, *Christianity as Old as the Creation* (London 1730).

Toland, John, *Christianity Not Mysterious: Text, Associated Works, and Critical Essays* (eds. Philip McGuiness, Alan Harrison, and Richard Kearney; Dublin: The Lilliput Press 1997).

Turnbull, George, *Christian Philosophy* (London 1740).

Turretin, Francis, *Institutes of Elenctic Theology* (ed. James T. Dennison Jr.; trans. George Musgrave Giger; 3 vols, Phillipsburg, NJ: P&R Publishing 1992–97).

Warburton, William, *Principles of Natural and Revealed Religion* (London 1753).

Watts, Isaac, *An Essay on the Freedom of Will in God and in Creatures* (London 1732).

Whitby, Daniel, *Discourse on the Five Points* (1735 edn, London: Aaron Ward and Richard Hett 1710).

Winder, Henry, *A Critical and Chronological History of the Rise, Progress, Declension, and Revival of Knowledge, Chiefly Religious . . .* (2 vols, London 1745–46).

Wollebius, Johannes, *Abridgement of Christian Divinitie* (trans. Alexander Ross; London: John Saywell 1650).

III Secondary Works

Abraham, William J., *Canon and Criterion in Christian Theology* (Oxford: Clarendon Press 1998).

—, *Revelation and the Limits of Historical Criticism* (Oxford: Clarendon Press 2000).

Aldridge, Alfred Owen, "Edwards and Hutcheson", *Harvard Theological Review* 44 (1951), 35–53.

—, *Jonathan Edwards* (New York: Washington Square Press 1964).

Allen, Alexander V.G., *Jonathan Edwards* (Edinburgh: T&T Clark 1889).

Anderson, Francis I., "We Speak . . . in the Words . . . Which the Holy Ghost Teacheth", *Westminster Theological Journal* 22(2) (1960), 113–32.

Anderson, Wallace E., "Editor's Introduction", in Wallace E. Anderson (ed.), *The Works of Jonathan Edwards, Vol. 6: Scientific Writings* (New Haven, CT and London: Yale University Press 1980).

—, "Editor's Introduction to 'Images of Divine Things' and 'Types'", in Wallace E. Anderson, and Mason I. Lowance with David H. Watters (eds.), *The Works of Jonathan Edwards, Vol. 11: Typological Writings* (New Haven, CT and London: Yale University Press 1993), pp. 3–48.

—, "Immaterialism in Jonathan Edwards's Early Philosophical Notes", *Journal of the History of Ideas* 25 (1964), 181–200.

Avis, Paul (ed.), *Divine Revelation* (Grand Rapids, MI: Eerdmans 1997).

Baird, William, *History of New Testament Research, Vol. 1: From Deism to Tubingen* (Minneapolis, MN: Augsburg Fortress Publishers 1992).

—, *History of New Testament Research, Vol. 2: From Jonathan Edwards to Rudolf Bultmann* (Minneapolis, MN: Fortress Press 2003).

Barr, James, *Old and New in Interpretation: A Study of the Two Testaments* (London: SCM Press 1966).

Barshinger, David, " 'The Only Rule of Our Faith and Practice': Jonathan Edwards's Interpretation of the Book of Isaiah as a Case Study of His Exegetical Boundaries", *Journal of the Evangelical Theological Society* 52(4) (2009), 811–29.

Battles, Ford Lewis, "God Was Accommodating Himself to Human Capacity", *Interpretation* 31 (1977), 19–37.

Beardslee, John W. III., "Editor's Introduction", in John W. Beardslee III (ed.), *The Doctrine of Scripture: Locus 2 of Institutio Theologiae Elencticae* (Grand Rapids, MI: Baker Book House 1981).

Bercovitch, Sacvan (ed.), *Typology and Early American Literature* (Amherst, MA: University of Massachusetts Press 1972).

Biehl, Craig, *The Infinite Merit of Christ: The Glory of Christ's Obedience in the Theology of Jonathan Edwards* (Jackson, MS: Reformed Academic Press 2009).

Bogue, Carl W., *Jonathan Edwards and the Covenant of Grace* (Cherry Hill, NJ: Mack Publishing Company 1975).

Bombaro, John J., "Jonathan Edwards's Vision of Salvation", *Westminster Theological Journal* 65(1) (2003), 45–67.

Brand, David C., *Profile of the Last Puritan: Jonathan Edwards, Self-Love, and the Dawn of the Beatific* (Atlanta, GA: Scholars" Press 1991).

Brown, Robert E., "The Bible", in Sang Hyun Lee (ed.), *The Princeton Companion to Jonathan Edwards* (Princeton, NJ: Princeton University Press 2005).

—, "Edwards, Locke, and the Bible", *The Journal of Religion* 79(3) (1999), 361–84.

—, *Jonathan Edwards and the Bible* (Bloomington, IN: Indiana University Press 2002).

—, "The Sacred and the Profane Connected: Edwards, the Bible, and Intellectual Culture", in Harry S. Stout, Kenneth P. Minkema, and Caleb J. D. Maskell (eds.), *Jonathan Edwards at 300: Essays on the Tercentenary of His Birth* (Lanham, MD: University Press of America 2005), pp. 38–53.

Buckley, Michael J., *At the Origins of Modern Atheism* (New Haven, CT: Yale University Press 1987).

Butler, Diana, "God's Visible Glory: The Beauty of Nature in the Thought of John Calvin and Jonathan Edwards'", *Westminster Theological Journal* 52(1) (1990), 13–26.

Byrne, Peter, *Natural Religion and the Nature of Religion: The Legacy of Deism* (ed. Stewart Sutherland; *Routledge Religious Studies*, London and New York: Routledge 1989).

Caldwell, Robert W. III., *Communion in the Holy Spirit: The Holy Spirit as the Bond of Union in the Theology of Jonathan Edwards* (*Studies in Evangelical History and Thought*, Milton Keynes: Paternoster 2006).

Carpenter, Frederic I., "The Radicalism of Jonathan Edwards'", *New England Quarterly* 4 (1931), 629–44.

Carrick, John, *The Preaching of Jonathan Edwards* (Edinburgh: Banner of Truth 2008).

Carse, James, *Jonathan Edwards and the Visibility of God* (New York: C. Scribner's Son's 1967).

Carson, D. A., and John D. Woodbridge (eds.), *Hermeneutics, Authority, and Canon* (Leicester: InterVarsity Press 1986).

Chai, Leon, *Jonathan Edwards and the Limits of Enlightenment Philosophy* (Oxford and New York: Oxford University Press 1998).

Chamberlain, Ava, "Brides of Christ and Signs of Grace: Edwards's Sermon Series on the Parable of the Wise and Foolish Virgins", in Stephen J. Stein (ed.), *Jonathan Edwards's Writings: Text, Context, Interpretation* (Bloomington, IN: Indiana University Press 1996), pp. 3–18.

—, "Editor's Introduction", in *The Works of Jonathan Edwards, Vol. 18: The 'Miscellanies' 501–832* (New Haven, CT and London: Yale University Press 2000).

—, "The Grand Sower of the Seed: Jonathan Edwards's Critique of George Whitfield", *New England Quarterly* 70 (1997), 368–85.

—, "Self-Deception as a Theological Problem in Jonathan Edwards's 'Treatise Concerning Religious Affections'", *Church History* 63(4) (1994), 541–56.

Champion, J. A. I., *The Pillars of Priestcraft Shaken: The Church of England and Its Enemies, 1660–1730* (eds. Anthony Fletcher, John Guy, and John Morrill; *Cambridge Studies in Early Modern British History*, Cambridge: Cambridge University Press 1992).

Cherry, Conrad, *Nature and the Religious Imagination: From Edwards to Bushnell* (Philadelphia, PA: Fortress Press 1980).

—, "The Puritan Notion of the Covenant in Jonathan Edwards' Doctrine of Faith", *Church History* 34 (1965), 328–41.

—, "Symbols of Spiritual Truth: Jonathan Edwards as Biblical Interpreter", *Interpretation* 39 (1985), 263–71.

—, *The Theology of Jonathan Edwards: A Reappraisal* (1990 edn, Bloomington, IN: Indiana University Press 1966).

Claghorn, George S., "Transcribing a Difficult Hand: Collecting and Editing Edwards' Letters over Thirty-Five Years", in D. G. Hart (ed.), *The Legacy of Jonathan Edwards: American Religion and the Evangelical Tradition* (Grand Rapids, MI: Baker Academic 2003), pp. 217–27.

Clark, Gordon H., *Religion, Reason and Revelation* (Philadelphia, PA: Presbyterian and Reformed Publishing Company 1961).

Clark, Stephen M., "Jonathan Edwards: The History of the Work of Redemption", *Westminster Theological Journal* 56(1) (1994), 45–58.

Colwell, John E., "The Glory of God's Justice and the Glory of God's Grace: Contemporary Reflections on the Doctrine of Hell in the Teaching of Jonathan Edwards'", *Evangelical Quarterly* 67(4) (1995), 291–308.

Conforti, Joseph A., *Jonathan Edwards, Religious Tradition, and American Culture* (Chapel Hill, NC: University of North Carolina Press 1995).

Cooey, Paula M., *Jonathan Edwards on Nature and Destiny: A Systematic Analysis* (*Studies in American Religion, Vol. 16*, Lewiston/Queenston/Lampeter: The Edwin Mellen Press 1985).

Copan, Paul, "Jonathan Edwards's Philosophical Influences: Lockean or Malebranchean?" *Journal of the Evangelical Theological Society* 44(1) (2001), 107–24.

Craig, Philip A., " 'And Prophecy Shall Cease': Jonathan Edwards on the Cessation of the Gift of Prophecy", *Westminster Theological Journal* 64(1) (2002), 163–84.

Crisp, Oliver D., "Jonathan Edwards's God: Trinity, Individuation, and Divine Simplicity", in Bruce L. McCormack (ed.), *Engaging the Doctrine of God: Contemporary Protestant Perspectives* (Grand Rapids, MI: Baker Academic and Rutherford House 2008), pp. 83–103.

—, *Jonathan Edwards and the Metaphysics of Sin* (Aldershot: Ashgate 2005).

—, "On the Theological Pedigree of Jonathan Edwards's Doctrine of Imputation", *Scottish Journal of Theology* 56(3) (2003), 308–27.

Crocco, Stephen D., "Edwards's Intellectual Legacy", in Stephen J. Stein (ed.), *The Cambridge Companion to Jonathan Edwards* (Cambridge: Cambridge University Press 2007), pp. 300–24.

Danaher, James P., "David Hume and Jonathan Edwards on Miracles and Religious Faith", *Southwest Philosophy Review* 17(2) (2001), 13–24.

Danaher, William J. Jr., "By Sensible Signs Represented: Jonathan Edwards' Sermons on the Lord's Supper", *Pro Ecclesia* 7 (1998), 261–87.

—, *The Trinitarian Ethics of Jonathan Edwards* (Louisville, KY and London: Westminster John Knox Press 2004).

Daniel, Stephen H., "Edwards as Philosopher", in Stephen J. Stein (ed.), *The Cambridge Companion to Jonathan Edwards* (Cambridge: Cambridge University Press 2007), pp. 162–80.

Daniel, Stephen, *The Philosophy of Jonathan Edwards: A Study in Divine Semiotics* (Bloomington, IN: Indiana University Press 1994).

Davidson, Bruce W., "Reasonable Damnation: How Jonathan Edwards Argued for the Rationality of Hell", *Journal of the Evangelical Theological Society* 38 (1995), 47–56.

Davidson, Edward H., *Jonathan Edwards: The Narrative of a Puritan Mind* (Cambridge, MA: Harvard University Press 1968).

Davies, Ronald E., "Jonathan Edwards, Theologian of the Missionary Awakening", *Evangel* 17(1) (1999), 1–8.

De Jaegher, Paul (ed.), *An Anthology of Mysticism* (London: Burns & Oates 1977).

De Prospo, R. C., *Theism in the Discourse of Jonathan Edwards* (Newark: University of Delaware Press 1985).

Delattre, Roland A., *Beauty and Sensibility in the Thought of Jonathan Edwards: An Essay in Aesthetics and Theological Ethics* (New Haven, CT and London: Yale University Press 1968).

—, "Religious Ethics Today: Jonathan Edwards, H Richard Niebuhr, and Beyond", in Sang Hyun Lee, and Allen C. Guelzo (eds.), *Edwards in Our Time: Jonathan Edwards and the Shaping of American Religion* (Grand Rapids, MI: Eerdmans 1999), pp. 67–85.

Demson, David E., *Hans Frei & Karl Barth: Different Ways of Reading Scripture* (Grand Rapids, MI: Eerdmans 1997).

Dillenberger, John, *Protestant Thought and Natural Science* (Garden City, NY: Doubleday 1960).

Donagan, Alan, "Spinoza's Theology", in Don Garrett (ed.), *The Cambridge Companion to Spinoza* (Cambridge: Cambridge University Press 1996).

Dowey, Edward A. Jr., *The Knowledge of God in Calvin's Theology* (3rd edn, Grand Rapids, MI: Eerdmans 1994).

Dulles, Avery R., *Models of Revelation* (Dublin 1983).

Dupre, Louis, *Passage to Modernity: An Essay in Hermeneutics of Nature and Culture* (New Haven, CT: Yale University Press 1993).

Dyrness, William A., *Reformed Theology and Visual Culture: The Protestant Imagination from Calvin to Edwards* (Cambridge: Cambridge University Press 2004).

Ehrhard, Jim, "A Critical Analysis of the Tradition of Jonathan Edwards as a Manuscript Preacher", *Westminster Theological Journal* 60(1) (1998), 71–84.

Elwood, Douglas J., *The Philosophical Theology of Jonathan Edwards* (New York: Columbia University Press 1960).

Erdt, Terrence, *Jonathan Edwards, Art and the Sense of the Heart* (Amherst, MA: University of Massachusetts Press 1980).

Fackre, Gabriel, *The Doctrine of Revelation: A Narrative Interpretation* (Edinburgh: Edinburgh University Press 1997).

Fairweather, Alan M., *The Word as Truth: A Critical Examination of the Christian Doctrine of Revelation in the Writings of Thomas Aquinas and Karl Barth* (London: Lutterworth Press 1944).

Faust, Clarence H., "Jonathan Edwards as a Scientist", *American Literature* 1 (1930), 393–404.

Fiering, Norman S., *Jonathan Edwards's Moral Thought and Its British Context* (Chapel Hill, NC: University of North Carolina Press 1981).

—, "The Rationalist Foundations of Jonathan Edwards's Metaphysics", in Nathan O. Hatch, and Harry S. Stout (eds.), *Jonathan Edwards and the American Experience* (New York and Oxford: Oxford University Press 1988), pp. 73–101.

Foster, Frank Hugh, *A Genetic History of the New England Theology* (Chicago, IL: University of Chicago Press 1907).

Frei, Hans W., "The Doctrine of Revelation in the Thought of Karl Barth, 1909 to 1922: The Nature of Barth's Break with Liberalism", Ph.D. Dissertation, Yale University, 1956.

—, *The Eclipse of Biblical Narrative: A Study in Eighteenth and Nineteenth Century Hermeneutics* (New Haven, CT and London: Yale University Press 1974).

—, *Types of Christian Theology* (eds. George Hunsinger, and William C. Placher; New Haven, CT: Yale University Press 1992).

Gay, Peter, *The Enlightenment: An Interpretation* (2 vols; Vol. 2, *The Science of Freedom*, London: W. W. Norton 1977).

—, *A Loss of Mastery: Puritan Historians in Colonial America* (Berkeley, CA: University of California Press 1966).

Gerrish, Brian A., "Biblical Authority in the Continental Reformation", *Scottish Journal of Theology* X (1957), 337–60.

Gerstner, John H., *Jonathan Edwards: A Mini-Theology* (Morgan, PA: Soli Deo Gloria Publications, Reprint 1996, 1987).

—, "Jonathan Edwards and the Bible", in John D. Hannah (ed.), *Inerrancy and the Church* (Chicago, IL: Moody Press 1984), pp. 257–78.

—, "Outline of the Apologetics of Jonathan Edwards (Four-Part Essay)", *Bibliotheca Sacra* 133(529–532) (1976), 3–10; 99–107; 95–201; 91–98.

—, *The Rational Biblical Theology of Jonathan Edwards* (3 vols, Powhatan, VA: Berea Publications 1991–93).

—, "The View of the Bible Held by the Church: Calvin and the Westminster Divines", in Norman L. Geisler (ed.), *Inerrancy* (Grand Rapids, MI: Zondervan 1979).

Gibson, Michael D., "The Integrative Biblical Philosophy of Jonathan Edwards: Empiricism, God, Being, and Postmillennialism", *Westminster Theological Journal* 64(1) (2002), 151–61.

Gilbert, Greg D., "The Nations Will Worship: Jonathan Edwards and the Salvation of the Heathen", *Trinity Journal* 23(1) (2002), 53–76.

Goen, Clarence Curtis, "Editor's Introduction", in Clarence C. Goen (ed.), *The Works of Jonathan Edwards, Vol. 4: The Great Awakening* (New Haven, CT and London: Yale University Press 1972).

Goen, Clarence Curtis, "Jonathan Edwards: A New Departure in Eschatology", *Church History* 28 (1959), 25–40.

Goppelt, Leonhard, *Typos: The Typological Interpretation of the Old Testament in the New* (trans. Donald H. Madvig; Grand Rapids, MI: Eerdmans 1982).

Guelzo, Allen C., "Learning Is the Handmaid of the Lord: Jonathan Edwards, Reason, and the Life of the Mind", *Midwest Studies in Philosophy* 28(1) (2004), 1–18.

—, "The Return of the Will: Jonathan Edwards and the Possibilities of Free Will", in Sang Hyun Lee, and Allen C. Guelzo (eds.), *Edwards in Our Time: Jonathan Edwards and the Shaping of American Religion* (Grand Rapids, MI: Eerdmans 1999), pp. 87–110.

Gunton, Colin E., *A Brief Theology of Revelation: The 1993 Warfield Lectures* (Edinburgh: T&T Clark 1995).

Gura, Philip, *Jonathan Edwards: America's Evangelical* (New York: Hill & Wang 2005).

Hall, David D., "The New England Background", in Stephen J. Stein (ed.), *The Cambridge Companion to Jonathan Edwards* (Cambridge: Cambridge University Press 2007), pp. 61–79.

Hardman Moore, Susan, "For the Mind's Eye Only: Puritans, Images and 'The Golden Mines of Scripture'", *Scottish Journal of Theology* 59(3) (2006), 281–96.

Haroutunian, Joseph, "Jonathan Edwards: Theologian of the Great Commandment", *Theology Today* 1(3) (1944), 361–77.

Harrison, Peter, *The Bible, Protestantism, and the Rise of Natural Science* (Cambridge: Cambridge University Press 1998).

—, '*Religion*' *and the Religions in the English Enlightenment* (2002 paperback edn, Cambridge: Cambridge University Press, Reprint 2002, 1990).

Hastings, W. Ross, "'Honouring the Spirit': Analysis and Evaluation of Jonathan Edwards' Pneumatological Doctrine of the Incarnation", *International Journal of Systematic Theology* 7(3) (2005), 279–99.

Hatch, Nathan O., and Harry S. Stout (eds.), *Jonathan Edwards and the American Experience* (New York and Oxford: Oxford University Press 1988).

Helm, Paul, *Divine Revelation: The Basic Issues* (ed. Peter Toon; *Foundations for Faith*, London: Marshall Morgan & Scott 1982).

—, *John Calvin's Ideas* (Oxford and New York: Oxford University Press 2004).

—, "John Locke and Jonathan Edwards: A Reconsideration", *Journal of the History of Philosophy* 7 (1969), 51–61.

Helm, Paul, and Oliver D. Crisp (eds.), *Jonathan Edwards: Philosophical Theologian* (Aldershot: Ashgate 2003).

Helm, Paul, and Carl Trueman (eds.), *The Trustworthiness of God: Perspectives on the Nature of Scripture* (Leicester: Apollos 2002).

Henderson, G. D., "Jonathan Edwards and Scotland", *Evangelical Quarterly* 16(1) (1944), 41–52.

Henry, Carl F. H., *God, Revelation, and Authority* (5 vols, Waco, TX: Word Books 1979).

Higton, Mike, *Christ, Providence and History: Hans W. Frei's Public Theology* (London and New York: T&T Clark 2004).

Holbrook, Clyde A., *The Ethics of Jonathan Edwards: Morality and Aesthetics* (Ann Arbor, MI: University of Michigan Press 1973).

—, "Jonathan Edwards and His Detractors", *Theology Today* 10 (1953), 384–96.

—, *Jonathan Edwards: The Valley and Nature: An Interpretative Essay* (Lewisburg, PA: Bucknell University Press 1987).

Holifield, E. Brooks, "Edwards as Theologian", in Stephen J. Stein (ed.), *The Cambridge Companion to Jonathan Edwards* (Cambridge: Cambridge University Press 2007), pp. 144–61.

Holmes, Stephen R., "Does Jonathan Edwards Use a Dispositional Ontology? A Response to Sang Hyun Lee", in Paul Helm, and Oliver D. Crisp (eds.), *Jonathan Edwards: Philosophical Theologian* (Aldershot: Ashgate 2003).

—, *God of Grace and God of Glory: An Account of the Theology of Jonathan Edwards* (Edinburgh: T&T Clark 2000).

—, "The Justice of Hell and the Display of God's Glory in the Thought of Jonathan Edwards'", *Pro Ecclesia* 9(4) (2000), 389–403.

—, "Triune Creativity: Trinity, Creation, Art and Science", in Paul Louis Metzger (ed.), *Trinitarian Soundings in Systematic Theology* (Edinburgh: T&T Clark 2005), pp. 73–85.

Illick, Joseph E. III., "Jonathan Edwards and the Historians", *Journal of the Presbyterian Historical Society* 39 (1961), 230–46.

Infante, Dominic A., Andrew S. Rancer, and Deanna F. Womack, *Building Communication Theory* (Prospect Heights, IL: Waverland Press 1990).

Israel, Jonathan I., *Radical Enlightenment: Philosophy and the Making of the Modernity 1650–1750* (Oxford and New York: Oxford University Press, Reprint 2002, 2001).

Jenson, Robert W., *America's Theologian: A Recommendation of Jonathan Edwards* (New York: Oxford University Press 1988).

Jinkins, Michael, "'The Being of Beings': Jonathan Edwards' Understanding of God as Reflected in His Final Treatises", *Scottish Journal of Theology* 46(2) (1993), 161–90.

Johnston, Charlotte, "Locke's Examination of Malebranche and John Norris", *Journal of the History of Ideas* 19(4) (1958), 551–58.

Kant, Immanuel, *The Critique of Pure Reason* (trans. Paul Guyer, and Allen W. Wood; Cambridge: Cambridge University Press 1998).

Kearney, John, "Jonathan Edwards' Account of Adam's First Sin", *Scottish Bulletin of Evangelical Theology* 15 (1997), 127–41.

Kimnach, Wilson H., "Jonathan Edwards's Pursuit of Reality", in Nathan O. Hatch, and Harry S. Stout (eds.), *Jonathan Edwards and the American Experience* (Oxford and New York: Oxford University Press 1988), pp. 102–17.

Klever, Wim N. A., "Spinoza's Life and Works", in Don Garrett (ed.), *The Cambridge Companion to Spinoza* (Cambridge: Cambridge University Press 1996).

Kloosterman, Nelson D., "The Use of Typology in Post-Canonical Salvation History: An Orientation to Jonathan Edwards' a History of the Work of Redemption", *Mid-America Journal of Theology* 14 (2003), 59–96.

Knight, Janice, "Learning the Language of God: Jonathan Edwards and the Typology of Nature", *William and Mary Quarterly* 48 (1991), 531–51.

—, "Typology", in Sang Hyun Lee (ed.), *The Princeton Companion to Jonathan Edwards* (Princeton, NJ and Oxford: Princeton University Press 2005).

Kroll, Richard, Richard Ashcraft, and Perez Zagorin (eds.), *Philosophy, Science, and Religion in England, 1640–1700* (Cambridge: Cambridge University Press 1992).

Kuhn, Thomas S., *The Structure of Scientific Revolutions* (Chicago, IL: Chicago University Press 1962).

Kuklick, Bruce, "Review Essay: An Edwards for the Millennium", *Religion and American Culture: A Journal of Interpretation* 11 (2001), 116–17.

Lambert, Frank, *Inventing the Great Awakening* (Princeton, NJ: Princeton University Press 2001).

Lampe, G. W. H., and K. J. Woollcombe, *Essays on Typology* (London: SCM Press 1957).

LaShell, John K., "Jonathan Edwards and the New Sense", *Reformation & Revival* 4(3) (1995), 87–97.

Laurence, David, "Jonathan Edwards, John Locke, and the Canon of Experience", *Early American Literature* 15(2) (1980), 107–23.

Lee, Sang Hyun, "Does History Matter to God? Jonathan Edwards's Dynamic Re-Conception of God's Relation to the World", in Harry S. Stout, Kenneth P. Minkema, and Caleb J. D. Maskell (eds.), *Jonathan Edwards at 300* (Lanham, MD and Oxford: University Press of America 2005).

—, "Editor's Introduction", in Sang H. Lee (ed.), *The Works of Jonathan Edwards, Vol. 21: Writings on the Trinity, Grace, and Faith* (New Haven, CT: Yale University Press 2003), pp. 1–106.

—, "Edwards on God and Nature: Resources for Contemporary Theology", in Sang Hyun Lee, and Allen C. Guelzo (eds.), *Edwards in Our Time: Jonathan Edwards and the Shaping of American Religion* (Grand Rapids, MI: Eerdmans 1999).

—, "God's Relation to the World", in Sang Hyun Lee (ed.), *The Princeton Companion to Jonathan Edwards* (Princeton, NJ and Oxford: Princeton University Press 2005), pp. 1–13.

—, "Jonathan Edwards on Nature", in Sang H. Lee (ed.), *The Philosophical Theology of Jonathan Edwards, Expanded Edition* (Princeton, NJ: Princeton University Press 2000), pp. 243–68.

—, *The Philosophical Theology of Jonathan Edwards* (Revised edn, Princeton, NJ: Princeton University Press 2000).

— (ed.), *The Princeton Companion to Jonathan Edwards* (Princeton, NJ and Oxford: Princeton University Press 2005).

Lee, Sang Hyun, and Allen C. Guelzo (eds.), *Edwards in Our Time: Jonathan Edwards and the Shaping of American Religion* (Grand Rapids, MI: Eerdmans 1999).

Lesser, M. X., *Reading Jonathan Edwards: An Annotated Bibliography in Three Parts, 1729–2005* (Grand Rapids, MI: Eerdmans 2008).

—, " 'So the People Rescued Jonathan': Edwards and His Readers", Paper Presented at the American Society of Church History Conference, Seattle, WA, January 2005.

Lesser, Wayne, "Jonathan Edwards: Textuality and the Language of Man", in William J. Scheick (ed.), *Critical Essays on Jonathan Edwards* (Boston, MA: G. K. Hall & Co. 1980), pp. 287–304.

Letham, Robert, *The Holy Trinity: In Scripture, History, Theology, and Worship* (Phillipsburg, NJ: P&R Publishing 2004).

Lewis, Edwin, *A Philosophy of the Christian Revelation* (New York: Harper 1940).

Lints, Richard, *The Fabric of Theology: A Prolegomenon to Evangelical Theology* (Grand Rapids, MI: Eerdmans 1993).

Loewinsohn, Ron, "Jonathan Edwards' Opticks: Images and Metaphors of Light in Some of His Major Works", *Early American Literature* 8(1) (1973), 21–32.

Logan, Samuel T., "The Doctrine of Justification in the Theology of Jonathan Edwards'", *Westminster Theological Journal* 46(1) (1984), 26–52.

—, "The Hermeneutics of Jonathan Edwards', *Westminster Theological Journal* 43(1) (1980), 79–96.

Louie, Kin Yip, "Jonathan Edwards' Theological Aesthetics", Ph.D. Dissertation, Edinburgh University, 2006.

Lowance, Mason I., "in Sacvan Bercovitch, *Typology and Early American Literature* (Amherst, MA: University of Massachusetts Press, 1972), pp. 139–60.

—, "Editor's Introduction to 'Types of the Messiah'", in Wallace E. Anderson, and Mason I. Lowance with David H. Watters (eds.), *The Works of Jonathan Edwards, Vol. 11: Typological Writings* (New Haven, CT and London: Yale University Press 1993), pp. 157–86.

—, "Images or Shadows of Divine Things; The Typology of Jonathan Edwards', *Early American Literature* 5(1) (1970), 141–81.

—, *The Language of Canaan: Metaphor and Symbol in New England from the Puritans to the Transcendentalists* (London: Harvard University Press 1980).

Lukasik, Christopher, "Feeling the Force of Certainty: The Divine Science, Newtonianism, and Jonathan Edwards's 'Sinners in the Hands of an Angry God'", *New England Quarterly* 73(2) (2000), 222–45.

Lyttle, David, "Jonathan Edwards on Personal Identity", *Early American Literature* 7(2) (1972), 163–71.

—, "Sixth Sense of Jonathan Edwards', *Church Quarterly Review* 167 (1966), 50–59.

Marsden, George M., *Jonathan Edwards: A Life* (New Haven, CT and London: Yale University Press 2003).

May, Henry F., *The Enlightenment in America* (Oxford and New York: Oxford University Press 1976).

McClymond, Michael J., *Encounters with God: An Approach to the Theology of Jonathan Edwards* (Oxford: Oxford University Press 1998).

—, "God the Measure: Towards an Understanding of Jonathan Edwards' Theocentric Metaphysics", *Scottish Journal of Theology* 47(1) (1994), 43–59.

—, "Review of Avihu Zakai, Jonathan Edwards's Philosophy of History", *The Journal of Religion* 85(1) (2005), 121–23.

—, "Sinners in the Hands of a Virtuous God: Ethics and Divinity in Jonathan Edwards's End of Creation", *Zeitschrift fur Neuere Theologiegeschichte* 2(1) (1995), 1–22.

—, "Spiritual Perception in Jonathan Edwards'", *Journal of Religion* 77(2) (1997), 195–216.

McDermott, Gerald R., "The Deist Connection: Jonathan Edwards and Islam", in Stephen J. Stein (ed.), *Jonathan Edwards's Writings: Text, Context, Interpretation* (Bloomington, IN: Indiana University Press 1996), pp. 39–51.

—, "Franklin, Jefferson and Edwards on Religion and the Religions", in Harry S. Stout, Kenneth P. Minkema, and Caleb J. D. Maskell (eds.), *Jonathan Edwards at 300: Essays on the Tercentenary of His Birth* (Lanham, MD: University Press of America 2005).

—, *Jonathan Edwards Confronts the Gods: Christian Theology, Enlightenment Religion, and Non-Christian Faiths* (Oxford and New York: Oxford University Press 2000).

—, "Jonathan Edwards, Deism, and the Mystery of Revelation", *Journal of Presbyterian History (Philadelphia, PA)* 77(4) (1999), 211–24.

—, *One Holy and Happy Society: The Public Theology of Jonathan Edwards* (University Park, TX: Pennsylvania State University Press 1992).

—, "A Possibility of Reconciliation: Jonathan Edwards and the Salvation of Non-Christians", in Sang Hyun Lee, and Allen C. Guelzo (eds.), *Edwards in Our Time: Jonathan Edwards and the Shaping of American Religion* (Grand Rapids, MI: Eerdmans 1999), pp. 173–202.

—, "Response to Gilbert: 'The Nations Will Worship: Jonathan Edwards and the Salvation of the Heathen'", *Trinity Journal* 23(1) (2002), 77–80.

McDonald, Hugh Dermot, *Theories of Revelation: An Historical Study, 1860–1960* (London: George Allen & Unwin Ltd. 1963).

McNeill, John T., "The Significance of the Word of God for Calvin", *Church History* XXVIII (1959), 131–46.

Metzger, Paul Louis, "Introduction: What Difference Does the Trinity Make?", in Paul Louis Metzger (ed.), *Trinitarian Soundings in Systematic Theology* (Edinburgh: T&T Clark 2005), pp. 5–8.

—, "The Relational Dynamic of Revelation: A Trinitarian Perspective", in Paul Louis Metzger (ed.), *Trinitarian Soundings in Systematic Theology* (Edinburgh: T&T Clark 2005), pp. 21–33.

— (ed.), *Trinitarian Soundings in Systematic Theology* (Edinburgh: T&T Clark 2005).

Miller, Perry, *Errand into the Wilderness* (Cambridge, MA: Harvard University Press 1956).

—, "From Jonathan Edwards to Emerson", *The New England Quarterly* 13(4) (1940), 589–617.

— (ed.), *Images or Shadows of Divine Things* (New Haven, CT: Yale University Press 1948).

—, *Jonathan Edwards* (New York: William Sloan Associates, Reprint, Lincoln: University of Nebraska Press 2005, 1949).

—, "Jonathan Edwards on the Sense of the Heart", *Harvard Theological Review* 41 (1948), 123–45.

—, *Nature's Nation* (Cambridge, MA: Harvard University Press 1967).
—, *The New England Mind: The Seventeeth Century* (Boston, MA: Beacon Press 1961).
Minkema, Kenneth P., "Jonathan Edwards: A Theological Life", in Sang H. Lee (ed.), *The Princeton Companion to Jonathan Edwards* (Princeton, NJ and Oxford: Princeton University Press 2005).
—, "Jonathan Edwards in the Twentieth Century", *Journal of the Evangelical Theological Society* 47(4) (2004), 659–87.
—, "The Other Unfinished 'Great Work': Jonathan Edwards, Messianic Prophecy, and 'The Harmony of the Old and New Testament'", in Stephen J. Stein (ed.), *Jonathan Edwards's Writings: Text, Context, Interpretation* (Bloomington, IN: Indiana University Press 1996), pp. 52–65.
—, "Personal Writings", in Stephen J. Stein (ed.), *The Cambridge Companion to Jonathan Edwards* (Cambridge: Cambridge University Press 2007), pp. 39–60.
Minkema, Kenneth P., and Richard A. Bailey, "Reason, Revelation, and Preaching: An Unpublished Ordination Sermon by Jonathan Edwards', *Southern Baptist Journal of Theology* 3(2) (1999), 16–33.
Mitchell, Louis J., *Jonathan Edwards on the Experience of Beauty* (Vol. 9, *Studies in Reformed Theology and History*, Princeton, NJ: Princeton Theological Seminary 2003).
Moody, Josh, *Jonathan Edwards and the Enlightenment: Knowing the Presence of God* (Lanham, MD: University Press of America 2005).
Morimoto, Anri, *Jonathan Edwards and the Catholic Vision of Salvation* (University Park, PA: Pennsylvania State University Press 1995).
—, "Salvation as Fulfillment of Being: The Soteriology of Jonathan Edwards and Its Implications for Christian Mission", *Princeton Seminary Bulletin* 20(1) (1999), 13–23.
Morris, William Sparkes, *The Young Jonathan Edwards: A Reconstruction* (Eugene, OR: Wipf and Stock Publishers 2005).
Muller, Richard, "Christ-the Revelation or the Revealer? Brunner and Reformed Orthodoxy on the Doctrine of the Word of God", *Journal of the Evangelical Theological Society* 26(3) (1983), 307.
—, *Post-Reformation Reformed Dogmatics: The Rise and Development of Reformed Orthodoxy, Ca. 1520 to Ca. 1725* (4 vols, Grand Rapids, MI: Baker Academic 1987–2003).
Murray, Iain H., *Jonathan Edwards: A New Biography* (Edinburgh: Banner of Truth 1987).
Nichols, Stephen J., *An Absolute Sort of Certainty: The Holy Spirit and the Apologetics of Jonathan Edwards* (Phillipsburg, NJ: P&R Publishing 2003).
Niebuhr, Richard R., "Being and Consent", in Sang Hyun Lee (ed.), *The Princeton Companion to Jonathan Edwards* (Princeton, NJ and Oxford: Princeton University Press 2005), pp. 34–43.
Nieuwenhove, Rik Van (ed.), *The Theology of Thomas Aquinas* (Notre Dame: University of Notre Dame Press 2005).
Noll, Mark A., *America's God: From Jonathan Edwards to Abraham Lincoln* Oxford: Oxford University Press, (2002).
—, "God at the Center: Jonathan Edwards on True Virtue", *Christian Century* 110 (1993), 854–58.

—, "The Irony of the Enlightenment for Presbyterians in the Early Republic", *Journal of the Early Republic* 5(2) (1985), 149–75.

—, "Jonathan Edwards and Nineteenth Century Theology", in Nathan O. Hatch, and Harry S. Stout (eds.), *Jonathan Edwards and the American Experience* (Oxford and New York: Oxford University Press 1988), pp. 260–87.

O'Higgins, J., "Archbishop Tillotson and the Religion of Nature", *Journal of Theological Studies* 24(1) (1973), 123–42.

Oliphint, K. Scott, "Jonathan Edwards on Apologetics: Reason and the Noetic Effects of Sin", in D. G. Hart (ed.), *The Legacy of Jonathan Edwards: American Religion and the Evangelical Tradition* (Grand Rapids, MI: Baker Academic 2003), pp. 131–46.

—, "Jonathan Edwards: Reformed Apologist", *Westminster Theological Journal* 57 (1995), 165–86.

Opie, John (ed.), *Jonathan Edwards and the Enlightenment* (Lexington, MA: D. C. Heath and Company 1969).

Parker, T. H. L., *The Doctrine of the Knowledge of God: A Study in the Theology of John Calvin* (Edinburgh: Oliver and Boyd 1952).

Partee, Charles, "Calvin's Central Dogma Again", *Sixteenth Century Journal* 18 (1987), 191–99.

Pauw, Amy Plantinga, "Editor's Introduction", in *The Works of Jonathan Edwards, Vol. 20: The 'Miscellanies,' 833–1152* (New Haven, CT and London: Yale University Press 2002).

—, " 'One Alone Cannot Be Excellent': Edwards on Divine Simplicity", in Paul Helm, and Oliver D. Crisp (eds.), *Jonathan Edwards: Philosophical Theologian* (Aldershot: Ashgate 2003), pp. 115–25.

—, *The Supreme Harmony of All: The Trinitarian Theology of Jonathan Edwards* (Grand Rapids, MI and Cambridge: Eerdmans 2002).

Peacock, Virginia A., *Problems in the Interpretation of Jonathan Edwards' the Nature of True Virtue* (*Studies in American Religion, Vol. 47,* Lewiston/Queenston/Lampeter: The Edwin Mellen Press 1990).

Pfisterer, Karl D., *The Prism of Scripture: Studies on History and Historicity in the Work of Jonathan Edwards* (Frankfurt: Peter Lang 1975).

Piper, John, *God's Passion for His Glory: Living the Vision of Jonathan Edwards; with the Complete Text of the End for Which God Created the World* Wheaton, IL: Crossway,(1998).

—, "Jonathan Edwards on the Problem of Faith and History", *Scottish Journal of Theology* 31(3) (1978), 217–28.

Preus, Klemet, "Jonathan Edwards: A Case of Medium-Message Conflict", *Concordia Theological Quarterly* 48 (1984), 279–97.

Proudfoot, Wayne,, "Perception and Love in *Religious Affections*", in Stephen J. Stein (ed.), *Jonathan Edwards's Writings: Text, Context, Interpretation* (Bloomington, IN: Indiana University Press 1996), pp. 122–36.

Quinn, Philip L., "Disputing the Augustinian Legacy: John Locke and Jonathan Edwards on Romans 5:12–19", in *Augustinian Tradition* (Berkeley, CA: University of California Press, 1999), pp. 233–50.

Rae, Murray A., *History and Hermeneutics* (London and New York: T&T Clark 2005).

Ramm, Bernard, *Special Revelation and the Word of God* (Grand Rapids, MI: Eerdmans 1961).

Ramsey, Paul, "Editor's Introduction and Appendices", in Paul Ramsey (ed.), *The Works of Jonathan Edwards, Vol. 8: Ethical Writings* (New Haven, CT: Yale University Press 1989).

Redwood, John, *Reason, Ridicule and Religion: The Age of Enlightenment in England, 1660–1750* (Cambridge, MA: Harvard University Press 1976).

Reedy, Gerard, *The Bible and Reason: Anglicans and Scripture in Late Seventeenth Century England* (Philadelphia, PA: University of Philadelphia Press 1985).

Rehnman, Sebastian, *Divine Discourse: The Theological Methodology of John Owen* (ed. Richard A. Muller; *Texts and Studies in Reformation and Post-Reformation Thought*, Grand Rapids, MI: Baker Academic 2002).

Reid, Jasper, "The Metaphysics of Jonathan Edwards and David Hume", *Hume Studies* 32(1) (2006), 53–82.

Reid, John Kelman Sutherland, *The Authority of Scripture: A Study of Reformation and Post-Reformation Understanding of the Bible* (New York: Harper and Brothers 1957).

Reventlow, Henning Graf, *The Authority of the Bible and the Rise of the Modern World* (trans. John Bowden; Philadelphia, PA: Fortress Press, Reprint 1985, 1980).

Rightmire, R. David, "The Sacramental Theology of Jonathan Edwards in the Context of Controversy", *Fides et Historia* 21 (1989), 50–60.

Rogers, Eugene F., *Thomas Aquinas and Karl Barth: Sacred Doctrine and the Natural Knowledge of God* (Notre Dame: University of Notre Dame Press 1999).

Rosengren, Karl Erik, *Communication: An Introduction* (London: Sage Publications 2000).

Rupp, George, "The 'Idealism' of Jonathan Edwards'", *Harvard Theological Review* 62 (1969), 209–26.

Sairsingh, Krister, "Jonathan Edwards and the Idea of Divine Glory: His Foundational Trinitarianism and Its Ecclesial Import", Ph.D. Dissertation, Harvard University, 1986.

Scheick, William J. (ed.), *Critical Essays on Jonathan Edwards* (Boston, MA: G. K. Hall & Co. 1980).

—, "The Grand Design: Jonathan Edwards' History of the Work of Redemption", *Eighteenth-Century Studies* 8(3) (1975), 300–14.

Schreiner, Susan, *The Theater of His Glory: Nature & the Natural Order in the Thought of John Calvin* (Grand Rapids, MI: Baker Academic 2001).

Schweitzer, William M., "Rage against the Machine: Jonathan Edwards Vs. The God of Deism", *Scottish Bulletin of Evangelical Theology* 25(1) (2007), 61–79.

—, "An Uncommon Union: Understanding Jonathan Edwards's Experimental Calvinism", *Puritan Reformed Journal* 2(2) (2010), 208–19.

Shea, Daniel B. Jr., "The Art and Instruction of Jonathan Edwards's *Personal Narrative*", *American Literature* 37 (1965), 17–34.

—, "Jonathan Edwards, Historian of Consciousness", in Everett Emerson (ed.), *Major Writers of Early American Literature* (Madison, WI: University of Wisconsin Press 1972).

Shultz, Walter, "Jonathan Edwards's *End of Creation*: An Exposition and Defense", *Journal of the Evangelical Theological Society* 49(2) (2006), 247–71.

Simonson, Harold P., *Jonathan Edwards: Theologian of the Heart* (Grand Rapids, MI: Eerdmans 1974).

—, *Radical Discontinuities: American Romanticism and Christian Consciousness* (Madison, NJ: Fairleigh Dickinson University Press 1983).

Smith, Claude, "Jonathan Edwards and 'the Way of Ideas'", *Harvard Theological Review* 59(2) (1966), 153–73.

Smith, John E., "Editor's Introduction", in *The Works of Jonathan Edwards, Vol. 2: The Religious Affections* (New Haven, CT and London: Yale University Press 1959).

Sommer, Andreas Urs, "Weltgeschichte Und Heilslogik: Jonathan Edwards' History of the Work of Redemption", *Zeitschrift für Religions und Geistesgeschichte* 53(2) (2001), 115–44.

Spohn, William C., "Sovereign Beauty: Jonathan Edwards and the Nature of True Virtue", *Theological Studies* XLII (1981), 394–421.

Stahle, Rachel Susan, "The Trinitarian Spirit of Jonathan Edwards' Theology", Ph.D. Dissertation, Boston University, 1999.

Stein, Stephen J. (ed.), *The Cambridge Companion to Jonathan Edwards* (Cambridge: Cambridge University Press 2007).

—, "Editor's Introduction", in *The Works of Jonathan Edwards, Vol. 5: Apocalyptic Writings* (New Haven, CT and London: Yale University Press 1977).

—, "Editor's Introduction", in *The Works of Jonathan Edwards, Vol. 15: Notes on Scripture* (New Haven, CT and London: Yale University Press 1998).

—, "Jonathan Edwards and the Rainbow: Biblical Exegesis and Poetic Imagination", *New England Quarterly* 47 (1974), 440–56.

— (ed.), *Jonathan Edwards's Writings: Text, Context, Interpretation* (Bloomington, IN: Indiana University Press 1996).

—, "Providence and Apocalypse in the Early Writings of Jonathan Edwards'", *Early American Literature* 13 (1978), 250–67.

—, "The Quest for the Spiritual Sense: The Biblical Hermeneutics of Jonathan Edwards', *Harvard Theological Review* 70 (1977), 99–113.

—, "The Spirit and the Word: Jonathan Edwards and Scriptural Exegesis", in Nathan O. Hatch, and Harry S. Stout (eds.), *Jonathan Edwards and the American Experience* (Oxford and New York: Oxford University Press 1988), pp. 118–30.

Stewart, M. A. (ed.), *English Philosophy in the Age of Locke* (*Oxford Studies in the History of Philosophy, Vol. 3,* Oxford: Oxford University Press 2000).

Stob, Henry, "The Ethics of Jonathan Edwards'", in Alvin Plantinga (ed.), *Faith and Philosophy: Philosophical Studies in Religion and Ethics; Essays Published in Honor of W Harry Jellema* (Grand Rapids, MI: Eerdmans 1964), pp. 111–37.

Storms, C. Samuel, "Jonathan Edwards on the Freedom of the Will", *Trinity Journal* 3(2) (1982), 131–69.

—, *Tragedy in Eden: Original Sin in the Theology of Jonathan Edwards* (London: University Press of America 1985).

Stout, Harry S., "Jonathan Edwards's Tri-World Vision", in D. G. Hart, Sean Michael Lewis, and Stephen J. Nichols (eds.), *The Legacy of Jonathan Edwards: American Religion and the Evangelical Tradition* (Grand Rapids, MI: Baker Academic 2003), pp. 27–46.

—, *The New England Soul: Preaching and Religious Culture in Colonial New England* (New York: Oxford University Press 1986).

—, "The Puritans and Edwards'", in Nathan O. Hatch, and Harry S. Stout (eds.), *Jonathan Edwards and the American Experience* (New York and Oxford: Oxford University Press 1988), pp. 142–59.

Stout, Harry S., Kenneth P. Minkema, and Caleb J. D. Maskell (eds.), *Jonathan Edwards at 300: Essays on the Tercentenary of His Birth* (Lanham, MD and Oxford: University Press of America 2005).

Studebaker, Steven M., "Jonathan Edwards's Social Augustinian Trinitarianism: An Alternative to a Recent Trend", *Scottish Journal of Theology* 56(3) (2003), 268–85.

Sullivan, Robert E., *John Toland and the Deist Controversy: A Study in Adaptations* (Vol. 101, *Harvard Historical Studies*, Cambridge, MA: Harvard University Press 1982).

Suter, Rufus, "The Strange Universe of Jonathan Edwards'", *Harvard Theological Review* 54 (1961), 125–28.

Sweeney, Douglas A., "Editor's Introduction", in *The Works of Jonathan Edwards, Vol. 23: The 'Miscellanies,' 1153–1360* (New Haven, CT and London: Yale University Press 2004).

—, "Edwards, Jonathan (1703–1758)", in Donald K. McKim (ed.), *Historical Handbook of Major Biblical Interpreters* (Leicester: Inter-Varsity Press 1998), pp. 309–12.

—, *Jonathan Edwards and the Ministry of the Word: A Model of Faith and Thought* (Downers Grove, IL: IVP Academic 2009).

—, " 'Longing for More and More of It'? The Strange Career of Jonathan Edwards's Exegetical Exertions", in Harry S. Stout, Kenneth P. Minkema, and Caleb J. D. Maskell (eds.), *Jonathan Edwards at 300: Essays on the Tercentenary of His Birth* (Lanham, MD: University Press of America 2005), pp. 25–37.

—, *Nathaniel Taylor, New Haven Theology, and the Legacy of Jonathan Edwards* (New York, Oxford University Press, 2003).

Sweeney, Douglas A., and Allen C. Guelzo (eds.), *The New England Theology, 1734–1852: America's First Indigenous Theological Tradition, from Jonathan Edwards and the New Divinity to Edwards Amasa Park* (Grand Rapids, MI: Baker Academic 2006).

Thiemann, Ronald, *Revelation and Theology: The Gospel as Narrated Promise* (Notre Dame: University of Notre Dame Press 1985).

Thuesen, Peter J., "Edwards' Intellectual Background", in Sang H. Lee (ed.), *The Princeton Companion to Jonathan Edwards* (Princeton, NJ and Oxford: Princeton University Press 2005).

—, "Jonathan Edwards as Great Mirror", *Scottish Journal of Theology* 50(1) (1997), 39–60.

Townsend, Harvey G., "Jonathan Edwards' Later Observations of Nature", *New England Quarterly* 13(3) (1940), 510–18.

Tracy, Patricia J., *Jonathan Edwards, Pastor: Religion and Society in Eighteenth-Century Northampton* (New York: Hill and Wang 1980).

Turnbull, Ralph G., *Jonathan Edwards the Preacher* (Grand Rapids, MI: Baker Book House 1958).

—, "Jonathan Edwards – Bible Interpreter", *Interpretation* 6 (1952), 422–35.

Tweyman, Stanley (ed.), *Hume on Natural Religion* (ed. Andrew Pyle; *Key Issues*, Bristol: Thoemmes Press 1996).

Valeri, Mark, "Jonathan Edwards in Modernity: A Review Essay", *Theology Matters* 9(6) (2003), 12–16.

van der Kooi, Cornelis, *As in a Mirror: John Calvin and Karl Barth on Knowing God* (ed. Robert J. Bast; trans. Donald Mader; *Studies in the History of Christian Traditions*, Leiden: Brill Academic Publishers 2005).

VanderMolen, Ronald J., "Puritan Philosophy of History: Providence as Mystery, Providence as Revelation", in Sacvan Bercovitch (ed.), *Puritanism in Old and New England* (Ft. Mitchell, KY: Thomas More College 1975).

Vanhoozer, Kevin J., *The Drama of Doctrine: A Canonical-Linguistic Approach to Christian Theology* (Louisville, KY and London: Westminster John Knox 2005).

Veto, Miklos, and Michael J. McClymond, "Spiritual Knowledge According to Jonathan Edwards'", *Calvin Theological Journal* 31 (1996), 161–81.

Voss, Geerhardus, *Biblical Theology* (Grand Rapids, MI: Eerdmans, Reprint, 2000 Banner of Truth 1948).

Wainwright, William J., "Jonathan Edwards and the Language of God", *Journal of the American Academy of Religion* 48 (1980), 519–30.

—, "Jonathan Edwards and the Sense of the Heart", *Faith and Philosophy* 7 (1990), 43–62.

—, "The Nature of Reason: Locke, Swinburne, and Edwards'", in Alan G. Padgett (ed.), *Reason and the Christian Religion: Essays in Honour of Richard Swinburne* (Oxford: Clarendon Press 1994).

Wallace, Ronald S., *Calvin's Doctrine of the Word and Sacrament* (Eugene, OR: Wipf and Stock Publishers 1997).

Walton, Brad, *Jonathan Edwards, Religious Affections and the Puritan Analysis of True Piety, Spiritual Sensation and Heart Religion* (Vol. 74, *Studies in American Religion*, Lewiston/Queenston/Lampeter: The Edwin Mellen Press 2002).

Ward, Keith, *Religion & Revelation: A Theology of Revelation in the World's Religions* (Oxford and New York: Oxford University Press 1994).

Warfield, Benjamin Breckinridge, *Calvin and Calvinism* (Oxford and New York: Oxford University Press 1931).

—, *The Inspiration and Authority of the Bible* (ed. Samuel G. Craig; Phillipsburg, NJ: Presbyterian and Reformed Publishing 1948).

Webber, Richard M., "The Trinitarian Theology of Jonathan Edwards: An Investigation of Charges Against Its Orthodoxy", *Journal of the Evangelical Theological Society* 44(2) (2001), 297–318.

Weddle, David L., "Jonathan Edwards on Men and Trees, and the Problem of Solidarity", *Harvard Theological Review* 67 (1974), 155–75.

Weinsheimer, Joel C., *Eighteenth-Century Hermeneutics: Philosophy of Interpretation in England from Locke to Burke* (New Haven, CT: Yale University Press 1993).

Werge, Thomas, "Jonathan Edwards and the Puritan Mind in America : Directions in Textual and Interpretative Criticism", *Reformed Review* 23(3) (1970), 153.

Westra, Helen Petter, "'Above All Others': Jonathan Edwards and the Gospel Ministry", *American Presbyterians* 67 (1989), 209–19.

—, "Jonathan Edwards and 'What Reason Teaches'", *Journal of the Evangelical Theological Society* 34 (1991), 495–503.

—, *The Minister's Task and Calling in the Sermons of Jonathan Edwards* (*Studies in American Relgion, Vol. 17*, Lewiston/Queenston/Lampeter: The Edwin Mellen Press 1988).

Whittemore, Robert C., "Jonathan Edwards and the Theology of the Sixth Way", *Church History* 35 (1966), 60–75.

Wilson, David S., "The Flying Spider", *Journal of the History of Ideas* 32 (1971), 447–58.

Wilson, John F., "History, Redemption, and the Millennium", in Nathan O. Hatch, and Harry S. Stout (eds.), *Jonathan Edwards and the American Experience* (Oxford and New York: Oxford University Press 1988), pp. 131–41.

—, "Jonathan Edwards as Historian", *Church History* 46 (1977), 5–18.

Wilson, Stephen A., *Virtue Reformed: Rereading Jonathan Edwards's Ethics* (Leiden and Boston, MA: Brill Academic Publishers 2005).

Winship, Michael P., *Seers of God: Puritan Providentialism in the Restoration and Early Enlightenment* (Baltimore, MD: Johns Hopkins Press 1996).

Winslow, Ola E., *Jonathan Edwards, 1703–1758: A Biography* (New York: The Macmillan Company 1940).

Withrow, Brandon G., "A Future of Hope: Jonathan Edwards and Millennial Expectations", *Trinity Journal* 22(1) (2001), 75–98.

—, "Jonathan Edwards and Justification by Faith", *Reformation & Revival* 11(2) (2002), 93–109.

Wolterstorff, Nicolas, *John Locke and the Ethics of Belief* (*Cambridge Studies in Religion and Culture*, Cambridge and New York: Cambridge University Press 1996).

Yarbrough, Robert W., "A Milestone in the History of New Testament Research: A Review Essay", *Journal of the Evangelical Theological Society* 46(2) (2003), 299–308.

Yarbrough, Stephen R., "Jonathan Edwards on Rhetorical Authority", *Journal of the History of Ideas* 47(3) (1986), 395–408.

Yarbrough, Stephen R., and John C. Adams, *Delightful Conviction: Jonathan Edwards and the Rhetoric of Conversion* (Westport, CT: Greenwood Press 1993).

Young, B. W., *Religion and Enlightenment in Eighteenth-Century England: Theological Debate from Locke to Burke* (Oxford: Clarendon Press 1998).

Zakai, Avihu, "Jonathan Edwards and the Language of Nature: The Re-Enchantment of the World in the Age of Scientific Reasoning", *Journal of Religious History* 26(1) (2002), 15–41.

—, *Jonathan Edwards's Philosophy of History: The Reenchantment of the World in the Age of Enlightenment* (Princeton, NJ: Princeton University Press 2003).

Index

Lightning Source UK Ltd.
Milton Keynes UK
UKOW03f1455020214

225730UK00003B/36/P